MARC PINCHERLE

VIVALDI

Genius of the Baroque

*Translated from the French
by Christopher Hatch*

The Norton Library
W · W · NORTON & COMPANY · INC ·
NEW YORK

W. W. Norton & Company, Inc. will soon issue *The World of the Virtuoso* by Marc Pincherle, and is also the publisher of current or forthcoming books on music by Howard Boatwright, Nadia Boulanger, Manfred Bukofzer, Alfred Einstein, Richard Franko Goldman, Donald Jay Grout, Charles Ives, Paul Henry Lang, Joseph Machlis, Arthur Mendel, Douglas Moore, Carl Parrish, Vincent Persichetti, Walter Piston, Gustave Reese, Curt Sachs, and Arnold Schönberg.

Contents

Foreword

THE AIM of this modest book is to guide the reader as well as possible through the life of Vivaldi and through his works, for which there is a growing audience created by radio and records, by the chamber orchestra revival, and by the belatedly awakened interest of the virtuosos.

My desire is that this book may be read without effort by those who are not specialists. Consequently, at the bottom of its pages one will not find those footnotes that both expand and adorn scholarly works. I have, however, devoted various articles and one voluminous book to Vivaldi, and these are supported by all sorts of references to which the interested reader can turn. In any case he would be convinced that imaginings on the part of the author make no contribution to the present work. What is only conjecture is presented as that.

I shall add that it is no great virtue to have escaped the temptation of writing a fictionalized biography. The truth in this instance is as good as a novel—a somewhat gloomy novel, if one considers the unfortunate end of the composer who had been so long overwhelmed with honors; an idealistic and moral novel, when we see that, after having been forgotten for almost two centuries, he is revived and received with as much enthusiasm as he had aroused in the best years of his own stay on earth.

I

Vivaldi: The Man and His Career

RECENTLY a treatise on the critical appraisal of music proposed that the value of a work should be measured by its success over a fixed period. This proposal took little account of the rather capricious way in which success is meted out. There are in all likelihood not so many unrecognized masterpieces buried in the crypts of history as some sanguine and anxious spirits have imagined. Most forgotten composers deserve nothing better than to be forgotten, as we demonstrate when we inopportunely try to bring them to light. But now and then it happens that an obvious injustice—sometimes one perpetrated for several centuries—is revealed, and that chance alone contrives to disclose and rehabilitate the neglected works. Witness the posthumous fortune of Vivaldi, which may profitably be recalled at this point by way of preamble.

He was famous and feted during his lifetime, and his music was performed and plagiarized throughout Europe. But soon after his death, or even a little before, he passed into a state of neglect that seemed final. His works disappeared from concert programs, and even in his own country his name was omitted from the gazettes, histories, and biographical dictionaries.

A century elapsed. Then in Germany came the rediscovery of Johann Sebastian Bach, who had been the victim of a similar fate, except that he had known neither so resounding a success nor so complete a repudiation. A small group of the faithful had kept the flame going until the memorable year 1829. In that year Mendelssohn presented Bach to a wider public by conducting the *Passion according to St. Matthew*. That performance marks the beginning of the movement that has resulted in the present worship of Bach.

One of the first concerns of the new admirers of Bach was to gather, with a view to publishing, the manuscripts scattered in public and private libraries. In the course of this work they came upon a collection dating from 1739, *XII Concerto* [sic] *di Vivaldi elaborati di J. S. Bach*, and also found a *Concerto del Sig*re *Ant. Vivaldi accomodato per l'Organo a 2 clav. e ped. del Sig*re *Giovanni Sebastiano Bach*.

Who was this Vivaldi, whom Bach had honored by transcribing? Information was sought, and a certain number of originals used by Bach were soon found in old engraved editions from Amsterdam. At first, with an assist from national pride, these originals were declared to be of slight value, and their transcriptions said to be of interest only because they exemplified academic exercises written by Bach just to keep his hand in. Then, on the strength of the transcriber alone, it was agreed to consider them, in their transcribed form, as works of art. It was not until the beginning of our own century that more enlightened and impartial scholars, foremost among them the German Arnold Schering, recognized in Vivaldi not only the precursor to whom J. S. Bach owed his initiation into new forms of instrumental music, but also a powerful innovator and the actual creator of the solo concerto prefigured by Torelli. Recent works assign him no less decisive a part in giving shape to the symphony.

We may marvel at the concurrence of circumstances thanks to which a musician of this stature was fortuitously brought to light in the train of J. S. Bach. We are reminded of the Egyptologists who, digging in the Valley of the Kings in search of a certain pharaoh's burial place, uncover an older, hitherto unsuspected tomb. But those of us who do not already know will soon learn that here it is not a question of mummified music.

Vivaldi's remote ancestors are unknown to us. The name is to be met with as early as the thirteenth century in Italian archives. It was borne by two fearless Ligurian navigators, the brothers Ugolino and Vadino Vivaldi, who rounded the Cape of Good Hope in 1291 and who were shipwrecked, as far as is known, in the region of Mogadiscio on the coast of Somaliland. They had many namesakes, especially at Genoa, from the fifteenth century on. One Raffaele de' Vivaldi was chosen in 1410 to negotiate concerning a tribute that the Genoese were to render to Venice. At about the same time a Cattaneo Vivaldi was one of the Council of Elders, and an Antonio Vivaldi also filled high posts. Yet another Vivaldi was the Doge of Genoa from 1559 to 1561.

As to the composer's immediate forebears, who were Venetians, the first precise information is given us in the unpublished work of the nineteenth-century historian Francesco Caffi: the father of our Antonio Vivaldi, Giovanni Battista, was a violinist at the ducal chapel of San Marco. He had sufficient talent to be cited in 1713 in *Guida dei Forestieri in Venezia*, a guidebook for the use of foreigners, under the title of virtuoso, on the same level as his son whose reputation was already great.

The family did not occupy a very lofty station in the social hierarchy, as what we know of the three other sons of Giovanni Battista will show. One, Bonaventura, is characterized for us only by a request for permission to contract marriage outside Venice, a request supported by testimonials from two barbers who had been raised with him. The second son, Francesco, was himself a barber; all that is known of him is that he got himself banished from the city for having indulged in an unseemly mimicry of a nobleman. The third, Iseppo, also incurred the penalty of banishment for a term of years; he had sported with a dagger at the stroke of two in the morning near the church of San Giovanni Crisostomo with a grocer boy, whom he lightly wounded, and then he had slipped away. There is little apparent reason to spend time on the next of kin of the man who was to make the name of Vivaldi immortal—Antonio, the only musician among Giovanni Battista's sons.

Antonio was probably born in 1678 or very shortly before. This date can be deduced with near certainty from the stages of his ecclesiastical career as it has been reconstructed from the Register of Ordinations preserved in the records of the Venetian patriarchate. Actually he who was later known by the nickname of the Red Priest (*il Prete Rosso*) was indeed a priest, just as he was redheaded. Italy from the sixteenth through the eighteenth

century offers a great many other examples of priests being involved in secular activities at least as much as Vivaldi was; one
example is Orazio Vecchi, composer of the well-known work
L'Amfiparnasso. It is possible that Legrenzi, the composer of
some twenty operas, and presumably Vivaldi's teacher, was also
of the Church. As for Vivaldi, having been tonsured on September 18, 1693, he received minor orders between the nineteenth
of the same month and September 21, 1696, and holy orders between April 4, 1699 (subdeacon), and March 23, 1703, the date of
his accession to the priesthood.

No one could be tonsured before the age of fifteen or ordained before twenty-three; hence Vivaldi's birth is to be placed
back at least as far as 1678. But it cannot be assumed to have
been long before this, because we know that he was still displaying great artistic activity around 1740. Frail as he was and
sickly during his early youth (a little further on his own testimony will be given), it is unlikely that he would have maintained
such an effort for long after his sixty-second year. (Sixty-two
is the lowest age fixed for 1740 by the date of his first tonsure,
1693.)

Regarding his musical training, little documentary evidence
exists. The above-mentioned manuscript by Francesco Caffi informs us that his father taught him the violin, and got him when
he was still very young a position in the ducal chapel, first as a
substitute, then as his possible successor. At the same time the
young Vivaldi learned the organ and completed his theoretical
studies, probably with Legrenzi.

Becoming a priest in 1703, he did not long thereafter carry on
his ministry. This soon caused surprising explanations. It was
claimed that he was never of the Church and that he owed the
title conferred on him to his activities as an instructor in a religious institution. The singularity of his ways gave rise to a different account. "One day when Vivaldi was saying mass, a fugue
subject came to his mind. He at once left the altar where he was
officiating and repaired to the sacristy to write out his theme;
then he came back to finish the mass. He was reported to the
Inquisition, which happily looked upon him as a musician, that is,
as a madman, and limited itself to forbidding him to say mass

from that time forward." It is thus that P. L. Roualle de Boisgelou around 1800 recounts this act. This version, appearing in his manuscript *Table biographique.* . . , has been reproduced by many biographers since then. But the anecdote was in circulation in Vivaldi's lifetime, and he himself was obliged to take the trouble of setting the record straight, though he failed to gain acceptance for the truth.

In the autumn of 1737 he was about to go to Ferrara in order to stage one of his operas when the papal nuncio Cardinal Ruffo forbade his admittance into the city on various grounds. One of these was that he failed to say mass. So Vivaldi wrote forthwith to one of his patrons, Marquis Guido Bentivoglio, to ask him for help. The letter of November 16, 1737, has been preserved. It reads in part as follows:

It was twenty-five years ago that I said mass for what will be the last time, not due to interdiction or at anyone's behest, as His Eminence can appraise himself, but by my own decision on account of an ailment that has burdened me since birth. When I had barely been ordained a priest I said mass for a year or a little more. Then I discontinued saying it, having on three occasions had to leave the altar without completing it because of this ailment.

For this same reason I nearly always live at home, and I only go out in a gondola or coach, because I can no longer walk on account of this chest ailment, or, rather, this tightness in the chest [*strettezza di petto*, commonly believed to refer to a kind of asthma]. No nobleman invites me to his house, not even our prince, because all are informed of my ailment. Immediately after a meal I can usually go out, but not ever on foot. Such is the reason I never say mass. I have spent three carnival seasons at Rome for the opera and, as Your Eminence knows, I never said mass; I played the violin in the opera house, and it is known that His Holiness himself wished to hear me play and that I received profuse thanks for it.

I have been called to Vienna and I never said mass. I was at Mantua for three years in the service of the exceedingly devout prince of Darmstadt with those same women who have always been treated by His Serene Highness with great benevolence, and I never said mass. My travels have always been very costly because I have always had to make them with four or five persons to assist me. . . .

A little earlier in the same letter Vivaldi had made allusion to the ladies who went with him on his travels; he pointed out to

Marquis Bentivoglio that the papal nuncio, as well as reproaching him for not celebrating mass, made the complaint that he had "the friendship of the cantatrice Girò." (This is Anna Giraud, a Mantuan singer whom we shall meet in Goldoni's *Memoirs;* undoubtedly she was accompanied by her mother and by her personal servants, or by those of the composer.) "What troubles me the most," the letter continues, "is the stain with which His Eminence Cardinal Ruffo marks these poor women; nobody has ever done that.

"Fourteen years ago we went together to a good many European cities, and their modesty was admired everywhere; Ferrara can give sufficient evidence of it. Every day of the week they made their devotions, as sworn and authenticated records can prove."

VIVALDI'S MUSICAL ENVIRONMENT

To come back to the beginning of Vivaldi's career, his withdrawal from the altar set him upon a new path. He rather quickly found an activity that reconciled music and religion, for he put his talents at the service of the conservatorio of the Pietà, more exactly the Seminario musicale dell'Ospitale della Pietà, one of the four musical institutes boasted by Venice—the Pietà, the Incurabili, the Mendicanti, and the Santi Giovanni e Paolo, more generally called the *Ospedaletto.* Like the conservatorios of Naples and of Palermo they were established as charitable institutions intended for invalids and foundlings. Later, schools (*scuole*) were annexed to them whose principal object became in time the teaching of music, so much so that around 1700 hardly anything concerning these four religious establishments is made mention of other than their *scuole*, which apparently engrossed the best part of their activity.

On these asylums, and music as practiced there in Vivaldi's time, we have quite an abundance of first-hand reports, all of which give the same general picture. Here is the testimony of the English traveler Edward Wright from his book *Some Observations Made in Travelling through France, Italy . . . in 1720–22* (1730):

Infants are received into these hospitals—into the Incurabili (originally destined to another use) not without a sum given with them,
into the Pietà, and the other two, as I take it, without any.

Those who would choose for a wife one that has not been acquainted
with the world go to these places to look for them, and they generally
take all the care they can, they shall be as little acquainted with the
world afterwards.

Those put into the Pietà are generally bastards. There are a prodi-
gious number of children taken care of in this hospital; they say they
amount sometimes to at least six thousand, and that before the erec-
tion of this charity multitudes used to be found which had been
thrown into the canals of the city. Every Sunday and holiday there
is a performance of music in the chapels of these hospitals, vocal and
instrumental, performed by the young women of the place, who are
set in a gallery above and, though not professed, are hid from any
distinct view of those below by a lattice of ironwork. The organ parts,
as well of those of other instruments, are all performed by the young
women. They have a eunuch for their master [here it seems that
someone took advantage of the traveler's naïveté], and he composes
their music. Their performance is surprisingly good, and many excellent voices are among them. And this is all the more amusing since
their persons are concealed from view.

Some years later, in August, 1739, the French jurist and
scholar Charles de Brosses wrote as follows:

The transcendent music is that of the asylums. There are four of
them, made up of illegitimate and orphaned girls and those whose
parents are not in a position to raise them. They are brought up at
the expense of the state and trained solely to excel in music. Moreover, they sing like angels and play the violin, the flute, the organ,
the oboe, the cello, and the bassoon; in short, there is no instrument,
however unwieldy, that can frighten them. They are cloistered like
nuns. It is they alone who perform, and about forty girls take part
in each concert. I vow to you that there is nothing so diverting as the
sight of a young and pretty nun in white habit, with a bunch of pome-
granate blossoms over her ear, conducting the orchestra and beating
time with all the grace and precision imaginable. (*Lettres familières
sur Italie,* ed. Bezard, 1931).

A well-known picture by Guardi in the Munich Pinakothek of a
concert in a convent excellently illustrates the traveller's description; in the act of playing, the young violinists seem to continue prattling as gay as can be, while the crowd below their
platform is an elegant and restless one.

I shall cite, further, a famous passage from J. J. Rousseau's *Confessions* (Part 2, Book 7), which dates from around 1743, that is, a little after Vivaldi's death.

Music of a kind that is very superior in my opinion to that of the operas and that has not its equal throughout Italy or perhaps the world is that of the *scuole*. . . . Every Sunday at the church of each of these four *scuole* during vespers, motets for a large chorus with a large orchestra, which are composed and directed by the greatest masters in Italy, are performed in barred-off galleries solely by girls, of whom the oldest is not twenty years of age. I can conceive of nothing as voluptuous, as moving as this music. . . . The church [I Mendicanti] is always full of music lovers; even the singers from the Venetian opera come so as to develop genuine taste in singing based on these excellent models. What grieved me was those accursed grills, which allowed only tones to go through and concealed the angels of loveliness of whom they were worthy. I talked of nothing else. One day I was speaking of it at M. le Blond's. "If you are so curious," he said to me, "to see these little girls, I can easily satisfy you. I am one of the administrators of the house, and I invite you to take a snack with them." I did not leave him in peace until he had kept his promise. When going into the room that contained these coveted beauties, I felt a tremor of love such as I never experienced before. M. le Blond introduced me to one after another of those famous singers whose voices and names were all that were known to me. "Come, Sophie"—she was horrible. "Come, Cattina"—she was blind in one eye. "Come, Bettina"—the smallpox had disfigured her. Scarcely one was without some considerable blemish. The inhuman wretch le Blond laughed at my bitter surprise. Two or three, however, looked tolerable; they sang only in the choruses. I was desolate. During the snack, when we teased them, they made merry. Ugliness does not exclude charms, and I found some in them. I said to myself that one cannot sing thus without soul; they have that. Finally, my way of looking at them changed so much that I left nearly in love with all these ugly girls.

These three accounts dwell annoyingly on the easy manners in these almshouses. To tell the truth, they did not have a monopoly on such behavior in that era. They came, some more, some less, under influences exerted to a degree throughout all of decadent eighteenth-century Venice. According to the historian Pompeo Molmenti (*Venice, its individual growth . . . from the earliest beginnings*, 1906–08), some of the thirty-five or so almshouses and convents in the city had strict sets of rules and observed them; in many others the nuns obeyed only their own whims. "They went to bed, arose, and prayed when they liked, and instead of fasting they ate all kinds of dainties and choice dishes. Some of them had taken the veil by coercion, and in the solitude of the cloister they cherished a thousand dreams of love and beauty. . . . Even after having declared their vows they maintained worldly practices and dressed elegantly, their hair curled and their bosoms only half covered by narrow-pleated bodices of silk. . . . The stillness of the cloister was broken sometimes by the sound of trumpets and fifes, sometimes by the merry shouts of the young aristocrats as they danced with the nuns, who would go so far as to stay out all night with their lovers." Charles de Brosses is more harsh when he claims that "the wicked conduct of the ladies of Venice has greatly lessened the gains of the nuns. . . ."

We probably should be on guard against accepting these allegations word for word. The scrupulous and usually trustworthy historian Francesco Caffi himself takes up the vindication of the orphans of the asylums. He lays stress on the bringing up that they received while they were being taught music; accomplished ladies initiated them in feminine occupations, pious matrons inculcated modesty and propriety, and the most exclusive families sought them out on account of their faultless conduct. In a letter to E. A. Cicogna, published in the latter's *Delle Inscrizioni veneziane* (1824-1853), he writes as follows: "It would not be irrelevant to remark that these young ladies, thanks to the allurements of their singing and playing and often also because of the attention from which the iron grills could not screen them—extolled as they were by all the city and listened to with rapture—frequently attracted the most respectable young men, from whom they received offers of marriage. Thus many of them gained deserved riches."

But contemporary paintings and sketches seem to give more support to the malicious. With Francesco Guardi, Pietro Longhi, and others, the convent reception room (*parlatorio*) was a favorite subject. A bright and accessible room is depicted with windows whose lattices permit the young and coquettishly dressed sisters to be seen without mystery. Within the room itself nobles and tradesmen, footmen passing food, and urchin showmen with a puppet show appear, with an altogether secular bustling.

Besides, such licence was not a purely Venetian affair. In the correspondence of the Abbé Conti with Madame de Caylus, owned by the San Marco library, one may read the story of the Neapolitan nuns who wished to enlarge their convent at the expense of the dormitory of the monks, their next-door neighbors. One night they made a sortie in a body, and, catching the monks unawares in their sleep, turned them out with great blows from cudgels without giving them time to dress. And their territorial gain was sanctioned by the city authorities.

To revert to the four Venetian ospedali, nothing so startling as this is associated with them, though austerity was not supposed to be their most conspicuous quality. As Wright observed, most of the students did not take vows. Therefore, in each of these houses professed nuns numbered fewer than members of the laity. For the latter the habit that de Brosses speaks of and that we see represented in a painting by Guardi and in Gabriele Bella's painting of a concert by the girls from the asylums— *Cantata delle putte degli Ospedali nella Procuratia dei Filarmonici* in the Querini-Stampalia Gallery, Venice—is only one more affectation. This last picture illustrates the accepted practice of taking the young *ospealiere* from their convent for musical purposes. They were occasionally taken very far away from Venice. Molmenti reports a night feast given around 1720 by the Contarini in their villa in the vicinity of Padua, at Piazzola, with the co-operation of more than thirty-six musicians from the *Ospedaletto*.

The very quality of the success that was created at their regular concerts smacks of the theater rather than of contemplative monasticism. On feast days the libretto of the oratorio that was going to be performed was distributed at the door of their church; the names of the solo singers were given, "objects of infatuation and intrigues, about which sonnets and songs were printed," as the nineteenth-century historian Taddeo Wiel says.

Applause being taboo on the holy premises, its place was taken by coughing, by loud nose-blowing, or by shuffling the feet. Could much better behavior be required of so mixed a public? All who wanted to could come in, so long as they remained in their seats. Only some aristocrats and distinguished visitors had access to the *coretti*, small reserved loggias that opened into the interior of the building.

Perhaps this is rather extended emphasis to put on the unconventional life led by the young women of the asylums. But it is important that their "conservatories" should not be identified with those that we know today. Moreover, the reader must be able to conceive the following three things: first, the task of the teachers charged with instructing this effervescent youth; next, the complications that could result from the work for Vivaldi, whom we shall see dividing his energies among a thousand cares and labors—and in a most weak state of health; and, finally, the authority that must have been his, if it is true that he succeeded in making unruly castoffs into what was reputed to be the best-disciplined orchestra in Italy.

The asylum of the Pietà, where Vivaldi was to serve for nearly forty years, was located on the Riva degli Schiavoni a little before one reaches the Ponte del Sepolcro coming from San Marco. The Instituto provinciale degli Espositi is on that site today, adjoining the modern church of the Pietà, which was reconstructed in 1745 at the location of the old one.

The beginnings of the institution date from the fourteenth century. Moved by the constantly increasing number of children abandoned in Venice, Brother Pieruzzo in 1346 founded the first asylum of the Pietà at San Francesco della Vigna, to which two years later he added an affiliate at San Giovanni di Bragora. Enlarged at various times from the end of the fourteenth century to the beginning of the eighteenth, the affiliate, administrated by the Congregazione del Luogo Pio, became one of the four main institutions of asylum in the city. It was there that Antonio Vivaldi began a career of multifarious duties—teacher, orchestra director, composer, violinist, and purchaser of instruments, without detriment to the tasks performed on the outside as theatrical musician, impresario, and virtuoso.

Music played an enormous part in the everyday life of the Pietà. It was directed by the *maestro di coro* (chorus taken here in the combined sense of singers and instrumentalists). This function was performed at one time by the Red Priest, at others, by different eminent composers—Porpora, Gasparini, Giovanni Porta —or by someone less well-known but of proved skill, such as Alessandro Gennaro, Pietro Grua, Pietro Scarpari, and Girolamo Bassani. It must be remembered that the four Venetian conservatorios (whose teachers included in the course of the century Lotti, Caldara, Tessarini, Domenico Scarlatti, Hasse, Traetta, Galuppi, and Pescetti, along with the above-named) together with those of Naples and one or two schools in the rest of Italy, were the only institutions of the peninsula that at that time actually turned out musicians of real ability.

The *maestro di coro* generally had a crushing amount of work. On the occasion of each feast he composed either an oratorio or one or more concertos, or lighter instrumental and vocal music of all kinds. He taught theory or the playing of an instrument or both. Under his command he had the performers, who were ranked in a fair and ingenious fashion.

Standing apart from the mass of the girls in the asylums (they were called, in the Venetian dialect, *ospealiere*) were the musicians or *figlie del coro* maintained by the state, which paid out, on the average, a hundred lire a year for each of them. In the archival documents the *ospealiere* may be seen frequently classified under two headings, *di coro*, designating the musicians as a group, and *di comun*, designating the nonmusicians. Thus the plain musicians constituted an aristocracy.

Above them came the elite musicians, the *privileggiate del coro*, who received the homage, the gifts, and the proposals of marriage. The Procurator Pietro Foscarini stipulated in his will (1745) a legacy of one hundred ducats for the "*figlie della Pietà*" provided they sang a mass and recited the Office of the Dead at his funeral ceremonies; he also left twelve ducats a year for life to six of the best singers and six of the best instrumentalists ("*sei figlie di coro più degne nel canto, e sei altre più degne nel suono*").

In everyday life they profited from minor privileges. Witness the following official report of the deliberations of December 14, 1744:

By your express command, venerable congregation, we the under-signed governors, who are put in charge of the management of the girls and their administration, have been required to hold an inquiry on the petition of Maestra Michieletta del Violin by which she implores the gift of a basket of wood each week for eight months, thanks to which, this basket being added to those that the charity of your venerable congregation has already granted to her, she would be able to provide for her daily needs. We shall make known further, as is our duty, that by the resolution of December 16, 1729, the aforesaid Michieletta has already profited from two baskets of wood by the week for the four winter months; after which the aforesaid congregation, continuing its kindness by another decision of January 13, 1735, bestowed on her the favor of another basket of wood each week for the remainder of the year.

The decision resulted in Michieletta's being granted the requested basket of wood for a period of eight months yearly.

The doctors of the asylum quite readily sent to the country musicians whose health inspired any anxiety; thus Doctor Domenico Bozzato affirmed under oath (June 6, 1741) that Apollonia "on account of her indispositions should be sent to the open air," and the same for Alina "because of all her indispositions, which result from hypersalinity of the blood."

Such care evoked much good will. From an official source we know, for example, that in September, 1737, the organists Bianca Maria and Antonia refused all payment for a long and tedious copying job.

Michieletta del Violin was referred to above as *Maestra*. The fact is that all the musicians—*figlie del coro* and *privileggiate di coro*—were subject to the authority of monitors, the immediate assistants to the *maestri;* these monitors or *maestre* were generally designated in the registers and official papers as well as in the journals by the indication of the instrument each taught, coupled with her Christian name—Maestra Lucieta della Viola, Maestra Cattarina dal Cornetto, Maestra Silvia dal Violino, Maestra Luciana Organista. Their role was above all to facilitate and lighten the task of the director. A resolution of July 2, 1723, charged them always to be present at the rehearsals so as to keep order. Their services were paid for; from 1738 to 1754 a *maestra* received eighty ducats a year. And not only did they rule over the young women of the choruses and orchestra, they also exerted, with regard to the administration, a downright control over their superiors, the *maestri;* the quarterly pay sheets, signed by them, certify that the teachers of organ, solfège, and so forth had conscientiously discharged their duties.

Some of them, independently of their teaching functions, distinguished themselves as virtuosos. As he recounts in his autobiographical contribution to Marpurg's *Historisch-kritische Beyträge* (1754), the famous German flutist J. J. Quantz, who places the Pietà first among the four asylums on account of the perfection of the music produced there, took note in 1726 of the aforementioned Apollonia ("a strong singer [*eine starke Sängerin*]," he writes). He also mentions an excellent violinist, whom he does not choose to name, and Angeletta, at one time the glory of the Pietà as a singer and organist, who had since married a banker.

In 1739 Charles de Brosses stated that Chiaretta "would certainly be the first violinist of Italy if Anna Maria of the Ospedaletto did not outdo even her." Indeed, he was not afraid to present Anna Maria to us as the equal of Tartini, saying that though she does not share with him the utmost technical precision, she eclipses him in all other regards.

The musicians of the Pietà were for a long time the ornament of the asylum and of the city. They had as much discipline in the orchestra as they had little outside. "What rigidity!" wrote de Brosses (in the sense of precision). "Only there is heard that crisp orchestral attack [*le premier coup d'archet*] so falsely boasted of at the Paris Opera." They enriched with their talent the ceremonies arranged for the rulers and dignitaries who visited Venice. Contemporary testimony makes us think that the orchestra of the Pietà succeeded in contesting the primacy of that of San Marco.

What we shall see further on of Vivaldi's life and works will enable us to estimate the influence on his genius of the long years that he devoted to the *ospealiere*. But even here we can safely establish certain particulars.

With its orchestra, its choruses, and its *maestre*, he had at his disposal a musical laboratory of extensive and manifold musical resources. The ardor of his students and their appetite for music matched their abilities. The account books of the asylum give proof of this. It is not only a question of the purchase and repair of instruments, of the copying expenses, of the costs of organizing concerts and *divertimenti musicali*, and of the acquiring of music, both Italian and foreign, the latter occasionally ordered from Paris. The English historian Burney, in a passage quoted later on, shows the constant rivalry of the young musicians, who competed with each other in virtuosity, even if the audience were sparse, and engaged among themselves and for themselves in a veritable contest of vocal acrobatics.

It is easy to imagine the responsiveness of such a group, dominated not by more or less blasé or hypercritical professionals, but by young students abounding in enthusiasm and curiosity. This was the group over which Vivaldi's personality was to have complete ascendancy. In this respect he was even more favored than J. S. Bach at the court of Cöthen, or Joseph Haydn at Esterház. He could experiment and study at his leisure the best way to apportion the orchestra; he could attack various comprehensive or detailed problems without being at the mercy of the clock, of an obstinate performer, or of the strict regulations of a labor union.

His agreement with the administration charged him with the supplying of a profusion of "fresh" music for all sorts of instruments. Some figures, quoted below, on the quantity of concertos and symphonies delivered literally by the dozen show how he met this obligation of ceaseless production. Whence comes the extreme hastiness of his handwriting, grossly observable in the autographs preserved at Dresden and Turin; their calligraphy seems to justify the boast of the Red Priest, in speaking to Charles de Brosses, that he could "compose a concerto with all its parts faster than a copyist could copy it." The notes, in fact, seem to lunge forward like those in certain rough drafts by Rimsky-Korsakoff, where the stems of the sixteenth notes bend like a field of wheat before the storm. Vivaldi's composition came so quickly that he continually invents abbreviations, achieving here and there a genuine musical shorthand.

How could it be otherwise when he had not only to provide for an orchestra and a chorus whose insatiable appetite for music I have just emphasized, but sometimes had to dash off three operas in less than three months or to make good that notice on the title page of *Tito Manlio*, a three-act opera, "Musica di Vivaldi, fatto in 5 giorni"—five days—or, say, one-third the time devoted by Handel to devising *Rinaldo*.

This speed is a Venetian tradition. There is the example of Cavalli and the finale of *Callistro* (1652), for which he had composed a certain duet. When the duet was nearly finished, he noticed that the librettist had three, not two persons speaking. He simply blotted out the duet and started over again on a trio. Of Vivaldi's contemporaries, more than one polished off three operas a season. During the year 1705 alone, Gasparini supplied the Teatro San Cassiano with four, without neglect of his other jobs. Marcello did not have to look very far for instances when in his *Teatro alla moda* (1720) he takes the composer to task: "If it happens that the impresario complains about the music, the composer ought to protest against such grave injustice, considering that he put a good third more notes into the score than usual and that it required fifty hours to compose."

As for Vivaldi, we know from his letters how, if pressed for time, he patched up some recitatives or arias from his old operas when he did not appropriate them from other composers. For example, an aria for Cino in the first act of *Il Teuzzone* repeats the exact text of an aria for Anastasio in *Il Giustino;* two arias from the first act of *Armida* are actually by Leonardo Leo, and several in *L'Olimpiade* have nothing but new words. The height of this breezy lack of restraint seems to be reached with *Rosmira*, dedicated in high-flown expressions to the Margrave of Brandenburg, in which Vivaldi is content to string together fragments of operas by Girolamo Micheli, G. A. Paganelli, Antonio Pampino, Antonio Mazzoni, Hasse, Handel, and others.

Of course he did not hesitate to transfer passages from his instrumental music to his vocal music and vice versa. The first

movement of the concerto *La Primavera* (Opus 8, No. 1, F. I, 22) [1]
was already in the oratorio *Juditha*, and the country dance of the
same concerto recapitulates Judith's aria *Vivat in pace*. It should
be noted that this was the general custom of Vivaldi's century.
Occasionally even Bach used the same aria or recitative in sacred
and secular compositions. And as late as 1784 we have a letter by
Mozart (July 21, to his sister) in which he asks that his oratorio
of 1771, *La Betulia liberata*, be sent to him so that he can transfer
several pieces from it to another oratorio on the same subject that
has just been ordered from him.

It should not be surprising that Vivaldi's purely instrumental
music also bears traces of the haste that marks his regular working regime. By going through the inventories of his symphonies
and concertos, it can be established that he was apt to use the
same largo twice, and to revert to the same tutti in three concertos, changing only the solos. (His publishers in Amsterdam,
carrying offhandedness further, printed in full the same concerto, note for note, in two different collections.)

Lack of time explains also why in a sinfonia *a quattro* (P. 175,
F. XI, 30) in the library of the Paris Conservatory the finale is
in only two parts, one written for the first and second violins in
unison, the other for the violas and cellos in unison. And we
have no reason to doubt that certain orchestral effects which
lighten the texture had their origin in a need for haste.

Counterbalancing this need for haste, the rapidity of Vivaldi's
conception and of its fulfillment is such that he just as frequently
cancels with a stroke of the pen several already orchestrated
pages and sets out again with new themes without trying to turn
to account those he had started to exploit. It even happened that

---

[1] Throughout this book, works by Vivaldi published with opus numbers
during his life are indicated by these numbers. Concertos not so published
are designated by numbers given them in the classification by keys to be
found in Marc Pincherle, *Antonio Vivaldi et la musique instrumentale*, 1948
(Vol. 2, *Inventaire thématique*); these numbers are preceded by a P. Those
works that have been issued thus far in the *Opere complete* (1947—), now
being published under the editorship of Gian Francesco Malipiero and
others, are also indicated by the numbers given them in the classification
drawn up by Antonio Fanna and used in this series; these numbers are
preceded by an F.

he would write out two movements for one, probably leaving freedom of choice to the interpreter (as Francesco Veracini did in his *Sonate accademiche*); a manuscript Dresden concerto in B-flat (P. 349; *cf.* F. I, 95) has two slow movements, a *grave* in g and a *largo* in E-flat, and either of these would have been sufficient for the equilibrium of the concerto. An even better example is the following: Having finished a finale in D for a concerto that begins in that key (P. 197, F. XI, 15), he was not satisfied with it and composed another. However, he wrote this last in g, contrary to the usage of the time and to his own practice, since the main key was D; the fact is that the middle *adagio* is in g and no doubt he neglected to refer further back before undertaking the finale. The same explanation is valid for the first concerto of Opus 7, Book 2, in B-flat with a *largo* in g that by a similar action sweeps the finale along in the same key.

Haste will explain to us many of the features of Vivaldi's techniques. Most of his weaknesses are due to the same cause, and it is a miracle that the robustness of his work was not compromised any more than it was.

If the Pietà holds the first place in the full development of the Red Priest's genius, it is impossible not to take account of the intense musical life that animated Venice everywhere and on every level of society at the beginning of the eighteenth century —a time, as is known, of marked political decadence, but for the arts, on the contrary, a period of intense and vigorous efflorescence.

The first home of instrumental polyphony in Italy, Venice maintained her concern for it in Vivaldi's time. The Venetian instrumental style, along with the orchestral coloring that is already so conspicuous in the work of both the Gabrieli, was to be renewed with increased intensity. And besides this taste for the imposing, the impress of which is still on Vivaldi's concertos for two *cori*, the innovating Venetian spirit is to be observed exalting monody over the older polyphony, to which the Roman school remained more attached. From this derives the following definition by the German theorist Mattheson in *Das neu-eröffnete Orchestre* (1713): "The Roman style is more sedate than the

Venetian; the latter is on the whole melodic, the former seeks a more continual harmony. The Venetian makes its way to the ear more quickly, but its spell continues for a shorter time than that of the Roman, which has more body. In the one is found more of the *galant*, in the other more of the substantial." At the time when he was writing, Mattheson could not yet take into account what Vivaldi had contributed to Venice, but he does at least give us some idea of what he received from her—not only directly from his teachers but also, and above all, from the environment, unique in Europe, in which he was a student.

I shall not try to reconstruct this environment; what is required, in the wake of so many others, is to recast the colorful picture of the life that surrounded San Marco and the Piazzetta. A few indications will suffice as to the main point, that is to say, the omnipresence of music, not only in the Ospedali but in the theaters, in the churches, and everywhere throughout the city.

The trait of Venetian character on which all historians agree (next to its sportiveness and taste for the exuberant and the burlesque) is its mania for music, attested as much by the ardor with which they give themselves to it as by the violence of the reaction it calls forth. "Contemporary memoirs," writes Molmenti, "recount for us how sometimes women would weep, cry out, and faint away when hearing the solemn chants of the church or the voice of some famous singer." And such was the love of this people for beautiful sounds that at the opera they could accept absurd librettos and plots of a complexity that deprived them of all hope of understanding, provided the music was to their taste.

In daily life there was neither a time nor a place where music was not present. The Venetians, alone or in groups, sang in the streets and on the canals. In front of San Marco "a man from the dregs of the populace, a shoemaker or a smith dressed in his work clothes, starts a tune; other people of his sort join in with him and sing this tune in parts with accuracy, precision, and taste that is scarcely to be met with in fashionable society in our northern lands." (P. J. Grosley, *Nouveaux mémoires ou Observations sur l'Italie . . . ,* 1764) Each guild had its own tunes. The

gondoliers' songs alone would fill numberless volumes. From
only one of these songs, which was written down by Tartini and
printed in Burney's *History of Music*, one can fancy what imagination and pathos they contained. This is one of those melodies
anonymously adapted to some fragments of Tasso's *Gerusalemme
liberata*, which were handed down in the guild by verbal tradition:

Aria del Tasso

Adagio quasi Recitativo

It was the custom among the gondoliers to improvise thus on texts drawn from this poem. Goethe relates in vivid terms one of those sessions of improvisation, and the Countess d'Agoult remarks in her *Mémoires* for 1838 that her gondolier Cornelio did not know how to sing Tasso "because he is not literate [*perche non è letterato*]."

Music was just as widespread among the aristocracy, in whose palaces and summer homes it took up residence. The villa of the Contarini at Piazzola was more than a conservatory and better than one, with its two theaters, its library where the best compositions, old and new, were brought together, and its collection of valuable instruments. The Venier, Morosini, Vendramin, Renier, Grimani, Tron, Mocenigo, and Giustiniani families were not satisfied with owning or supporting opera houses. They were passionately musical; they were practical musicians. In Venice there was no trace of the scorn that French and English nobility made a show of feeling about instrumental players; a Mocenigo, a Venier, a Giustiniani, and a Marcello (Alessandro) are numbered among the best violinists trained by Tartini. Albinoni, Domenico Alberti, and Benedetto Marcello, who became distinguished composers, styled themselves amateurs. The aristocracy devotedly attended the concerts that were given by Legrenzi.

Music was the essential element in nearly all the festivities which followed one another at a rate that was all the more lively because those who governed saw in them an excellent means of turning their people away from the political preoccupations which they meant to reserve for themselves. Therefore, there were celebrations for the election of the doge, of a procurator, or of a patriarch, for the arrival of a sovereign or of an ambassador, or for the anniversary of an illustrious birth. For want of something better, they fell back on the commemoration of the end of an epidemic—in 1730 they celebrated the centenary of the plague of 1630.

The sea and the canals permitted nautical rejoicings, such as the solemn wedding of the Adriatic by the doge, or the more lively festivals of the Fresco, processions of hundreds of gondolas that took place every Sunday and holiday from Easter Monday to the end of September. Returning at nightfall, the gondoliers made the lagoon ring with serenades.

The unceasing parade from all lands of sovereigns and princes, several of whom kept small lodgings in Venice and usually travelled with their favorite singers and instrumentalists, multiplied the opportunities for concerts. The Saxon and Bavarian princes were especially taken with Venice and its music; Charles Albert of Bavaria in January, 1725, is known to have been present at four opera performances in the space of three days.

And the composers! All who were of consequence in Europe came to this privileged climate at some time. In 1707 Alessandro Scarlatti directed two of his works there, and such was the prestige of Venice that in the first, *Mitridate Eupatore*, composed for the Teatro San Giovanni Crisostomo, he produced not only his biggest work up to that time but a work that obviously strives to conform to the traditions of Venetian opera, even to the minute details of orchestral color. There is, for example, his use of the marine trumpet (*tromba marina*), a bowed instrument that has nothing in common with the trumpet and was obsolete outside of Venice, but an instrument that Vivaldi would still be using in 1740 and that Marcello ironically recommends for the composer to use if he wants to captivate the crowds.

Handel, likewise, hit the tastes of his listeners so successfully with *Agrippina* (1709), an opera on a libretto by the Venetian cardinal Grimani, that he achieved a triumph whose echoes reverberated across Europe. It was in Venice that he got to know Domenico Scarlatti, who had come to work with Gasparini. And perhaps Corelli was there at the same time. Handel returned in 1729 for a longer stay. In 1714 Francesco Veracini was there, and, still in Venice, he set the date 1716 on a sonata dedicated to the elector Frederick Augustus of Saxony.

Tartini heard Veracini at the home of the Mocenighi in the spring of the same year (1716), and such was his astonishment that he felt it advisable to retire for the purpose of perfecting his technique. He was often to be seen in Venice, where he had pupils in the noble houses, as indicated above, and also in the Ospedali—at the Mendicanti, Antonia Cubli and Anna Lombardini (the future Madame Sirmen); and, at the Incurabili, Giaccomina Stromba. He maintained connections with the directors of the conservatorios; in January, 1735, he received from the coffers of the Pietà the sum of 800 lire, a present from one of the administrators in thanks for the dedication of his first collection of sonatas. He was heard at San Marco, where it had been customary at least since 1692 for a virtuoso to perform a violin solo during the Offertory.

During Vivaldi's lifetime innumerable composers, and not Venetians alone, lived in or passed through Venice—Gluck, Pergolesi, Legrenzi, Albinoni, Caldara, Porpora, Antonio Bononcini, Galuppi, Hasse, G. B. Somis, Pisendel, Domenico Alberti, and others. And then there were the singers—Bernacchi, Farinelli, Carestini, Faustina Bordoni-Hasse, Santa Stella (wife of Antonio Lotti), Cuzzoni, Tesi, and Miniati. A single opera cast might bring together the marvelous names of Faustina, Cuzzoni, and Carlo Scalzi, or, again, of Bernacchi, Cuzzoni, and Tesi.

Musical theater was one of the major preoccupations of the city, which was proud to have opened in March, 1637, the first opera house in Europe with a paying public, the San Cassiano. Venice had at least five or six theaters in full activity during each of the three opera seasons—the winter season or Carnival, from December 26 to March 30; the spring season or Ascension, from the day following Easter until June 30; the fall season from September 1 to November 30.

Despite the rapid progress of the Neapolitan school, the prestige of the Venetian opera remained great. In 1699—Alessandro Scarlatti had already been famous for quite a while—the poet and dramatist Andrea Perucci proclaimed in his own fief, Naples, his praise of "that most serene and superb Venice, which coordinates the efforts of the best composers of Italy, the most learned *maestri di cappella*, the most ingenious stage designers, and the most experienced choreographers."

Most of the theaters were controlled from above by the patricians; an account addressed by a traveler to a friend at the end of the seventeenth century tells us in what sort of spirit. "There are in Venice," writes M. Chassebras de Cramailles, "eight theaters, which take their names from the churches nearest to the places where they are erected. Almost all of them belong to

Venetian nobles who had them built or who have them by inheritance. The small ones [two out of the eight, the writer specifies further on] are rented by troupes of comedians, who betake themselves to Venice from the month of November on; and the large ones are reserved for operas that are ordered and paid for by these nobles or others. But it is rather for their entertainment than for their profit, because they do not take in enough to defray half the cost."

During the first half of the eighteenth century the following theaters were in operation: the San Cassiano, the property of the Tron family; the Santi Giovanni e Paolo, the Grimani's property, as were also the San Giovanni Crisostomo and the San Samuele; and the San Moise and San Salvatore, owned by the Giustiniani and the Vendramin families respectively. The Sant'Angelo, which staged two-thirds of Vivaldi's operas, had been founded by Santorini, the impresario of the San Moise. To these permanent opera houses were added, now and again, the Sant'Apostoli, the San Fantino, and the Santa Margherita.

The number of operas performed takes one's breath away: 150 between 1680 and 1700, with Legrenzi, M. A. Ziani, Caldara, Lotti, Albinoni, and Draghi as the chief composers; 432 between 1700 and 1743, among them notable works by Handel, Alessandro Scarlatti, M. A. Bononcini, Vinci, Porpora, Galuppi, Hasse, Pergolesi, and Gluck. Of the seventy operas he produced, C. F. Pollaroli gave sixty-four of them in Venice; and it was for Venice that Vinci, Hasse, and Porpora wrote their first dramatic scores.

As for religious music, it had two principal homes. There was, on the one hand, the Basilica of San Marco, which has been thoroughly studied by Francesco Caffi. Its role is sufficiently well-known to make it needless to go over it again here; it will be enough to recall that Vivaldi could be in touch there with organists, composers, and *maestri di cappella* of the stature of Legrenzi, Lotti, Antonio Biffi, Antonio and C. F. Pollaroli, Francesco Veracini, Pietro Ziani, and others. On the other hand, there were the famous asylums, including the Pietà, which we are going to meet again in taking up the account of the Red Priest's life where we left off.

VIVALDI'S CAREER

Vivaldi's activities at the Pietà began in 1703, the same year in which his health forced him to stop celebrating mass. He did not, however, doff the cassock, as has been so persistently repeated. For a long time it was thought that he had not entered upon his duties at so early a date, some historians placing the event as late as 1713. But I have discovered in the records of the asylum the mention of a payment of thirty ducats on March 17, 1704, as remuneration for services rendered during the half-year terminating at the end of February. This takes us back to September, 1703, in establishing the beginning of a career that was to be continued on the Riva degli Schiavoni for thirty-seven years, with now and again some brief absences.

Again, payments, corresponding to a monthly stipend of five ducats, appear in May and June, 1704. After August, Vivaldi was paid twenty ducats quarterly, then twenty-five in 1706–07. Over and above the sixty ducats that were allocated to him in 1709 as violin instructor, he undoubtedly received other emoluments by virtue of his roles as *maestro de' concerti* and *maestro di coro*. And while, on the title page of his first book of sonatas, published in 1705, he was simply "D. [Don] Antonio Vivaldi, Musico di Violino Professore Veneto," beginning with his Opus 2 (1709) he styles himself "Maestro de' Concerti del Pio Ospedale della Pietà di Venezia," and does so to the end of his days, adding only, from Opus 8 on, his titles of *maestro di cappella* (in Italy) to Count Morzin and to Prince Philip of Hesse-Darmstadt. (We shall discuss these titles later.)

From the varying designations under which he appeared in the records of the Pietà, it is difficult to deduce anything precise as to his material situation. Although the reports of the administrators' deliberations hardly ever allude to his being maintained in a post previously occupied by him, it is generally a question of simply renewing his mandate. Adding to the obscurity of this hierarchy for us are the great numbers of teachers employed, the vagueness of the terminology denominating them (*maestro di cappella, maestro di coro, maestro de' concerti,* not to speak of the teachers of instruments, of singing, and of solfege), and a sort of "musical chairs" occurring among the personnel because of trips and illnesses. What is certain is that during the whole of his time with the Pietà, Vivaldi taught the violin, and intermittently, but on a number of occasions, filled the offices of orchestral director and of composer in ordinary.

His repute as a composer was not slow in spreading beyond the asylum, and soon beyond Venice. His first printed collection left the press of his fellow-townsman Giuseppe Sala in 1705. (I am indebted to Gian Francesco Malipiero for having pointed out this collection, which was later reprinted at Amsterdam by Estienne Roger.) His Opus 2 likewise was published first in Venice, by Antonio Bortoli in 1709. After that, the first edition of his published works was to be reserved for Estienne Roger and his successors, and several were to be reproduced by London and Paris publishers without prejudice to those that circulated nearly everywhere in manuscript copies.

Two manuscript concertos that are preserved at Dresden and whose titles specify that they were composed in 1712, the one for the feast of the "Santa Lingua di S. Antonio in Padua" (P. 165), the other for the church of San Lorenzo in the same city (P. 169), lead us to believe that Vivaldi sojourned at Padua in that year; however, there is no other evidence of this. The date 1712 can also be assigned almost surely to the first, Dutch edition of the famous Opus 3, *L'Estro armonico*, on which Vivaldi's European reputation was founded.

In 1713 the administration of the Pietà granted him a vacation so that he might turn his talents to account (*"le sue vertuose applicazioni"*) outside the city. This point is worth being weighed with care; might it not have reference to a certain journey to Darmstadt that many biographers say occurred in this period? This hypothesis is probably to be rejected. On the one hand, some thirty years ago Dr. Voltz, Director of the Landesbibliothek of Darmstadt, went to the trouble of carrying out very searching investigations in the local archives which yielded up no trace of Vivaldi's having visited that city. On the other hand, the letter of November 16, 1737, which is quoted above, informs us that the Red Priest had been at Mantua for three years in the service

of the very devout prince of Darmstadt, Philip of Hesse-Darmstadt, who was governor of Mantua in 1707–08 and again from
1714 to 1735.

It is in the course of this second period that the three years of
service that Vivaldi speaks of may be placed, almost certainly
around 1720–23. At that time his dramatic output for the Venetian theaters lagged considerably—only two operas between 1718
and 1725 against one or two annually during the four preceding
years and the ten following. Besides, the title of "Maestro di
Cappella di Camera di S.A. il Sig. Principe Filippo Langravio
d'Hassia Darmistath" was to appear for the first time in the
libretto of *La Verità in Cimento*, dated 1720. Vivaldi maintained
the title in all his later publications, instrumental as well as dramatic, evidence that indicates the beginning of a long collaboration. Off and on he called himself by other titles also: once
"Maestro in Italia" of "Venceslao Conte di Marzin [Morzin],"
hereditary prince of Hohenelbe; another time "Maestro di Cappella di S. A. S. il Duca di Lorena." The latter title, used on his
opera *Adelaide*, which was presented in 1735, led some historians
to conjecture a stay by Vivaldi at Florence, where the duke
resided and where another opera of his, *Ginevra principessa di
Scozia*, was given in 1737. It is more likely that the meeting
should be placed in Vienna in the course of the sojourn that
Vivaldi must have made there in 1728; Francis III of Lorraine
had by then been living in that city for five years.

If we take up the thread of our biography at 1713—the question of the trip to Darmstadt having been decided in the negative
—we see Vivaldi launching into dramatic composition with
Ottone in Villa, a three-act opera on a libretto by Domenico
Lalli, which was produced that year, not in Venice, but in Vicenza. During the ensuing years other operas were to follow in
close succession in Venice itself, where the composer probably
had permanent residence until 1718. In the fall season of 1714 the
Teatro Sant'Angelo staged his *Orlando finto pazzo*. In 1715 the
same theater, to which Vivaldi supplied eighteen operas, saw the
production of *Nerone fatto Cesare*, written by several musicians
in collaboration, Vivaldi being one of them. From 1716 to 1718
we find him represented at the Sant'Angelo and at the San

Moise by *six* different operas, not to mention *Scanderbegh*, which served as the show for the reopening of the Teatro della Pergola in Florence on June 22, 1718.

Nevertheless, the Pietà was not neglected. While going on with his teaching duties, he also furnished two oratorios for the students to put on—*Moyses Deus Pharaonis* (1714), of which only the libretto is extant, and *Juditha triumphans* (1716), of which both the text and music have been preserved. Its publication and recording have made it available to the audience of to-day. In maturity and sumptuousness this work fully equals the concertos, which by that time had carried the fame of Vivaldi far and wide.

We know indeed that as early as 1714 in the little German town of Pirna, J. J. Quantz, who was to become illustrious as a flutist, teacher, and composer at the court of Frederick the Great, but who had begun by working at the violin, had already been deeply impressed by Vivaldi's concertos, which were probably circulating in manuscript copies. "I was eager," he relates in his autobiography, "to accumulate a good number. Their magnificent tutti subsequently constituted good models for me." We also know that during these same years of 1713–18 several German and Czech virtuosos—Gottfried Heinrich Stölzel, Johann David Heinichen, and Jan Dismas Zelenka—studied in Venice, and they undoubtedly brought home with them mannerisms learned from Vivaldi. Finally, we know from J. A. Hiller that in 1718, at Dresden, Franz Benda, the future founder of the Berlin school, played Vivaldi concertos with an orchestra that the choir-boys had formed for their own amusement.

But this period supplies us with more direct and suggestive testimony. Among such are the extracts recently published by Eberhard Preussner (*Die musikalischen Reisen des Herrn von Uffenbach*, 1949) from a travel diary kept from 1712 to 1716 by an architect from Frankfurt am Main and a great lover of music, Johann Friedrich Uffenbach, whose peregrinations led him to Venice on February 2, 1715, at the height of the Carnival season. Around San Marco there was the joyousness, the excitement, the swarm of maskers usual during such occasions. They sang to the guitar and improvised verses about the bystanders, while two steps away from this unrestraint there was a different world; at the Incurabili on the Grand Canal the nuns sang vespers "with truly angelic voices [mit rechten englischen Stimmen]," such as Uffenbach had never heard, and some of them gently played instruments. The audience was large; the traveler, a man endowed with a sturdy sense of the practical, observed that the asylum profited from this, since the seats were charged for.

The opera immediately attracted his attention. I shall return further on, when we come to Vivaldi's dramatic music, to the account he gives of Venetian performances, which appear to have been rather different from the notion of them that we get from the standard handbooks. The *Prete Rosso* was there, conducting the orchestra, on February 4 (the title of the opera is not mentioned; perhaps it was a revival of *Orlando finto pazzo*), and it was as a violinist that he stood out. "Toward the end of the work," Uffenbach relates, "Vivaldi performed a solo accompaniment admirably, and at the end he added an improvised cadenza [*eine Phantasie*] that quite confounded me, for such playing has not been heard before and can never be equalled. He placed his fingers but a hair's breadth from the bridge so that there was hardly room for the bow. He played thus on all four strings, with imitations [*mit Fugen*] and at unbelievable speed. Everyone was astonished, but I cannot say that it captivated me, because it was more skillfully executed than it was pleasant to hear."

On February 19 Uffenbach heard another of Vivaldi's operas, *Agrippina* (another title for *Nerone fatto Cesare*). The performance disappointed him; to make matters worse, "Vivaldi himself played solo on the violin only a very slight aria." On the other hand, a little later in the same theater on an unspecified date between February 28 and March 3, *Agrippina* was given again, and Vivaldi's playing this time left the writer in unreserved rapture. The rest of his stay in Venice was devoted wholly to the *Prete Rosso*. So that he might judge him better, he returned once again to the opera. He also sought to make his personal acquaintance. He sent his servant to him to request an appointment, which his journal recounts as follows:

Wednesday, March 6, 1715. After dinner Vivaldi, the famous composer and violinist, came to my home, for I had sent invitations to him a number of times. I spoke of some concerti grossi that I would like to have from him, and I ordered them from him. For him, since he belonged to the Cantores [here meaning church musicians], some bottles of wine were ordered. He then let me hear some very difficult and quite inimitable improvisations [*Phantasien*] on the violin. From close to, I had to admire his skill all the more, and I saw quite clearly that he played unusual and lively pieces, to be sure, but in a way that lacked both charm and a *cantabile* manner.

Saturday, March 9, 1715. In the afternoon Vivaldi came to me and brought me, as had been ordered, ten concerti grossi, which he said had been composed expressly for me. [From the sixth to the ninth of March, in three days?] I bought some of them. In order that I might hear them better he wanted to teach me to play them at once, and on that account he would come to me from time to time. And thus we were to start this very day.

Two years later, in 1717, a fellow-countryman of Uffenbach, Johann Georg Pisendel, a professional violinist who already had a considerable reputation, came at the expense of his sovereign, the Elector of Saxony, to ask for some lessons from the Venetian master.

Little is known of Vivaldi's students outside of those whom he trained for the orchestra of the Pietà. Julius Rühlmann, writing in the *Neue Zeitschrift für Musik* (1867), postulated a real center of musical studies at Mantua before 1713, of which Vivaldi was the prime mover. "There were young German artists already in Mantua, such as Handel, Hesse (the viola da gamba player from Darmstadt), and others in great numbers who had come to attach themselves to Vivaldi so that they might fathom his style to the full. The number of his admirers enlarged again when he took up residence in Venice." As a matter of fact, no item of information is possessed with regard to Vivaldi's stay in Mantua other than the few lines in the aforementioned letter, in which he says he lived there for three years. He does not specify the period, but there are good reasons for placing it around 1718–1722. The rest is pure imagination.

I have already named some pupils that Vivaldi had, beginning with these years. To these must be added the singers whom he trained for the opera, and the amateur violinists, such as Uffenbach, who passed through Venice, as well as those who were in-

habitants of that city. One of the latter was the aristocrat Vettor
Delfino, to whom Vivaldi's *Stravaganza*, published around 1713,
was dedicated. In his dedication the composer renders hyperbolic
homage. He states that the musical attainments of this gentleman
are so extensive that there is no virtuoso who would not be
honored to have him as his teacher, and he declares himself to
have been to him "a companion rather than a director of studies."

Among the professionals Pisendel is the violinist whose work
most openly bears the impress of Vivaldi's teaching. There was
undoubtedly a pre-established harmony between their personalities. Through its possession of something inspired and genuine,
the personality of the young Saxon must have compelled the
interest of the master. Their relations were exceedingly cordial;
witness the concertos dedicated to Pisendel by Vivaldi or the
adagio ornamented by the pupil, the manuscripts of which are
still preserved in the library of Dresden.

In 1717, at the instigation of the Elector of Saxony, Pisendel
had occasion to play a concerto by Vivaldi as the entr'acte of an
opera performed at the Teatro Sant'Angelo or the Teatro San
Giovanni Crisostomo. This gave rise to a curious incident that
J. A. Hiller in 1767 recounted in his journal of weekly musical reports. "In the last part of the concerto [in *F*, P. 268] the solo
begins *cantabile* but at the end reaches a thirty-two measure
section of passage work completely in the high register. In this
section the musicians of the orchestra, all Italians, sought to
mortify Pisendel by rushing the accompaniment. But he did not
let himself be at all troubled by their way of hurrying; on the
contrary, he forced those who wished to set a trap for him to
abate by strongly marking the tempo with his foot, so much that
they were confounded. The prince had great glee from it. With
much delight he himself forthwith related this act of Pisendel's
presence of mind to Madame Angioletta." Later, in his *Lebensbe-
schreibungen berühmter Musikgelehrten* (1784), Hiller tells us
of an occurrence that befell the young German one day in the
same year (1717) while he was walking in the Piazza di San
Marco with Vivaldi. The latter abruptly interrupted the con-
versation and in a low voice directed Pisendel to return immediately with him to his residence. Once under cover, he explained

to him why they had got out of sight. It was because four constables had for a long time been following and scrutinizing the young Pisendel. Had he perpetrated any deed or uttered any remark that was reprehensible? Upon his denials Vivaldi asked him not to leave before he had cleared up the matter. He saw one of the Inquisitors and finally learned that a malefactor was being sought who had some resemblance to Pisendel, but the house where he was hiding had only just been discovered. So the innocent man who had been unjustly suspected was allowed to resume his walk.

From 1718 to 1722 Vivaldi does not appear in the records of the Pietà. If, as may be conjectured, he was then at Mantua in the service of the Landgrave of Hesse-Darmstadt, it must be conceded that his new duties did not prohibit him from returning himself to his native city. There two of his operas, *Artabano re de' Parti* and *Armida al Campo d'Egitto*, were given during the winter season of 1718. During the autumn of 1720 *La Verità in Cimento* was produced there, and during the winter of 1721 *Filippo Re di Macedonia*. Also, on June 22 in Florence, he had his *Scanderbegh* performed for the reopening of the Teatro della Pergola, an opera of which no trace remains. Likewise, in 1718 *La Costanza trionfante*, which had been performed for the first time in Venice two years earlier, was given at the Munich court.

On the other hand, the Englishman Edward Wright, who traveled through Italy in 1720–22, saw Vivaldi take part in orchestral performances in Venice. (The composer undoubtedly directed the other musicians and played the solo violin, unless he was supervising from the harpsichord or organ.) "It is very usual," wrote the traveler, "to see priests play in the orchestra. The famous Vivaldi, whom they call the *Prete Rosso*, very well known among us for his concertos, was a topping man among them at Venice."

To the evidences of his wide repute at this time there was added one in 1930 that is rather odd. An annotated copy of Marcello's *Teatro alla moda* recovered by Francesco Malipiero enabled him to interpret the frontispiece of the pamphlet, which is full of allusions that contemporaries probably found very plain but which for two centuries no one had understood in the least.

In the frontispiece there is pictured a large Venetian gondola, a *peota*. At the prow stands a bewigged bear carrying a flag whose staff rests on his shoulder. At the stern perches a little angel, wearing a priest's hat and playing a violin, one foot on the tiller, one foot in the air. Underneath is the following inscription:

Stampato ne BORGHI di BELISANIA per ALDIVIVA
LICANTE all'Insegna dell'ORSO in PEATA.
Si vende nella STRADA del CORALLO alla
PORTA del PALAZZO d'ORLANDO

Printed in the SUBURBS of BELISANIA for ALDIVIVA
LICANTE at the Sign of the BEAR in the BOAT
For sale in CORAL STREET at the
GATE of ORLANDO'S PALACE

Now, the annotations in the copy discovered by Francesco Malipiero indicate, in addition to the exact date of publication (December, 1720), the celebrities referred to by the words printed in capital letters. All these words refer to theatrical people— several singers and impresarios and at least one composer. Vivaldi is defined as follows: "Aldiviva: Vivaldi, the celebrated violin virtuoso and composer of operas at the Sant'Angelo. [*Aldiviva: Mon.r Vivaldi virtuoso celebre di violino e compositore delle opere in Sant'Angelo.*]" Further on, the anonymous writer informs us that the violin-playing angel represents both the Teatro Sant'Angelo and Vivaldi, who regularly supplied it with operas.

Through the angel in the shape of the protector or guardian of the boat we are given to understand the theater of which the aforesaid Signor Modotto [the rower of the boat] is the impresario, but through the hat on its head and the violin held by the angel, who has its foot in the air, it comes to signify Vivaldi, in whom the aforesaid Modotto puts his entire trust. So does Vivaldi play the violin and have him going with two oars, and so, with his foot in the air, does he push as well as beat time.

[*"Per 'l'Angelo' in figura di protettore, o custode del bastimento si dà intendere il teatro di cui è impresario il sopradetto signor Modotto: ma per il cappello in testa, e violino in mano, toccato dall' 'Angelo' con piede in aria, si viene a significare Mon.r Vivaldi, al quale il detto*

Modotto s'è interamente affidato. Mon.r Vivaldi adunque ghe la suona, lo fa andar a due remi, e col piede in aria, oltre il far la battuta, gli dà la spinta."]

On the strength of this it would be right to suppose that Marcello's lampoon was directed above all at Vivaldi.

In 1723 Vivaldi reappears in the archives of the Pietà. The Notatorio stipulates in the entry of July 2 that the composer shall, during the time when he will be in Venice, guarantee two concerts a month, for the remuneration of a sequin for each concert, and that he shall direct three or four rehearsals preceding each concert for the purpose of getting the young performers "in good condition to play properly." This text clearly indicates the state of affairs for Vivaldi. He had become famous, a man to be reckoned with. The asylum had recourse to his talents as often as possible, but it gave him license to subordinate his teaching to the needs of his career as a dramatic composer and a touring virtuoso. He appears intermittently in the cashbooks of 1724 and 1725. From 1725 to 1735 there is nothing.

This is the period of distant expeditions, coupled with reappearances in Venice for the purpose of staging one or another new opera. Concerning these long trips, the letter of November 16, 1737, quoted above, leaves no room for doubt. "Fourteen years ago [that is, before 1737] we went together [with Anna Giraud] to a good many European cities. . . . I have spent three Carnival seasons at Rome for the opera. . . . I have been called to Vienna," and so on.

With regard to the three opera seasons at Rome, one of the three has not been definitely ascertained. The other two were those of 1723 and 1724. On January 23, 1723, the Teatro Capranica gave Vivaldi's *Ercole sul Termodonte* under his direction. The Vatican library owns an amusing sketch by Ghezzi discovered by the esteemed Professor Alberto Cametti. (I published it with his co-operation in the *Revue de Musicologie* of November, 1930.) It carries this inscription: "The Red Priest, the composer who did the opera at the Capranica in 1723. [*Il prete rosso comp. di musica che fece l'opera a Capranica del 1723.*]" In the following year the performances of *Il Giustino* and *La Virtù trionfante dell'amore e dell'odio ovvero Tigrane* took place. The excitement created was great enough for the Holy Father to manifest a desire to hear Vivaldi play the violin; he did not spare his commendations.

Vivaldi's style became the style of the moment. Especially copied was a certain kind of rhythmic movement that he had not in fact invented but had established. It is what was called Lombard rhythm or *manière lombarde;* essentially it consists of the reversing of the very common pattern ♩. ♪ into ♪ ♩. .

J. J. Quantz was struck by this craze upon his arrival at Rome in July, 1724. He was later to write, calling up his memories for his autobiography, "What came most often to my ears was the Lombard style [*lombardischer Geschmack*]. Vivaldi had just imported it to Rome with his operas and had, thanks to that style, captivated the Romans to such an extent that they would no longer, as it were, endure what was not conceived in that style."

Quantz met with Vivaldi again, in 1726 in Venice, conducting the orchestra at the Teatro Sant'Angelo, which had already presented his *Inganno trionfante in amore* and that year gave no less than four of his operas. The Abbé Conti, writing to Madame de Caylus from Venice on February 23, 1727, at the end of the season, indicated to her that "Vivaldi has brought forth three operas in less than three months, two for Venice and the third for Florence; the last has re-established the theater of that city and brought in much money."

In 1727 Vivaldi certainly returned, if indeed he had absented himself during so active a season, for the purpose of producing *Orlando.* And it may be conjectured that he directed the concert of his works that took place on September 19, at the festivities given by the French ambassador in honor of the birth of the royal princesses of his country. Around eight o'clock in the evening there was, said the *Mercure de France,* "a very beautiful instrumental concert, which lasted nearly two hours; the music for this as well as for the *Te Deum* was by the famous Vivaldi."

It was probably in 1728 that he made the trip to Vienna to which he refers in his letter of November, 1737. This would explain the dedication that appears on the manuscript parts—they are not autographs—of *La Cetra,* Opus 9, concertos preserved at the Nationalbibliothek; the dedication reads *La Cetra Con-*

certi Consecrati alla Sacra, Cesarea, Cattolica, Real Maestà di Carlo VI Imperadore [sic] . . . *l'anno 1728.* Again through the Abbé Conti we learn that in this same year (1728) the emperor Charles VI, an ardent music lover, met Vivaldi at Venice or Trieste (on this point the wording is ambiguous). "The Emperor remained for two days at Trieste, but he came neither to Bucari or Fiume. . . . Give my compliments to the count your son; tell him that the Emperor gave a large sum of money to Vivaldi along with a chain and a gold medallion and made him a chevalier." And again the Abbé Conti writes, "The Emperor was not too satisfied with his Trieste. . . . The Emperor conversed for a long time with Vivaldi on music; they say that he talked longer to him alone in fifteen days than he has talked to his ministers in two years." Perhaps Vivaldi was at this time attached to the imperial court, but the presentation of *Rosilena ed Oronta* during the winter season must have brought the traveler to his native city for a time.

Then comes a space of three years concerning which we are bereft of all information. His dramatic output breaks off, and the records of the Pietà tell us nothing of him. We do not know whether to charge these lacks to illness or to absence. However, in the Venetian archives Rodolfo Gallo in 1938 came upon the deliberations of September 30, 1729, in which it appears that Giovanni Battista Vivaldi, the father of Antonio, asked for permission to leave the service of the ducal chapel for a year so that he might accompany his son to Germany—most certainly Antonio, for one can hardly see how the two barber brothers could have had business abroad, except when they had gotten themselves banished from the city.

There is reason to believe that Vivaldi was absent or ill in 1731, since in that year the Teatro Sant'Angelo had recourse to the good offices of the arranger Galeazzi in order to give an adaptation of a Vivaldi opera under the title of *L'Odio vinto dalla costanza.* This was *La costanza trionfante degli amore e degli odi,* performed in 1716, and already recast by its composer as *Artabano re de' Parti.* Likewise in 1731, the Teatro Santa Margherita staged *Armida al campo d'Egitto* with music by several composers, whereas the original, produced at the Teatro San Moise in 1718, had a score wholly written by Vivaldi.

In 1732 his dramatic production resumed with *Semiramide*, played at Mantua, and *La Fida Ninfa* at Verona. Until 1739 his operas were parcelled out at the rate of one or two a year among Venice, Florence, Verona, and Ancona.

The deliberations of the administrative council of the Pietà mark his reappearance in 1735 as *maestro de' concerti* at the annual salary of one hundred ducats. At that time he again took up his job of supplying instrumental music; on September 6 he was paid forty-four lire for some "*sonate di musica*," which could be, in truth, concertos or symphonies, for the terminology of the time was something less than precise. And the Notatorio reinstated him in his duties as *maestro de' concerti* while specifying that he carry on "with no idea of leaving any more as has been his practice in past years [*senza idea di più partire come aveva praticato negli anni passati*]." Later, in a well-known passage from Goldoni's *Memoirs*, we shall see another evidence of his activities in 1735. For 1736 payments made to Vivaldi by the Pietà are again recorded.

From the following year dates the first performance of *Catone*, which occurred in Verona, where Vivaldi was on May 13. Charles Albert, the Elector of Bavaria, and his wife were to hear this work on March 26, and it "did not fail to please." They were also present in June at a concert by the Pietà, whose orchestra struck them as admirable, whereas the voices "did not have anything extraordinary about them."

In 1738 there took place the only trip outside Italy on which we are informed, although Vivaldi had undoubtedly made others. The governors of the theater of Amsterdam had decided to commemorate the centenary of that institution. They arranged a solemn spectacle for January 7, and wanting to put a composer of European reputation in charge, they called upon Vivaldi, who came to organize personally the musical part of the spectacle. He was already very well-known in Holland, where all his instrumental work had been printed by Estienne Roger and Michel Charles Le Cène; perhaps he had even come there previously to meet with them. He was always received as a distinguished guest, and so it was in this instance.

What the ceremonies consisted of we learn from the Dutch musicologist Daniel François Scheurleer, who in 1909 reported on his recovery of the complete account of the festivities in a record drawn up by a contemporary amateur with all the original documents as support, bound in two sumptuous volumes. The spectacle included two plays set off with music—a tragedy by Pieter Langendijk, *Caesar and Cato,* and an occasional piece by Jean de Marre, *Het Eeuwgetijde van den Amsteldamschen Schouwburg (The Centenary of the Amsterdam Theater).* The music, which is preserved in its entirety, comprised ten numbers and included nine sinfonie for strings, two by Chinzer and one each by Agrell, Hubfelt (Bernard Hubfeld, a pupil of Agrell), Fesch, Temanza, and three unidentified composers.

These sinfonie were preceded by a more ample work that would have served as an overture, a concerto grosso by Vivaldi in three movements (*allegro-grave-allegro*) "*a 10 Stromenti*" (P. 444), the instruments being a solo violin, two oboes, two hunting horns, the four-part string ensemble, and timpani. The Venetian directed the orchestra, probably with bow in hand, because the harpsichord was played by an Amsterdam organist, Jan Ulhorn.

It was in this year or the next that Vivaldi, in the presence of Ferdinand of Bavaria, the brother of the Elector Charles Albert, conducted the performance of his *Mopso,* "a piscatorial eclogue for five voices [*egloga pescatoria a cinque voci*]." According to Caffi's historical manuscripts in the Marciana Library of Venice, the prince, who wished to especially honor the young women of the Pietà by paying them a visit, highly appreciated the cantata and particularly praised "the brilliant and very full orchestral accompaniment, which has always made for the fame of the institution." On that occasion the Prete Rosso was showered with honors and presents.

A good observer, Charles de Brosses, met him in August, 1739. "Vivaldi became my intimate friend," he wrote to his correspondent M. le Blancey, "for the purpose of selling me some very costly concertos. He was partly successful in this, and I was successful in what I wanted, which was to hear him and have frequent and good musical diversion. He is a *vecchio*, who composes furiously and prodigiously. I have heard him undertake to compose a concerto with all its parts more quickly than a copyist could copy it. I found to my great astonishment that he was not as esteemed as he deserves in this country where all is fashion, where his works have been heard for a long time and the music of the preceding year no longer brings in receipts." We shall probably never know at what price this French traveler was willing to acquire the concertos for which he considered he had paid "very dearly." But the purchase price that the administrators of the Pietà accorded to the *vecchio* for his compositions is known; I shall come back to it a little further on.

A valuable collection of the Dresden Landesbibliothek contains scores of the following:

Concertos for several instruments played by the girls of the charitable asylum of the Pietà before His Royal Highness the Most Serene Frederick Christian, Royal Prince of Poland and Electoral Prince of Saxony. Music by Don Antonio Vivaldi, *maestro de' concerti* at the aforesaid asylum. In Venice in the year 1740.

[*Concerti con molti Istromenti Suonati dalle Figlie del Pio Ospitale della Pietà avanti Sua Altezza Reale Il Serenissimo Federico Cristiano Prencipe Reale di Polonia et Elettorale di Sassonia. Musica di D. Antonio Vivaldi Maestro de Concerti dell'Ospitale Sudetto. In Venezia nell'anno 1740.*]

On December 19, 1739, Prince Frederick Christian, son of Frederick Augustus, King of Poland and Elector of Saxony, arrived in Venice. He came from Naples, then the home of his sister, who the year before had married Don Carlos, the future Charles III of Spain. Lodged in the Foscarini Palace, honored with an escort of four very select aristocrats, the young prince had a most eventful stay. There were entertainments of all sorts —masquerades, opera performances, jousts, serenades, nautical amusements, wrestling, bull fights, visits to public buildings, churches, arsenals, and famous factories, such as the glassworks of the islands.

Throughout these festivities much music was performed; and, judging from the place they occupy in the official records, the three soirées got up by the young women of the Pietà, the Mendicanti, and the Incurabili, on March 21 and 29 and April 4, respectively, undoubtedly gained the greatest honor. For the first of these, that given by the Pietà, a spacious hall, hung with gold brocade and damask, was used. Dazzling light played on the crystal chandeliers. In the neighborhood of the Ospedale even the canal was lighted. On a stage ingeniously fitted up with mechanical contrivances, the *ospealiere* performed a cantata, *Il Coro delle Muse*, in which Melpomene and her companions extol the attainments of the illustrious visitor. Singing it were Apollonia, Bolognese, Giuletta, Ambrosina, Fortunata, Margherita, Teresa, Albetta, and Chiaretta, whom de Brosses praised as a violinist and who accordingly combined the talents of an instrumentalist and a singer.

At the end of the first part of the cantata the libretto mentions that the *Concerto di Viola d'Amore e Leuto col ripieno di moltissimo Strumenti* follows. This is the third concerto of the Dresden collection (P. 266). At the end of the second part the *Concerto a Violini obbligati con Eco* (P. 222) is called for, this being the second concerto in the same collection. The first concerto (P. 16) and the sinfonia that completes this volume were to be performed as an overture and a piece to close the ceremonies.

Now, I have found in the records of the Pietà the payment that corresponds to these four works—fifteen ducats, thirteen lire, placed to the credit of Vivaldi on April 27, a little more than a month after the entertainment, "for three concertos and a sinfonia." Another document specifies their character as occasional works; "*Antonio Vivaldi maestro di concerti per haver composto trois* [sic] *concerti ed una sinfonia . . . duc*[*ati*] *15.13.*"

Shortly after this settlement, on May 12, 1740, he received the sum of seventy ducats, twenty-three lire, for a series of twenty concertos. One gets the impression that, on the verge of quitting his position at the Pietà, he was selling off pieces that formed part of a previously constituted repository. From that time on, he is no longer spoken of.

Both the date and place of Vivaldi's death remained mysterious up until recent years. Nearly all historians and lexicographers considered that he died in 1743, relying on a phrase in Lacombe's *Dictionnaire portatif des Beaux-Arts* (1753 edition) that sets his death at "about ten years" back. More explicitly, Gerber, in his new dictionary of 1814, states, *"Er starb im J. 1743."* It was tacitly accepted that he died in Venice, although the necrology that is extant in the state archives does not mention it.

Only in 1938 did Rudolfo Gallo present in the *Ateneo Veneto* an exact documentation by which he established that Vivaldi died in Vienna, not Venice, at the end of July, 1741. Before then Giuseppe Ortolani, in his preface to an edition of Goldoni's complete works (1935), had named Vienna as the place of Vivaldi's death, perhaps following a passage in the *Commemoriali Gradenigo:* "173 . . . Antonio Vivaldi, the incomparable violin virtuoso, called the Red Priest, was very highly regarded for his compositions and had earned at one time more than 50,000 [5,000?] ducats, but his inordinate extravagance caused him to die poor, in Vienna."

Starting from this information, Signor Gallo did some research in Vienna and found in the necrology of the parish of St. Stephen for the year 1741 the precise details that until then had remained unknown. Vivaldi had died in the house of a certain Satler in the parish of St. Stephen near the Kärntnertor; he was buried on July 28, 1741, in the cemetery of the Bürgerspital, a cemetery for indigents, which has since disappeared. The necrology refers to his capacity as a priest (*"Weltl. Priester"*). The accounts of the parish indicate in a rather vague way that he died of an internal inflammation. They furnish information as to the costs deducted for his humble obsequies—nineteen florins, forty-five kreutzer. He was entitled only to the *"Kleingleuth [Kleingeläut]"* or ringing of bells for the poor, which cost two florins thirty-six, to six pallbearers, and to six choirboys; whereas a nobleman buried by night had the knell at four florins twenty, eight pallbearers, twelve choirboys, and six musicians, with the rest in keeping, the expenses totaling 102 florins.

It cannot be said that Vivaldi's contemporaries realized the loss represented by the passing of such a master. It is unaccountable to us that this sad close to a few years of resounding triumph should have caused so little stir. Let us add that, beginning in 1740, the administrators of the Pietà replaced this genius with *maestri di*

coro and *di cappella* of slight repute. (Several of them, such as
Alessandro Gennaro, had already been appointed to temporary
duties.) It was only in 1742 that a name was to appear that was
worthy of succeeding Vivaldi's, that of Nicolo Porpora. On the
fourteenth of March, Porpora received ninety-five ducats as payment for two months of service, and payments continued down
to November 6, when he reached the sum of forty-seven ducats,
seventeen lire, monthly. This was a much larger amount than
Vivaldi had received after a comparable length of service.

The glittering exception of Porpora does not, however, change
the fact that Vivaldi's death marks the beginning of a slow decline for the Pietà. If, moreover, we again have recourse to the
letters and memoirs of the time, we get the sense of a general
regression in taste during the second half of the eighteenth
century; only in the performing talent of the Venetian asylums
might we see on the whole an exception to this. The picture of
customs remains the same. "In these conservatorios, administered
with earnestness by some elderly Senators, orphans and foundlings
are raised, supported, and endowed with considerable means. . . .
Music makes up the fundamental part of an education that appears
more appropriate to form Laises and Aspasias than nuns or moth-
ers of families." Thus wrote P. J. Grosley in his *Nouveaux
mémoires* (1764) of observations made in 1758.

Such is the dominant note, and most of the observers connect
this gradual disintegration with a growing perversion of style.
At the Incurabili in 1764 Dittersdorf heard a commonplace oratorio performed inharmoniously and inaccurately; he records his
great disappointment in his autobiography (1801). The *Re-
marques sur la musique et la danse, ou Lettres de M. G. à Milord
P.* [Pembroke], published in 1773, speaks mockingly of the
oratorios having become "the storehouse for performers who
excel in singing to side drums, timpani, and trumpets," and of
their instilling not piety but the wish "to dance a rigadoon or to
glide through a minuet." Incidentally, this lampoon could well
have been written by the anonymous author—unquestionably to
be identified as Ange Goudar—who wrote *Le Brigandage de la
musique italienne* (1777). There the same features are found, more
fully developed. "The church, changed into the pit of a theater, is

always filled with spectators, most of them foreigners. A ticket, which is taken at the door, costs only *due soldetti;* therefore, the hall is always full. The violinist, the flutist, the oboist, the timpanist, the organist, and the chalumeau player are of the feminine gender. They pray to God with a great deal of gaiety, that is, always in the style of a rigadoon or a minuet. The players in the spiritual show are always seen through a screen. Nevertheless, the Venetian nobles who are their governors keep them under lock and key, since the organist of these conservatorios who directed the orchestra was found to be pregnant to the great horror of those who had not yet been."

The Pietà cut perhaps a better figure than the three rival houses. Among its other claims to fame was that the great violinist Regina Strinasacchi had been trained there. With his customary precision Burney gave a description of this institution in the month of August, 1770, some thirty years after Vivaldi's death. Despite the objection of repetitiveness, I shall reprint an extensive extract from his account, which permits us to gauge accurately the road traveled.

I went to . . . the Pietà the evening of my arrival, Saturday, August 4. The present *maestro di cappella* is Signor Furlanetti, a priest, and the performers, both vocal and instrumental, are all girls; the organ, violins, flutes, violoncellos, and even French horns, are supplied by these females. It is a kind of foundling hospital for natural children, under the protection of several nobles, citizens, and merchants, who though the revenue is very great, yet contribute annually to its support. These girls are maintained here till they are married, and all those who have talents for music are taught by the best masters of Italy. The composition and performance I heard tonight did not exceed mediocrity. . . .

Then, for August 11 he wrote the following:

This afternoon I went to the Pietà; there was not much company, and the girls played a thousand tricks in singing, particularly in the duets, where there was a trial of skill and of natural powers, as who could go highest, lowest, swell a note the longest, or run divisions with the greatest rapidity.

A little after this, in 1786, the young composer Gyrowetz was no less disappointed than was Dittersdorf by the undistinguished musical atmosphere of Venice and the general debasement of taste. "The musical conservatorio for young women gave a concert from time to time consisting almost solely of vocal music. It indeed possessed several gifted orchestral directors, but these masters were almost continually absent, having been called to other cities in Italy for the purpose of composing operas" (*Autobiographie*, 1848).

Johann Christian Maier's *Beschreibung von Venedig* (1789) supplies us afresh with a detailed picture of the musical activities of the asylums. Particulars are to be found there as to the quality of interpretation and the abundance of beautiful voices—sopranos whose range covered nearly three octaves, contraltos able to sing bass parts. Among the latter was a certain Capitona of the Ospedaletto, who, when she was heard, could be taken for a man, which did not prevent her marriage to an aristocrat. Contrary to Rousseau, Maier found the voices less moving than they were beautiful and well-trained. According to him, this results from the fact that the young women sing in Latin without understanding the text, and "even when they perform the most emotional opera arias, one can, without being a great connoisseur, discern in their most vehement tones not the native character of the emotion but a wretched imitation."

From that time the period of brilliance is indeed no more. The conservatorio of the Incurabili ceased to exist in 1782. In 1796 it was the turn of the Mendicanti, soon followed by the Ospedaletto. The Pietà outlived the three other asylums, but it was a diminished, lackluster existence. Fétis in 1831 records it in melancholy terms for the *Revue Musicale*. "The Pietà, the only [conservatorio] that exists until this day, although it is no more than a shadow of what it formerly was, is now under the direction of Perotti." To this comment an echo is made a dozen years later (1843) in a statement from Francesco Caffi's letter to his friend Cicogna; it seems to close the history of the institution in all that relates to its artistic life. "The Pietà still exists, but from the musical point of view it is no more than an empty semblance."

VIVALDI THE MAN

Having reconstructed Vivaldi's career after a fashion, let us return and try to rediscover the man. As to outward appearance we can summon up a rather exact image of him without too much difficulty. Five portraits are extant, two of which are worth describing in detail:

1) There is the very lively sketch made by P. L. Ghezzi in 1723, which was mentioned above. The Prete Rosso appears in profile, half-length. He is portrayed as having long and curly hair, a somewhat receding forehead, a prominent, arched nose, widely dilated nostrils, a large mouth, half open, and a pointed chin. His glance is lively, his expression interested and willful.

2) The engraving by François Morellon de La Cave, a Dutch artist of French origin, done two years later than the Ghezzi sketch, is much more formally worked out but also much less expressive. The composer is seen firmly planted before his writing desk; he holds in his right hand, which is brought up against his chest, a notebook of music paper where some measures typical of Vivaldi may be read. The features of the face are vague and a little sheeplike, the hair so well-groomed that it may be taken for a wig. The full, round cheeks give Vivaldi the look of a nice young man, well fed and happy to be alive. Nevertheless, to express the turbulence of inspiration the portraitist has opened wide the collar of his shirt and put in a ribbon that floats from it untied.

James Caldwell's engraving, printed in Hawkins' *History of Music*, and that of the younger Lambert in the *Galerie des violons et luthiers célèbres* (1818) copy La Cave's portrait while weakening it. Finally, Francesco Vatielli published and annotated in the *Rassegna Musicale* (1938) a portrait preserved in the Liceo Musicale of Bologna, which comes, it is believed, from the Martini collection. Vivaldi is here represented full face, half-length. He is dressed with starchy formality, and he wears a wig and lace ruffles. In his left hand he holds a violin, in his right a quill pen. A sheet of music paper is before him. The expression of his face is serious and a little stiff.

Ghezzi's drawing has our confidence more than La Cave's or his plagiarists' or the anonymous artist's at Bologna. All save Ghezzi were working on behalf of the general public, if not for posterity; they try above all to be decorative. Ghezzi had no ulterior motive in dashing off a likeness of his prominent contemporary on a loose piece of paper. Besides, that determined and headstrong look is much more in line with Vivaldi's character than the unctuous smile of the academic portraits.

It is known that he could at times express himself sharply. On the manuscript of the concerto in *A* dedicated to Pisendel (P. 228), he believed that in measures 61–66 of the finale he had to indicate by figures some simple harmonies that should have been self-evident. And to show clearly to the recipient that this precaution was not directed to him and was aimed only at blockheads, he added in large letters, "*Per li Coglioni.*"

He also knew how to be playful. Caffi, in the material lodged unpublished in his *Storia della Musica teatrale*, mentions a certain number of humorous compositions—*Concerto de' Cucchi* (*Concerto of the Cuckoos*), *Coro delle Monache* (*Choir of Nuns*), and others—designed to serve as entertainment to the aristocrats.

If we cannot safely accept as accurate the kindly facial expression given to Vivaldi by La Cave and those who copied him, we can place no more confidence in the air of robust health that they have bestowed on the composer. We have seen already that he was weakly, having been afflicted from birth with a serious illness. Indeed this prohibited all physical effort to such a degree that he could not travel without a retinue of four or five persons.

He was not, however, prevented from being uncommonly hard working and from combining the manifold activities of virtuoso, teacher, composer, and impresario. Those of his letters that have been preserved give an exact and picturesque idea of this last aspect of his personality. They deal with a single opera season at Ferrara. Vivaldi recruited the virtuosos and the dancers, discussed the tickets, adjusted the length of the show to the nature of its expected public, had the copies made, and resisted the whims of the dancers who held it their right to do as they pleased. In all this correspondence there is evidence of a good dose of practical common sense. Quotations made above from the letters of Charles de Brosses and the diary of J. F. von Uffenbach have given indications of this trait.

Also recorded in Vivaldi's letters is much docility and humbleness before the great. In this the composer conformed to established practice. The few dedications of his that have lasted down to our time do not hesitate to push eulogy to the point of patent flattery. This, it is true, was apparently still the absolute rule at the close of the eighteenth century as it had been ever since the sixteenth. Vivaldi chose well the recipients of each of his dedications—at one time (for Opus 2) Frederick IV of Denmark; at another (Opus 3) His Royal Highness Ferdinand III, "*gran prencipe di Toscana*"; for Opus 8, "*l'Illustrissimo Signor Venceslao conte di Marzin* [Morzin], *Signore Ereditario di Hohenelbe, Lomnitz, Tschista, Krzinetz, Kaunitz, Doubek e Sowoluska, Cameriere Attuale, e Consigliere di S.M.C.C.*"; and for Opus 9, the "*Sacra, Cesarea, Cattolica, Real Maestà di Carlo VI Imperadore* [sic] *e Terzo Re delle Spagne di Bohemia di Ungaria. . . .*"

The first of these dedications, the one to Frederick IV, portrays for us a ruler "*Grande per Nascita, ma più Grande per Virtù*" and goes on to acknowledge the following: "You descended from the throne and your humility put aside the trappings of your exalted position so as to console all who bowed down to confess themselves unworthy of even kissing the lowest step of your throne . . . [*Voi scendeste dal Trono e l'humiltà tolse gli impedimenti della Vostra Altezza per consolare chi tutto inchinato confessasi indegno di nè pur baciare l'ultimo gradino del Vostro Soglio*]."

The dedication of *L'Estro armonico* (Opus 3) is just as humble. The "*sopraggrande*" merit of the recipient, the unworthiness of the work offered to him, and notwithstanding this the "*somma Benignità*" of an "*Animo Eccelso*" that disdains nothing and receives everything kindly—these touches are repeated with an insistence that may entertain those who read on the following leaf these few lines addressed, again by Vivaldi, "To the Lovers of Music."

The generous indulgence that up till now you have granted to my weaknesses induces me to apply myself to please you by bringing forth a collection of instrumental concertos. I confess that, if in the past my compositions have had beyond their own shortcomings the misfortune of bad publication, today their greatest advantage is to have been engraved by the famous hand of Monsieur Estienne Roger. This is one of the reasons I have for laboring to please you by having these concertos printed, and it encourages me shortly to offer to you another series of concertos *a quattro*. Retain your kind regard for me. I wish you well.

Thus the prudent composer honored both the public and the publisher, whereas, as he puts it in the dedications of Opus 3 and Opus 4, the power of the eminent patron, the recipient of the work, ought to cut short in advance "the prattling of the malicious and the pedantic severity of the critics."

He offers the sponsorship of Opus 4 to the aristocrat Vettor Delfino, who was his pupil but whom he hastens in a spirit of boundless generosity to declare his equal. Addressing himself to Count Morzin, Vivaldi acknowledges that he is having Opus 8 printed in order to bring it humbly to the feet of his most illustrious lordship. The customary hyperbolical compliments follow. But perhaps the most characteristic document in this connection is the dedication of *Rosmira*, a work performed at the Teatro Sant'Angelo in 1738. The inscription is addressed to Frederick, Margrave of Brandenburg. We may be permitted to quote it in its entirety because of its interest as well as because of the rarity of the document.

Your Most Serene Highness:

Whatever may be the tribute that my very devout respect offers with an audacious boldness to Your Highness, I hope to see it accepted. Princes of a merit as distinguished as yours do not proportion their approval to the humbleness of the gift, but to the greatness of their spirit. Receive then, O magnanimous one, this drama, which, coming from the felicitous pen of the renowned Silvio Stampiglia, is dedicated to you by me not to point out to you the direction of your future actions by delineating those of some past hero; you have no need to take examples from somewhere else when you have such frequent and illustrious ones in YOUR GREAT FAMILY. The glory of your father's family, that of your house, suffices for you, and you are too well aware of the privilege of your birth and of your endowments to go and search for better in times gone by and among foreign peoples. It is to entertain you that this opera has been composed; it happens that great princes have welcomed these pleasant entertainments with benevolence, thus providing rest for their souls from the grave cares of power. Such is my design; happy if I have realized it and if I at some time obtain pardon for my rashness, to be envied always even if I fail. I believe that it would, at any rate, be an honored blunder to which I owe the glory of putting at Your Highness' feet the testimony of my most profound respect, in this way declaring myself to be

of Your Royal Highness

the most humble, devoted, and respected servant,

Don Antonio Vivaldi

This very secular demeaning of oneself, a custom of the age, was allied in the Red Priest with an unfeigned piety. Gerber in his first *Lexicon* (1790–92) depicts him around 1730 as "exaggeratedly devout," to the point of letting go of his rosary only when he takes up his pen to write an opera. No one puts this most mercurial disposition in a more curious light than Goldoni in the famous passage of his *Memoirs* which I cannot resist reprinting here (taken from the first edition, published in French in 1787 at Paris).

Griselda had been chosen, an opera by Apostolo Zeno and Pariati, who worked together before Zeno left for Vienna in the service of the Emperor, and the composer who was to put it to music was the abbé Vivaldi, who is called, because of his hair, *il Prete Rosso* (the Red Priest). He was better known by this nickname than by his family name.

That clergyman, an excellent violin player and a middling composer, had taught Mlle. Giraud [this is the Anna Giraud mentioned in the letter of November 16, 1737] and given her training in singing; she was a young singer born in Venice, the daughter, however, of a French wigmaker. She was not pretty, but she had charms—a delicate figure, beautiful eyes, beautiful hair, a charming mouth, and not much of a voice, but much acting ability. It was she who was to portray the role of Griselda.

M. Grimani sent me to the musician's home in order to make the necessary changes in the opera, be they to shorten the drama or to change the position and the nature of the arias to suit the wishes of the actors and the composer. Therefore, I went to the home of the abbé Vivaldi, I presented myself on behalf of His Excellency Grimani, I found him surrounded by music and with his breviary in hand. He got up, he made a complete sign of the cross, he put his breviary aside, and made me the usual compliments. "What is the cause of my having the pleasure of seeing you, Monsieur?"

"His Excellency Grimani has entrusted me with the alterations that you think necessary in the opera of the Carnival. I have come to see, Monsieur, what your intentions are."

"Ah! Ah! Are you entrusted, Monsieur, with the alterations in my opera *Griselda?* Then M. Lalli is no longer connected with M. Grimani's productions?"

"M. Lalli, who is very elderly, will always profit from the dedicatory letters and the sales of the librettos, which does not concern me. I have the pleasure of busying myself in work that ought to amuse me, and I have the honor of beginning under the commands of M. Vivaldi." The abbé took up his breviary again, made another sign of the cross, and did not answer.

"Monsieur," I said to him, "I do not wish to distract you in your religious pursuit; I shall come back at another time."

"I am well aware, my dear sir, that you have a talent for poetry; I have seen your *Belisario*, which gave me great pleasure. But this is very different. One may be able to create a tragedy or an epic poem, if you please, and not be able to fashion a musical quatrain."

"Do me the honor of showing me your drama."

"Yes, yes, I am willing. Where then is *Griselda* tucked away? It was here. . . . *Deus in adjutorium meum intende . . . Domine . . . Domine . . . Domine. . . .* It was here just now. *Domine ad adjuvandum.* . . . Ah! Here it is. See, Monsieur, this scene between Gualtiere and Griselda; it is an interesting and moving scene The author has put a pathetic aria at the end, but Mlle. Giraud does not like the languid style of singing. She would like a piece with expression and excitement, an aria that expresses emotion by different means, by interrupted words, for example, by heaved sighs, by action and agitation; I don't know if you understand me."

"Yes, Monsieur, I quite clearly understand you. Moreover, I have had the honor of hearing Mlle. Giraud and I know that her voice is not very strong."

"Why, Monsieur, do you insult my pupil? She is good at everything; she sings everything."

"Yes, Monsieur, you are right. Give me the book and allow me to do it."

"No, Monsieur, I cannot give it up, I need it, and I am very hard pressed."

"Very well, Monsieur, if you are in a hurry, give me a moment and I shall gratify you at once."

"At once?"

"Yes, Monsieur, at once."

The abbé, while scoffing at me, held out the drama to me and gave me paper and a writing desk, again took up his breviary and recited his psalms and hymns while walking about. I reread the scene, with which I was already acquainted. I made a summing up of what the musician wanted, and in less than a quarter of an hour I wrote down the text for an aria of eight lines divided into two parts. I called the clergyman and showed him my work. Vivaldi read it and smoothed the wrinkles from his brow; he read it again and uttered cries of joy; he threw his prayer book on the ground and summoned Mlle. Giraud. She came.

"Ah!" he said to her, "Here is an unusual man, here is an excellent poet. Read this aria. It is this gentleman who has done it here without hedging and in less than a quarter of an hour." And coming back to me, he said, "Ah! Monsieur, I beg your pardon." And he embraced me and swore that he would never have another poet but me.

He entrusted me with the drama and ordered the alterations from me. He was always satisfied with me, and the opera succeeded excellently.

So it is that Vivaldi appears to us, when we have collected all the scattered testimony, as a man composed of contrasts—weak and sickly, yet of a fiery temperament; quick to become irritated, quick to become calm; quick to pass from worldly thoughts to a superstitious piety; tractable when necessary, but persevering; mystical, yet ready to come down to earth again when a specific concern was at issue, and by no means unskillful in handling his affairs. But above all, he was possessed by music and moved, in the words of de Brosses, "to compose furiously and prodigiously." As we shall see, it is no exaggeration to describe Vivaldi thus.

II

Vivaldi's Music: Style and Form

UNTIL the discovery some thirty years ago of the manuscripts bequeathed to the Biblioteca Nazionale in Turin by the Foà and Giordano families, Vivaldi was considered of importance only in the realm of instrumental music. As far as his dramatic music was concerned, of which the only available samples were a few isolated arias, old opinions prevailed that underestimated it outrageously. Finally, there was no awareness of his prolific output of sacred music, though several masterpieces in this category have since been popularized by records.

However, it remains true that it is chiefly through his instrumental music that Vivaldi's role is decisive. It is appropriate to begin with this, establishing first of all an outline of its chronology. In the beginning of the eighteenth century when the symphony and the concerto were being evolved, a difference of a few years greatly alters the perspective. At the time when the Red Priest was just being discovered, Luigi Torchi, in an article in the *Rivista Musicale Italiana* (1899), dates the publication of *L'Estro armonico* as 1740–1750 (actually it dates from 1712); in so doing he made Vivaldi a follower of J. S. Bach, Handel, Tartini, Locatelli, and Leclair, all of whom were actually in his debt to some extent. On the other hand, Fausto Torrefranca in his article on Vivaldi in the *Enciclopedia Italiana* (1937) relies on a daring interpretation of the catalogues of the Dutch publishers Roger and Le Cène, and antedates Vivaldi's first concertos by some ten years; this falsifies their relationship to the concertos of Torelli and Arcangelo Corelli among others, thus depriving these composers of a part of their originality.

I have discussed these questions of chronology at length in my earlier book on Vivaldi. I confine myself here to the results. I shall discuss only the published works, since with two or three exceptions the manuscripts do not carry dates and Vivaldi's handwriting developed in too capricious a fashion for a classification to be risked. Here then is a list of the printed collections of his instrumental music:

Opus 1: (12) *Suonate da Camera a Tre, Due violini, e Violone o Cembalo Consacrate All'Illustrissimo et Eccelentissimo Signor Conte Annibale Gambara Nobile Veneto. . . , Da D. Antonio Vivaldi Musico di Violino Professore Veneto Opera Prima. In Venetia. Da Gioseppe Sala MDCCV* (1705). Republished at Amsterdam by Estienne Roger *ca.* 1712–13, numbered 363.

Opus 2: (12) *Sonate A Violino, e Basso per il Cembalo Consagrate A Sua Maestà Il Re Federico Quarto di Danimarka. . . , Da D. Antonio Vivaldi Musico di Violino e Maestro de' Concerti. . . , (1709) Appresso Antonio Bortoli.* Republished at Amsterdam by Roger *ca.* 1712–13 under the same title with the addition of the words *opera Seconda*, the publication being numbered 2.

Opus 3: *L'Estro Armonico Concerti Consacrati All'Altezza Reale Di Ferdinando III Gran Prencipe di Toscana da Antonio Vivaldi. . . , Opera Terza Libro Primo A Amsterdam Aux dépens d' Estienne Roger Marchand, Libraire N° 50.* (*Libro Secondo* under the same title is indicated as No. 51.) Beginning with this collection, the first editions of all Vivaldi's printed works were published by Estienne Roger, his associates, or successors. The title of the collection may be taken to mean "the harmonic spirit" or, better, "harmonious inspiration" (compare the English word *oestrus* or the French *oestre*, which the dictionary defines as a vehement impulse or excitation). The work appeared in 1712 in two series of six concertos each, bound together.

Opus 4: *La Stravaganza Concerti Consacrati a Sua Eccellenza Il Sig. Vettor Delfino Nobile Veneto da Antonio Vivaldi. . . , Opera Quarta Libro Primo.* Amsterdam, Roger, No. 399. (*Libro Secondo* under the same title is indicated as No. 400.) *Ca.* 1712–13. Walsh's edition, which was undoubtedly put out a little after

1720, comprises only six concertos instead of twelve, Nos. 1, 2, 4, 9, and 11 of the Amsterdam publication with, for the sixth and last concerto, a work that does not appear in the above Amsterdam edition.

Opus 5: *VI Sonate Quatro a Violino Solo e Basso e due a due Violini e Basso Continuo di Antonio Vivaldi Opera Quinta O Vero Parte Seconda del Opera Seconda A Amsterdam chez Jeanne Roger*, No. 418, ca. 1716. These six sonatas are numbered 13 through 18, forming, as the title indicates, a continuation of the twelve sonatas of Opus 2.

Opus 6: *VI Concerti a Cinque Stromenti, Tre Violini Alto Viola e Basso Continuo di D. Antonio Vivaldi. . . , Opera Sesta A Amsterdam chez Jeanne Roger*, No. 452, *ca.* 1716–1717.

Opus 7: (12) *Concerti a Cinque Stromenti, tre Violini, Alto Viola e Basso Continuo di D. Antonio Vivaldi. . . , Opera Settima. Libro Primo. Uno è con Oboe. A Amsterdam chez Jeanne Roger*, No. 470 (*Libro Secondo* indicated as No. 471), *ca.* 1716–1717.

Opus 8: *Il Cimento* [*cimento* indicating a trial or venture] *dell'Armonia e dell'Inventione Concerti a 4 e 5 Consacrati All'Illustrissimo Signore Il Signor Venceslao Conte di Marzin. Da D. Antonio Vivaldi Maestro in Italia dell'Illustrissimo Conte Sudetto, Maestro de' Concerti del Pio Ospitale della Pietà in Venetia, e Maestro di Cappella di S.A.S. il Signor Principe Filippo Langravio d'Hassia Darmistath. Opera Ottava. Libro Primo*, Amsterdam, Le Cène, No. 520 (*Libro Secondo* indicated as No. 521), *ca.* 1725.

Opus 9: *La Cetra* [the lyre] *Concerti Consacrati Alla Sacra, Cesarea, Cattolica, Real Maestà di Carlo VI Imperadore e Terzo Re delle Spagne di Bohemia di Ungaria. . . , da D. Antonio Vivaldi, Opera Nona Libro Primo*, Amsterdam, Le Cène, No. 533 (*Libro Secondo* indicated as No. 534), 1728.

Opus 10: *VI Concerti a Flauto Traverso Violino Primo e Secondo Alto Viola Organo e Violoncello di D. Antonio Vivaldi. . . , Opera Decima*, Amsterdam, Le Cène, No. 544, *ca.* 1729–30.

Opus 11: *Sei Concerti a Violino Principale, Violino Primo e Secondo, Alto Viola, Organo e Violoncello di D. Antonio Vi-*

valdi. . . , *Opera Undecima*, Amsterdam, Le Cène, No. 545, *ca.* 1729–30.

Opus 12: Same title as the preceding except for the words *Opera Duodecima*, Amsterdam, Le Cène, No. 546, *ca.* 1729–30.

Opus 13: *Il Pastor Fido* (6) *Sonates, pour la Musette, Viele, Flûte, Hautbois, Violon avec la Basse Continüe Del Sigr Vivaldi. Opera XIIIe A Paris chez Me Boivin, Mde, rue St-Honoré à la Règle d'or, ca.* 1737.

Opus 14 (?): *VI Sonates Violoncello Solo col Basso da d'Antonio Vivaldi Musico di Violino e Maestro de' Concerti del Pio Ospidale della Pietà di Venezia gravé par Mlle Michelon,* Paris, Le Clerc, Le Clerc the younger, and Madame Boivin, *ca.* 1740. This publication, of which the only example that I know of is to be found in the Henry Prunières collection, does not carry an opus number. But several Paris publishers had around 1740 asked for and obtained licenses to transcribe and publish an Opus 14 by Vivaldi. This, if I am not mistaken, ought to be identified with those cello sonatas whose announcement appeared in the *Mercure de France* in December, 1740.

On the basis of the most thorough investigation, Vivaldi's instrumental work amounts to 554 pieces: 75 sonatas or trios (to the 74 listed in my *Inventaire thématique*[1] there is added a flute sonata acquired in 1940 by the library of Cambridge University); 2 organ pieces, the existence of which G. F. Malipiero was kind enough to point out to me (he recently discovered them at the end of a manuscript containing some works of Pescetti); 23 sinfonie; and 454 concertos.

Regarding the concertos, my *Inventaire thématique* lists 447. There is reason to subtract 2; one, P. 360, F. XII, 6, duplicates a sonata for five instruments that is found in the Dresden library, the other, P. 447, the attribution of which was conjectural, is actually by G. B. Sammartini and is found in the Blancheton collection of the Paris Conservatory. But 9 concertos are to be added: a concerto for violin and strings in *E*-flat discovered by

---

[1] The *Inventaire thématique* is the second volume of Marc Pincherle, *Antonio Vivaldi et la musique instrumentale*, 1948. The present work designates Vivaldi's works by numbers drawn from this *Inventaire* and from the *Opere complete*; see footnote, page 29 above.

Bence Szabolcsi in the Conservatorio San Pietro a Majella in
Naples (described by him along with two other concertos, which
were already known) in *Musica*, Rome, 1947; and 7 concertos for
cello and 1 for oboe, recently discovered in German libraries, for
the description of which I am obliged to Dr. Kolneder, director of
the Luxembourg Conservatory.

Ninety-six of the concertos were printed in the eighteenth
century. Of these, 71 are solo concertos for violin with string
orchestra, 2 are for violin or oboe, 2 for violin *scordatura*, 4 for
two violins, 4 for two violins and a solo cello, 2 for four violins,
2 for four violins and cello, 3 for oboe, and 6 for flute.

The 454 concertos as a whole present an exceedingly wide
variety of instrumentation. Nearly 300 are for one or more solo
violins joined with various combinations of string instruments,
sometimes with flutes, oboes, horns, or bassoons in addition.
There are 7 concertos for viola d'amore, 27 for cello, 22 for solo
flute, two flutes, or piccolo, and 37 for bassoon. A dozen are for
a real symphony orchestra which includes three or four desks of
woodwinds by two, nearly always with a solo violin predominat-
ing, while the concerti ripieni—some fifty of them—are, on the
contrary, actually symphonies for strings such as were to appear
a little later. Vivaldi's instrumental output is as impressive in its
diversity as in its abundance. To an outstanding Italian composer of today, Luigi Dallapiccola, is attributed the telling estima-
tion of Vivaldi as "the composer not of six hundred concertos
but of one concerto written six hundred times over." Such
phrases, too well put, must arouse our distrust. (Who has not, for
example, amused himself by turning the maxims of La Roche-
foucauld inside out, with the resulting reversed version being
nearly always as good as the original?) As regards Dallapiccola's
sally, nothing more supremely unfair can be imagined.

In so huge an output it is, to be sure, easy to expose examples
of negligence, to point out passages that may cause monotony because of the composer's letting down. First, there is the music of
others that the composer, pressed for time, appropriates for his
own use. I have already called attention to this common practice
of the time; be it noted that J. S. Bach did not deny himself this
resource. And then, above all, there is too extensive a use of

harmonic sequences, customarily by conjunct steps, which to our ears lack the element of the unexpected. But it should be observed that Vivaldi has recourse to this almost exclusively in passages designed to show off the soloist; at such moments, according to the musical customs of the times, the attention of the listeners was concentrated on the performance, while the constructive aspect receded from prominence. Attention was paid to how the virtuoso might manage this sequential passage work, to the ease and speed and the diversity of bowing he displayed, and to the ability he possessed to outdo himself in improvising new difficulties. Considered in the light of that time, the *rosalias* of Vivaldi are neither more nor less bearable than the cadential formulas readily accepted in the recitatives of the Bach Passions and in the Brandenburg Concertos.

And then, once granting these repetitions, of what weight are they in the face of the overflowing invention that characterizes the basic elements of Vivaldi's music—the melody, the rhythm, the harmonic and contrapuntal writing—as well as his orchestration and his manner of constructing a work? In *Antonio Vivaldi et la musique instrumentale* I investigated these particulars at great length. I shall take them up more briefly here, beginning with the nature and treatment of his themes.

THEMES, RHYTHM, DYNAMICS

At the time when the Red Priest wrote his first concertos, two styles were in open conflict—the old polyphonic style in which no one voice predominates, each being conceived to complete a whole in which its course is conditioned by that of its fellows; and, opposed to this, the newer monodic style in which the top voice monopolizes attention, the others being reduced to the simple function of accompaniment. Now, Vivaldi employs both styles of writing, which obviously govern very dissimilar melodic outlines. But above all he unites them, as very few of his contemporaries know how to do, in the course of a single work or even of a single concerto movement. It may occur to him to begin an *allegro* in the strict style; then imitation may be heard less and less, disappearing in favor of vertical harmony and per-

sisting only to the extent necessary to secure unity of construction.

Although Vivaldi's themes answer a variety of purposes, a certain number of essential features makes them as easy to recognize
as those of Mozart, Franck, or Fauré. They are marked by firmness of tonality, animation and ingenuity of rhythm, and breadth
of melodic phrasing, be it in an *allegro* or a *largo*.

The characteristic that compels recognition from the very
first is the strength of tonal feeling in the modern sense of major-
minor—what Maurice Emmanuel, ardent defender of the old
modes as he is, has called the "tyrant tonic." In studying Vivaldi's
forms we shall see how constantly they submit to its ascendancy.
Not only are the majority of the themes in the first movements
generated from the tonic triad or the tonic scale, but many among
them use only these elements. When Beethoven comes to build the
allegro of his *Eroica* with its well-known rudimentary theme as
the basis, he is far from being an innovator.

This insistence by Vivaldi upon establishing a tonality is found
pushed to its farthest limit as early as Opus 3. In the eleventh concerto, the first 5 measures of the *allegro* are made up solely of a
d chord; the following 14 measures continue over a pedal point
on *D* the persistent assertion of the same key in broken chords
and in diatonic patterns that grow more and more closepacked
and insistent. Opus 4, No. 11, begins in a similar spirit, with 10
measures on a *D* chord. In many themes having the characteristics
of a trumpet fanfare the opera overture is suggested. Others are
limited to brief calls of a few notes, which develop into less
schematic motives but which are at the outset nothing but the
three degrees of the scale that make up the tonic triad.

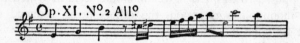

It is not surprising that J. S. Bach, so familiar with this music,
opens his violin concerto in *E* in the very same way—*E*, *G*-sharp,
B. Some such opening is met with throughout the eighteenth
century in a considerable number of violin concertos up to Viotti
and beyond. To cite only Mozart, whose instrumental music

abounds in themes of this kind, all his violin concertos from the second on begin with a tutti whose initial motive is none other than an arpeggiated tonic triad.

Vivaldi has other ways of simplifying the nature of symphonic themes, going so far as to be content with a tonic tone repeated in a sturdy rhythmic pattern:

or with the consonances of the fifth and octave, or, again, with fragments of the scale. These thematic patterns were to be adopted by the Italianized composers of France—Senaillé, Aubert, and even Leclair—and by all the Mannheim school, not to speak of Joseph Haydn, more than twenty of whose symphonies begin with a tonic triad spread out over one or two measures. Although very numerous in Vivaldi's work, such themes escape monotony by their brisk and varied rhythms. Because of this especially, he surpasses his precursors, Corelli and Torelli, and his contemporary, Albinoni.

Curiously enough, this emancipation, so manifest with the first collection of concertos, Opus 3, did not appear in the sonatas Opus 1 and Opus 2, although these were nearly contemporary with Opus 3. Unquestionably they do possess points of real beauty, but the composer's personality is scarcely released in them. Whereas the sonatas from the years of full maturity are typical of their composer—I am thinking of the four delightful sonatas for two violins and *basso continuo* in the Giordano collection at Turin, which can with the assent of the composer be played on two violins alone—Opus 1 and Opus 2 are clearly related to Corelli's work.

Not only does Opus 1 close with a *folia* based on a theme used by Corelli, but several movements in the same collection, for example the prelude of No. 8, also draw their inspiration from it. The celebrated gavotte in *F* from Opus 5, which Tartini was to vary in his *Arte dell'arco*, seems to have made even more of a mark. It is evoked rather naively in the prelude of the seventh

sonata, and is met with again in the allemande of the fourth sonata
of Opus 2:

We see it also in the gavotte with variation that terminates the
sonata in *F* dedicated to Pisendel, now owned by the Paris Conservatory. The same model, in more or less diluted form, is still
found in five or six concertos where other Corelli influences have
penetrated.

But in the concertos what there is in the way of reminiscences
—and on the whole they are rare—is swept away by a rhythmic
drive ever so much more imperative in Vivaldi than in the "sub-
lime Arcangelo." Here the *allegros* start off with an irresistible
pace. At times the opening themes have an incisive, somewhat
archaic stiffness and bear a resemblance to some that are found in
the overtures of Badia, M. A. Ziani, and M. A. Bononcini, or
in the concertos of Albinoni. At other times the *allegro* begins
with something borrowed from the same models, principally
Albinoni—a fixed pattern of repeated notes whose dynamic quality is so unmistakable that Vivaldi does not hesitate to use a good
half-dozen variants of it:

Op. III. Nº 6

These repeated notes in units of four or eight are not, as might
be expected, bound up with a systematic employment of phrasing
that groups measures by twos, fours, and eights. Not that Vivaldi's
phraseology is antipathetic to this, but it is far from being a slave
to it. Some vigorous tuttis are made up of ternary motives (measures grouped by threes), or of a mixture of ternary and binary.
Even when square phraseology seems to be adhered to, it is made
flexible by asymmetrical subtleties.

One peculiarity of Vivaldi's rhythm is the intimate association
of binary and ternary in themes that are written in four-beat meas-

ures but split up into groups of three measures; the stress comes in the first beat of each measure, so that the three accents following one another at a rather fast tempo give the impression of one measure in triple time.

(P. 53)

(Aside from Vivaldi, somewhat exceptional examples are also to be found, for instance, in Albinoni and Gaetano Maria Schiassi.)

More often ternary rhythm is brought about by accents that are not placed unvaryingly on the first beat, but come alternately on the first beat of one measure and the third of the following.

(P. 431, F. I, 79)

In reduced note values this would come out if taken down from dictation thus:

It can be seen that Vivaldi is less tied down to the barline than is ordinarily the case among the classical composers.

We have still to consider another rhythmic device that Vivaldi uses extensively—syncopation, and its corollary wherein rests fall on the strong beats. He calls on it for the most diverse effects—at one time for that rather feverish impulse, like a scarcely controllable agitation, which symphonists later on often imparted to the beginning of their *allegros:* Opus 8, Book 1, No. 9, F. VII, 1, opening of the first *allegro:*

At another time on the contrary, for an incontestable resolution:
P. 285, F. II, 17:

Or, again, for a kind of odd, disjointed swaying: Opus 12, No. 2, *allegro:*

The piquancy of this last effect may be emphasized by a persistent rhythmic pattern in the bass:

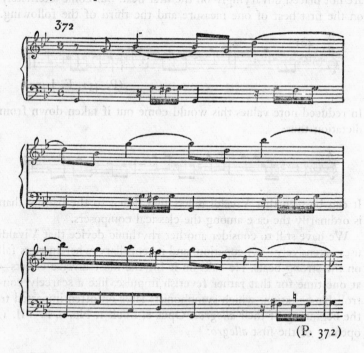

(P. 372)

Quite apart from the rhythm, the variety of Vivaldi's melodic inspiration is attested to by the greatly differing lengths of his themes—from a few measures or, indeed, notes, to long periods of a breadth unequaled in this era. The slow movement, which is nearly always free of old-fashioned counterpoint, suggests an opera aria or an arioso still more free in its progress. I call to mind the *larghetto* of Opus 3, No. 9, with its smoothly unfolding phrase of 22 measures, which pours forth in a continuous stream with neither repetition nor recapitulation. Here is another less well-known example, all the more significant in that it is taken not from a slow movement but from an *allegro*:

(P. 235, F. XI, 4)

The alternation of major and minor in this passage is to be noted, as is the inflection of the melody, which takes on here and there a singing character rather removed from the majesty that ordinarily marks the opening *allegro*.

As opposed to this plasticity, certain motives which are indubitably of dramatic intent have a savage violence that could without much exaggeration be termed Beethovenian. With due allowance, an inkling both of the scherzo of the Seventh Symphony and of the *allegro vivace* of the Fourth may be seen in the following:

(P. 317, F. I, 88)

Other traits to be noticed include Vívaldi's exploitation of the large intervals of the seventh and ninth, generally for expressive reasons, and, in certain concertos (among others, Opus 4, No. 8; Opus 10, No. 6, F. XII, 13; Opus 11, No. 1, F. I, 89), his pioneering activity in the so-called cyclic method of composition which was later codified by Franck and his school. This method consists of establishing a family relationship both melodically and rhythmically among the themes of the different movements of a work.

Finally, as for thematic origins, certain themes, especially in finales, assuredly have a popular source, quite possibly Slavic. It should be recalled that Vivaldi had patrons among the Bohemian nobility, in particular Count Morzin, to whom Opus 8 is dedicated. In the dedication Vivaldi says that he knew the *"virtuosissime"* orchestra of this lord, and it is possible that either in Italy or during his sojourns in Austria he heard it perform tunes descended from Central European folk music.

Though not employing expressly French themes, Vivaldi does appropriate from that country the rhythm of the minuets which bring most of his concertos and sinfonie to a close. Twice, to my knowledge, the indication *alla francese* appears in his instrumental music, applied to pieces with a strongly marked rhythm in the manner of Lully's French overtures.

This discussion of various aspects of Vivaldi's themes will be concluded with the mention of some details of performance (*manières*) indicated explicitly or left for the performer to improvise. The most characteristic of these is the Lombard rhythm, which is described in Quantz's *Versuch* in these words:

It is said of him [Vivaldi] that he was one of those who invented the Lombard style, which consists of the following: where there are two or three short notes one occasionally shortens the note that comes on the beat and puts a dot after the note that comes between the beats. This style began around the year 1722. But it seems to resemble Scottish music somewhat as certain features of this style reveal. Some German composers made use of it before it was popular in Italy, so that it may be said that the Italians only imitated them. [Actually, examples of this from as early as the sixteenth century are known.]

The fact remains that Vivaldi started the vogue of this rhythmic device and that he also conceived some interesting variants such as this one in the finale of a concerto at Turin; the same melodic pattern and bowing are kept up for six measures, and the composer has taken care to specify, "Pay attention to the slur [guardate la legatura]":

(P. 293)

Then again there is to be found in Vivaldi's works an abundance of most of the melodic formulas whose creation the historians of the Mannheim school now and then credit to Johann Stamitz, F. X. Richter, and their emulators, men who merely systematized their use. Italians and Germans—Buxtehude, Caldara, Jommelli, and others—from the end of the seventeenth century on used the appoggiatura (*Vorhalt*) in a most expressive way. In France, J. F. Rebel, Senaillé, Louis Francoeur, and Jacques Aubert also employed it. Gossec wrote tremolos from which higher notes are struck off like sparks (*Funken*) and grace notes and trills evoke the twittering of little birds (*Vögelchen*) in pages that antedate all Mannheim influence.

But Vivaldi makes use of these resources in a less fragmentary way. The whole arsenal of Mannheim devices exists already in his concertos—arpeggiated chords that rocket upwards (*Raketen*), *portamenti* or "sighs" (*Seufzer*), and *Vögelchen*. These last are numerous both in the concerto *La Primavera* and in Opus 10, No. 3, F. XII, 9.

More significant are the melodies outlined in notes that spout up over a bed of sixteenth or thirty-second notes (*Funken*). Torelli already had recourse to them, and Vivaldi welcomed them into his work beginning with *L'Estro armonico* (Opus 3, No. 9, finale). He uses them especially in his sinfonie and concerti ripieni. The collection of the Paris Conservatory is full of such characteristic touches as the following:

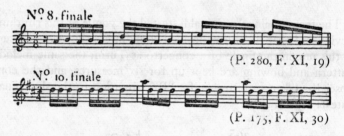

(P. 280, F. XI, 19)

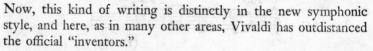

(P. 175, F. XI, 30)

Now, this kind of writing is distinctly in the new symphonic style, and here, as in many other areas, Vivaldi has outdistanced the official "inventors."

His dynamics are just as modern. Well in advance of Johann Stamitz he used the crescendo, more often than not without taking the trouble to indicate it when he could not have doubted that gradation of loudness would be observed. This is the case for the introduction of Opus 3, No. 11—the pseudo-concerto of Friedemann Bach—which can only be a broad crescendo of nineteen measures. But the third concerto of Opus 10 (F. XII, 9) presents the succession *f*, *piu f*, *ff*. The decrescendo is several times expressed by the nuances *piano*, *piu piano*, and *pianissimo*, or by *p*, *pp*, and *pianissimo* (for *pp* then meant *piu piano* and not *pianissimo* as nowadays). Attention has already been called to *cres.* and *decrescendo* in the dramatic works of Stradella. Vivaldi once more has transferred into the symphony a procedure previously tested in opera, where in his day it had become established practice. On that we have the testimony of Charles de Brosses, writing in 1740 to his friend Maleteste. "It is there especially [in opera duets] that the voice and also the violins use this chiaroscuro, this scarcely perceptible swelling of tone that grows in strength from note to note up to the highest degree and then returns to a gentle and affecting nuance."

An analysis of Vivaldi's harmonic and contrapuntal writing would be as interesting as one of his themes and his rhythms, but it would pass beyond the technical level at which this brief book purposes to remain. Besides, a little further on, a study of forms will give us an opportunity to bring out the dominant characteristics of that writing, which are—I may indicate them now—variety, plasticity, and a throwing off of the yoke of rigid rules once and for all. In passing by subtle transitions from vertical chordal writing to an imitative style, Vivaldi commands such flexibility that sometimes it is a puzzle whether homophony or polyphony is primarily involved. But let us first look into the mediums that he has at his disposal and study how he makes up his orchestra and how he utilizes it.

THE ORCHESTRA IN VIVALDI'S TIME

In the chapter "Histoire de l'orchestration" of the *Encyclopédie de la Musique et Dictionnaire du Conservatoire* (Part 2, Vol. 4) Vivaldi's orchestra is described. But the authors have taken as their example an exceptional score, which is, as far as one can determine from the obviously unreliable description they supply, one of the concertos performed at the Pietà in March, 1740, in the presence of the Elector of Saxony. It is said to have been written for "two flutes, two theorbos, two mandolins, two *valeurs* [here the artless historian, the victim of a badly copied index card, asks, "Ought this to be read as two viols?"], two marine trumpets [*trombe marine*], two *violettere*, two cellos, basses, and organ." This commentary follows: "This constitutes a rather strange combination. As we have already remarked, *composers at that time gave scarcely any attention to timbre or to the effect of groupings.* It is very evident that they composed in accordance with the number and types of instruments that were put at their disposal without taking into account the more or less felicitous quality of the sonority."

This point of view is not a new one. Romain Rolland in his

Haendel (1910) adopts the opinion of Karl Mennicke, according to whom "Neutral orchestral coloring characterizes the age of Bach and Handel. Instrumentation corresponds to registration for the organ." And Rolland adds, "The basic constituents of the symphony orchestra are the strings. The winds are useful in the ripieno. When obbligato woodwinds are employed, it is for the full duration of a piece and not to add a touch of color here and there."

Now, the use of wind instruments *on account of* their tone color is, on the contrary, a specialty, if one may use that term, of Bach for descriptive effect. And earlier than Bach the composers of opera in the seventeenth century knew how at some stated point to characterize such and such an episode—a hunt, a solemn procession, a combat, or a *sommeil*—by bringing in the trumpets, flutes, and oboes. It is certainly not "orchestration" in the modern sense of the word. But perhaps it would be fitting to take into account traditional practices about which Georg Muffat (1645–1704), among others, has amply informed us. Uniform writing does not mean uniform performance, because the performers have a large share of initiative. A proposed musical outline is treated by each performer in a way that is appropriate to his instrument; the flute does not realize the musical outline like the violin, the trumpet, or the lute. So a way of orchestration comes to be established by the constant collaboration of the composer and the interpreters.

Material conditions differed greatly from those of today, a point which must also be considered in evaluating an older method of orchestration. For reasons of pure parsimony, Walsh, the publisher of Handel, neglected to provide figures for the instrumental parts in the score, though these would occur in the performance. Vivaldi, for reasons not of economy but of haste, more than once resorted to the same practice in his manuscripts.

To be sure, the masters at the beginning of the eighteenth century appear opportunistic when compared to the Classical composers, as do these latter in turn when compared to Wagner and even more to contemporary masters. Often the choice of instruments for which they wrote depended less on their inspiration than on external limitations. But we shall see how Vivaldi makes the best of such constraints; he understood the various timbres and used them with sureness and economy of means, with boldness when innovating and when renewing a practice already known.

Everything we know about Vivaldi's work shows that it was dominated at the outset by Corelli's influence, which was felt as much in his orchestration as in, say, his formal methods. The concertos that he wrote during the first decade of the century and even a little beyond employ only strings and keyboard instruments entrusted with realizing the bass—the medium called for in Corelli's Opus 6. It is true that from Opus 3 on, Vivaldi's treatment of the four-part string ensemble indicated a tremendous advance over that of any and all of his predecessors. However, as to the instruments called upon, not only is there no new contribution, but rather there is a retreat to be noted in comparison with examples left by Torelli. Francesco Vatielli in his *Arte e vita musicale a Bologna* [1927] has described a large number of works by the Bolognese master, preserved in the archives of San Petronio of Bologna, the form of which constitutes an intermediary step between the concerto and the symphony. (This is shown in Vivaldi's work as well.) It is in these pieces that numerous wind instruments are employed. The most noteworthy is a *Sinfonia a quattro*, actually a symphony *by* fours, conceived for the following:

Trumpets 1, 2, 3, 4	Double-basses (Violone) 1 and 2
Oboes 1 and 2 (*di concertino*)	Bassoon 1 (*di concerto*)
Oboes 3 and 4 (*di ripieno*)	Bassoon 2 (*di ripieno*)
Violins 1 and 2 (*di concertino*)	Trombone
Violins 3 and 4 (*di ripieno*)	Timpani
Violas	Thorough-bass
Cellos 1 and 2	

Vatielli's investigation attests not only that Torelli sought to set up a concertino over against a concerto grosso but that he tried out manifold combinations of timbres, now uniting and now separating the oboes and the violins, or, again, displaying the trumpets alone, or setting the oboes of the concertino with two cellos, the double-basses and the bassoon—in short, "orchestrating" in the modern sense of the word.

In this Torelli probably let himself be somewhat influenced by the example of dramatic music, where the necessity for the picturesque and the pathetic involve calling on all known instrumental resources. Vivaldi was not slow to react with intensified vigor in this direction. His temperament inclined him to it, and he had before him the example of the Venetian school starting with Legrenzi, whose instrumental music exhibits a dramatic character.

Precisely at this time a new hierarchy of instruments was beginning to establish itself. The composers of operas, without renouncing the riches put at their disposal by the wind instruments, gradually became aware of the advantages offered by the strings, the balance of which was a less risky business. The center of gravity in the orchestra progressively came to be in the four or five sections of strings.

Henry Prunières, in his *Nouvelle histoire de la musique* (1936), attributes this innovation to Alessandro Scarlatti, starting with his one hundred and sixth opera, *Tigrane* (1715). But well before this, especially in the works of the Venetian masters or those influenced by Venice, the handling of the orchestra was often based on four or five string parts treated as the main body of the orchestra to which flutes, trumpets, and bassoons are joined from time to time to emphasize some picturesque feature. Such is the case in the serenade in Don Remigio Cesti's opera *Il Principe Generoso* (1665), in *Il Pomo d'Oro* (1667) by M. A. Cesti, and in the operas and oratorios of Antonio Sartorio, Legrenzi, and others.

As a matter of fact, the role of the orchestral quartet of strings is more than foreshadowed by many composers of the seventeenth century. At the beginning of the eighteenth it was made explicit, and Vivaldi was one of the principal champions of the change. But at the same time he maintained and even magnified the coloristic gifts by which the Venetians could always be distinguished from other Italian musicians.

One wonders why Henry Prunières has on various occasions denied the existence of a Venetian style after the death of Cavalli. "Though there was a school of librettists working for Venice there was not, strictly speaking, a Venetian school of musicians. Venice with its six or seven opera houses attracted the best musicians from all over Italy, but the music that was sung there did not differ in any specific quality from that which could be heard elsewhere. Until the powerful individuality of Alessandro Scarlatti established the Neapolitan school, local characteristics could scarcely be observed, and the unity of style [throughout Italy] was remarkable."

Perhaps the purely vocal portions of Venetian operas differ little from those of Roman or Florentine operas. This is certainly not true for the symphonic episodes—the ritornellos and overtures—or even for the instrumental accompaniment, whose brilliant, bold, and diversified tone colors are most distinctive.

Venice maintained other characteristic features, apart from orchestral coloring, that were still clearly perceptible during the first ten or twenty years of the eighteenth century. Fausto Torrefranca in his *Origini italiane del romanticismo musicale* (1930) notes "certain predilections in matters of tonality, of melody, of successions of sounds, that to the experienced ear differentiate the Venetian school from the Neapolitan, whereas any specific character for the others [Florentine and Roman] is less marked." He adds, in substance, that in the realm of instrumental music it is Venice that predominates, with Vivaldi taking the lead. Between Naples and Venice a rivalry was to continue for a long time; the Neapolitans on principle nicknamed all the composers of the opposing school "Signor Barcarolo," meaning by this to scoff at the Venetians' preference for their pliant and melancholy *andantes*. "But it is from these quiet melodies, which a rapid quivering of notes crowding close together agitate this way and that, like fine wrinkles stirring the surface of placid water, that the modern *adagio* will gradually come."

Knowing these models, let us now see how Vivaldi's orchestra is constituted. A quick examination of his instrumental music will establish the fact that he uses all the components of the Classical orchestra with the occasional addition of lute, theorbo, mandolin, or viola d'amore, and without the percussion. (Timpani appear only in the oratorio *Juditha* and in the concerto grosso P. 444, played in 1738 at Amsterdam under his direction.)

But whereas the make-up of the Classical orchestra remained in essence pretty much the same from Haydn and Mozart on, for Vivaldi the orchestra is unstable, as much in the number of instruments as in their distribution. And this is easily explained; the differences were governed by the exceedingly diverse circumstances for which his works were designed. Some, like the *Concerto for the Orchestra of Dresden* (P. 383, F. XII, 3), were expressly conceived for large ensembles, while the greater number were written for the use of the Pietà. Now, in that laboratory where Vivaldi was allowed all manner of experiments, sometimes he made use of the whole of his resources, sometimes of only one part. Certain concertos were written for accomplished virtuosos, the *maestre*, or Vivaldi himself. Others, much easier to perform, very likely including the sinfonie and certain concertos for orchestra (concerti ripieni), were intended for the students.

What description of the orchestra of the Pietà can be given? No doubt it resembled the one that Guardi painted so vividly in his "Concert in a Convent," now in the old Munich Pinakothek. Choristers and instrumentalists are represented in a gallery of three tiers; in the top row thirteen singers; below them, ten violinists and violists; still lower down, two players of bass instruments, a cello and a violone, framed by eight more violinists—in all, twenty instruments. No organ, harpsichord, or theorbo, nor any wind instrument is to be seen. Perhaps they are beyond the frame of the picture, for the whole gallery is not depicted; perhaps they occupy another loggia, one for the instruments that realize the bass, the use of wind instruments not being invariable. The way in which the orchestra is centered on the canvas certifies that one sees the greater part of it and that the whole does not exceed some thirty virtuosos. During the eighteenth century, the complement of performers increased. In 1770, when Burney visited the Pietà, there were seventy in the chorus and orchestra.

We have a good example of a Vivaldi orchestra in the one that the Red Priest directed in 1738 in Amsterdam. According to the document already referred to, this orchestra comprised seven first violins, five second violins, three violas, two cellos, two doublebasses, two trumpets or horns, two bassoons, with probably an oboist, a timpanist, and an accompanying harpsichord playing as well—in all, say, twenty-five players.

An examination of the scores confirms the extreme variety of the ensembles employed by Vivaldi, as to both number and proportion. It would be wrong to rely on the size of the performing body to establish a classification, by genre, of the symphonies and concertos. *In general* the chamber concerto is well suited to a small number of interpreters, and the important religious ceremonies could be enhanced by an imposing orchestral deployment. A well-known engraving portrays Frederick the Great at Sans Souci performing a flute concerto accompanied only by a harpsichord, six violins and violas, and two cellos; this is a typical example of what Quantz calls "*kleine Kammermusik*" or "*petite musique de chambre*," an expression applying not only to the solo concerto but to nearly all that then constituted the purely orchestral repertory. Concert orchestras of the mid-eighteenth century, excluding only those of the Paris Concert Spirituel, of Mannheim, and two or three others in Europe, did not exceed the complement of the chamber orchestra of today, that is, twenty to thirty musicians. Only exceptionally were colossal formations brought together—one hundred and forty musicians at the time of a feast at San Petronio of Bologna in 1722, two hundred in the papal hall of Monte Cavallo on Christmas Eve, 1739.

But the flexibility of traditions concerning performance is such that one can add or subtract instrumentalists to the point of making a trio into a symphony or vice versa. Torelli, the precursor of Vivaldi in the elaboration of the concerto form, explicitly indicates this in the forewords to his Opus 5 (1692), Opus 6 (1698), and Opus 7 (1709, a posthumous publication).

Muffat, a follower of Corelli after having been Lully's disciple, indicates in the preface to his concerti grossi of 1701 that these pieces could be performed by three players, using only the soloists of the concertino; or that it was possible to add one, two, or three instruments in order to obtain a quartet, a quintet, or sextet; or that as a supplement a first violin, a second, and a cello of the concerto grosso could be brought into play. Finally, the concerto grosso might be enlarged "according to the dictates of reason and of the number of your people" and even the solo parts in the concertino might be doubled "when the concerto grosso was extremely full."

More significant, because it is exactly contemporary with Vivaldi and refers to Venetian usage, is this quotation from Alessandro Marcello, the brother of Benedetto. It is taken from the preface of his collection *La Cetra* (1738). "To achieve the full effect of these concertos, two oboes or transverse flutes, six violins, three violas, two cellos, and one violone or bassoon are necessary. Nevertheless, in the absence of oboes and flutes, one will take note to reinforce the solo violins by uniting two colleagues with them. Although, to provide their full effect and express the thought of the composer, these concertos need the aforesaid fifteen instruments, one can—with more convenience although with less effect —perform them without oboes or flutes, with only six violins or even four, if absolutely necessary. Also one can have only a solo cello, and a second violin instead of a viola."

Vivaldi, too, employed and authorized instrumental substitutions. The ninth and twelfth concertos from Opus 8 (respectively, F. VII, 1, and F. I, 31) are for violin or oboe; the sixth concerto of Opus 11 is only a transcription for oboe of Opus 9, No. 3 (F. I, 52). In the manuscripts *ad libitum* indications abound— mandolin replaceable by violins pizzicato, oboe by bassoon or cello, and like substitutions. The advantage of so flexible a system is that it allows a wide use for works written for a rare instrument in honor of a touring virtuoso or some princely dilettante. The recipient of the thirty-seven bassoon concertos in the Turin library having passed from sight, it was of interest to the composer to try to get a double profit by using the oboe. Similarly, he was moved to transfer into the ordinary repertory for string orchestra a concerto for mandolin that was originally composed for Marquis Bentivoglio (P. 134, F. V, 1).

For the way in which the orchestra was grouped we have a model in the aforementioned picture by Guardi. There were other arrangements. J. J. Quantz indicates the most common in his *Versuch*, which was issued in both German and French versions in 1752. Quantz discusses the orchestral layout in a theater, which was breadthwise like that of today, but with one harpsichord in the center, its keyboard toward the audience, and one at the left as support to the cello group. He then goes on to describe the concert orchestra as follows:

In music for a large number which is performed in a hall or in another large place where there is no theater, the harpsichord may be put so that its point is toward the audience. In order that none of the players shall have his' back to the audience, the first violins may be placed in a row one beside the other next to the harpsichord. He who directs is to be at the right hand of him who plays the harpsichord; the latter has on either side the bass instruments who play from the same part along with him. The second violins are to be placed behind the first, and then behind the second violins may come the violas. Next to the latter, to the right in the same line, are placed the oboes, and behind that row the horns and the remaining bass instruments. If the flutes have something to play that is conspicuous, they best find their places next to the point of the harpsichord in front of the first violins or to the left of the wing of the harpsichord. Were they placed further back they would not be heard, because of the weakness of their tone.

For small chamber works the harpsichord can be placed toward the wall to the left of the player. Nevertheless, he ought to be far enough away so that all accompanying instruments except the cellos can take their places between him and the wall. If there are only four violins, all of them as well as the viola can be put in the same row parallel to the keyboard. But if there are as many as six or eight violins, it would be better to place the second violins behind the firsts and the violas behind that so that the middle voices will not rise above the principal voices; that would make a very bad effect. Those who play as the concertino can in any case take their places in front of the wing of the harpsichord; in this way they will be able to see sideways those who accompany them.

In the case of those compositions for double choir, the two bodies of sound were to be separated as much as the dimensions of the hall permitted so as to give the audience the clearest impression of their duality. This was the usual practice throughout Italy. André Maugars noted it in Rome a century earlier, and Charles de Brosses speaks also in 1740 of concertos played "by two choirs in two galleries, which answer back and forth from one aisle of the church to the other." The Venice of the Gabrieli had long ago set the example.

The directing of the orchestra was no more strictly codified

than the number, proportion, or respective places of its performers. The duties of directing sometimes devolved upon the composer seated at the harpsichord, sometimes—and more commonly
—upon the solo violinist (*primo violino*, the *Konzertmeister* of
the Germans). Quantz defines at length the functions of the solo
violinist. His most important duty was the thorough preparation
of the concert by previous study of the bowing, nuances, and
ornamentation—in short, all that makes a perfect leader who is
concerned that nothing be left to chance. After this, it remained
for him only to guide, stimulate, or restrain according to the
circumstances, whether or not he had recourse to beating time.
De Brosses relates in 1740 that in Rome "one beats time in church
during Latin music but never at the opera, however numerous the
instrumentalists, however laden with parts the aria performed."
At Venice for the Feast of the Assumption in 1758 (sixteen years
after Vivaldi's death) there was no one beating time. "The composer was occupied like the general of an army only in animating
by word and gesture those whom he had in charge" (P. J. Grosley, *Nouveaux mémoires ou Observations sur l'Italie*, 1764). On
the other hand, the same narrator was present, again in Venice
during the same year, at an oratorio performance in a convent;
that performance, he tells us, was a disaster because the leader
beat time in the Neapolitan way, "that is, employing the upbeat
where other Italians employ the downbeat."

As for Vivaldi, Burney, in his *History of Music*, tells us that
he conducted the opera orchestra but without specifying how.
He could, to be sure, have taken his place at the organ or harpsichord, both of which he had studied in his youth. We might
better picture him flourishing his bow, his hair disheveled, as by
his own example he sweeps along those about him and conveys
to them the spirited rhythm that should animate his tutti.

VIVALDI AS VIOLINIST

The core, the very heart of Vivaldi's orchestra was, as one
would expect, the string section. Nowhere better than in Venice
was it known how to draw from a string ensemble the effects of
fullness and of color that were elsewhere sought by means of

diversified timbres; witness Cavalli and Legrenzi. Vivaldi, however, with his marvelous intuition of what was permissible to the four-part string ensemble was able to secure unforeseen returns from it. He did not do this by passage work of transcendent virtuosity; for indeed it was his merit rather to discipline and restrain fresh virtuosity and to base it on a classical technique, as Corelli had done on a more modest plane a generation earlier. Even in *La Stravaganza* we do not find any spectacular acrobatics designed to astonish the layman. Vivaldi's daring is of a musical order, and it is his musical inspiration that entails technical innovations.

But it must not be forgotten that the Red Priest was one of the most astounding virtuosos of his time. As was seen above, the princely courts sought him out, the Holy Father and the Emperor of Austria asked to hear him, and the engagements that called him from Venice were at least as often the concern of the virtuoso as of the opera composer.

How was this talent formed? It is known only that Giovanni Battista Vivaldi, who was himself a gifted performer, had had his son as a pupil. But the artistic ancestry of the father is still unknown. The certain thing is that any Venetian would have been born to a violin school that was long-established and ever-thriving. The first of the great violinist-composers of the seventeenth century, Biagio Marini, had contributed to its founding. In the title of his first work (1617) he calls himself *"Musico della Serenissima Signoria di Venetia."* Of the great virtuosos that follow— G. B. Fontana, Massimiliano Neri, Martino Pesenti, Tarquinio Merula, and the rest—some are Venetians, and others who were published in the city of the doges stopped there for more or less extended sojourns.

Vivaldi had also been influenced by Torelli, Corelli, and the Bologna school, as the study of his themes plainly shows. Now, this Bologna school goes back in large part to Venetian sources. One of its founders, Maurizio Cazzati, had had seventeen collections published in Venice before he settled in Bologna. One of Corelli's two teachers was Leonardo Brugnoli, *"detto il Veneziano."*

Finally, the very unusual musical situation in his **native city** allowed Vivaldi to read or hear all the works of interest that were written for the violin throughout Europe; while close at hand during his beginning years his fellow townsman Albinoni published worthwhile models of rhythm, bowing, and various kinds of themes.

Besides what he owed to the tradition of the violinist-composer, Vivaldi was stimulated mightily by the opera, even in his manner of writing for the violin. In particular, his way of handling cadenzas and ornamenting melodies stems from dramatic music rather than from the early concerto as it appears in the works of Corelli, Torelli, and Albinoni. Music written for the theater was more tricked out than was concert music. Marcello, in his humorous and savage *Teatro alla moda*, administers a verbal drubbing to embellishments—improvised or supposedly so. He depicts the violinists as refusing to obey their leader, and embellishing according to their own whims; while the solo violin, entrusted with accompanying a castrato [*musico*], botches the rhythm and launches into an interminable "improvised" cadenza which he had made up in advance, seasoned with arpeggios, double stops, and the like.

Vivaldi found bold and brilliant virtuoso passages in the ritornellos of Scarlatti's scores that sounded well on the instrument and made a greater impression, while presenting more difficulties, than do those of Torelli's best concertos. Drawn as he was toward the theater, he could not ignore such suggestions. So it happened that his violinistic skill, like his compositional craft, synthesized two elements, one coming from pure instrumental music, the other from opera and oratorio; the one linked to the classicism of Corelli, the other to the fantasy of the Neapolitans and Venetians, men who worked sometimes for their own theaters and sometimes for the Vienna opera. The result was a singularly cunning skill, indeed.

Virtuosos, when they let their hair down and forgo fine words, are in the habit of distinguishing between the virtuosity that pays and that which does not. What pays is obviously that which, with the least cost to the performer, in other words at the price of a minimum of effort, extracts the highest sonorous profit from the instrument and stirs the audience the most.

If in our day we compare the concerto cadenzas written by Kreisler with those of such violinists as Joachim and Leonard, we find that those of Kreisler (I think especially of his cadenza for the first movement of the Beethoven concerto) spare the public the wheezing and sawing and other customary accessories of the cadenza and yet give it the same feeling of difficult heights surmounted, perhaps to an even greater extent. The cleverness of the composer inspires him to astonishing polyphonic effects, which are, to tell the truth, within the reach of any experienced instrumentalist.

Vivaldi's violinistic skill is similarly oriented. Differing greatly from that of Tartini or Locatelli, for whom the virtuoso's difficulties do not seem to be taken into account, he seeks out or, rather, by instinct hits upon, the runs that lie best under the fingers, the multiple stops in which the open strings supply the surest points of support, and the most sonorous registers.

As for the matter of left-hand position, it would seem, if we confine ourselves to the printed and manuscript scores, that he never ventured beyond the eighth. Nevertheless, the fragment of Herr von Uffenbach's journal that I have already quoted proves that from 1715 on Vivaldi, when performing his own music, indulged in ascensions to perilous heights. When "he placed his fingers but a hair's breadth from the bridge, so that there was hardly room for the bow" (and it is a violinist who verifies this), it means that he evolved the thirteenth, fourteenth, and fifteenth positions to which, it had been believed, only Locatelli approached.

Perhaps Vivaldi must also be credited with the initiative of putting the second position to use, which occurs often in his passage work. According to Burney's *History*, "Geminiani used to claim the invention of the half-shift [second position] on the violin, and he probably brought it to England; but the Italians ascribed it to Vivaldi; and others to the elder Mateis [Nicola Matteis], who came hither in King William's time."

Vivaldi's ingenuity also manifests itself in certain *brisures* (formulas involving large melodic skips and requiring special dexterity with the bow, which must leap from one string to another not adjacent to it); in these we see the influence of Locatelli, who, in the dedication of his Opus 3 (1733) to "Girolamo Michiellini, Patricio Veneto," tells us in exact terms that he had performed his concertos in Venice. His emulator would not have missed a chance to hear him. In Vivaldi's works there are jumps over strings going from the G-string to the E that would require a bow no less deft than the left hand.

He knows and uses double stops, but does not extend his researches very far in that direction. He seldom aspires to carry into effect polyphony like that employed by the German masters of the late seventeenth century or even by Corelli, in this field their rather cautious imitator. Vivaldi aims at the effect of accompanied song—a voice standing out in the foreground with the other serving as its harmonic support. He also asks of double stops those fanfare-like sonorities to which the Venetians were so attached and of which examples may be found in his concertos for "*violino in tromba*," that is, for a violin in the manner of a trumpet. This is the way he begins a concerto for solo violin, which is exposed for six measures without any bass (P. 171, F. I, 45).

Passages written from end to end in double stops make wide use of open strings and "comfortable intervals," the sixths and sevenths in third position for which the hand places itself, so to speak, by instinct, and also the fourths, whose slightly hollow sonority has a very special bite—and here again Vivaldi heralds Kreisler.

In the same spirit of simplification for the sake of the performer he has recourse in several concertos to *scordatura*, the artifice of modifying the normal tuning of the violin. By using *scordatura*, playing on open strings or with easy fingerings produces chords of three or four tones that would be complicated or impossible with normal tuning. Biagio Marini had employed it as early as 1629; the Germans, Czechs, and Austrians had extended the practice, influenced especially by Biber. Vivaldi hardly uses any but three particular *scordature*.

Where he shows a talent for unrivalled invention is in a violinistic and, above all, musical exploitation of the arpeggio. In the section devoted to his orchestra we shall see striking examples of sonorous or harmonic effects founded entirely on the arpeggio.

He was able to find among the Germans and, in his country, in Torelli—and would likewise have found in Bonporti if he knew him—highly interesting precedents. It seems that none outstripped him either in daring or in flexibility; this is due as much to the diversity of his bowings as to the harmonic arpeggiations that he ventures (see Opus 11, No. 5).

The same skill is seen in the use of that particular instance of the arpeggio known as the *bariolage*, in which one open string continues like a pedal through a series of chords achieved by a seesawing of a high, delicate bow. It is untrue that Vivaldi invented this, as Andreas Moser supposes (*Geschichte des Violinspiels*, 1923). Biber had made use of it well before him, as had Alessandro Scarlatti in an oft-cited cadenza in *Mitridate Eupatore*. But Vivaldi uses it with an unequaled authority and pertinence. In Opus 8 the *presto* of *L'Estate* (F. I, 23) contains a descending run that has to be played entirely in the fifth position to attain a *bariolage* on the third and fourth strings. Vivaldi specifies, "*Sopra il Tenore e Basso*."

As for his bowing technique, it is brilliant, incisive, and diversified, not only in the arpeggios and *brisures* on three or four strings, but also in the glitteringly rapid passages, some of which call for a very dry *sautillé* bowing; other passages call for a swift staccato notated as it still is today, sometimes with as many as twenty-four notes in a single stroke of the bow.

There are many other interesting details to which attention might be called on the subject of handling the bow, despite the lack of indications. Several *forte* passages of quarter notes are designated *con l'arco attaccato alle corde*, that is, a *grand détaché* on the string; others must have a *grand détaché* with a more marked attack, sometimes a really biting sound (see in the concerto *La Primavera* the episode of the goatherd sleeping, where the viola, *molto forte, e strappato*, conveys the barking of the dog). On the other hand, passages—either melodic or of decorative figurations—that are performed *pianissimo* are also numerous.

Sometimes, as in Corelli, the long time values carry indications such as *arcate lunghe* or *come stà*. From this we could learn, if we did not know it from other sources, that it was the custom to embroider the written text, and that if the composer wished it to be performed without an additional burden of parasitical ornamentation, he had to request this most clearly.

Among Vivaldi's contemporaries, Marcello, in a bantering vein, and Quantz, as seriously as possible, give us information on the practice of orchestral violinists in decorating their parts, each for himself, at the risk of fearful cacophony. Quantz writes, "Above all, one ought to perform the ritornellos without any arbitrary additions. That is allowed only to the soloist. Some people have the bad habit indeed of putting all manner of frivolity in the ritornello [the tutti] and neglect in the course of this to read the notes aright." On the other hand, for the soloist (the "*Concertist*" or "*joueur du concert*") it is not merely allowable; it is obligatory. Judgment of him and of his technique, of his faculties of improvisation and expression, depended on the way in which he enriched the sketch furnished by the composer. Quantz himself assures us of it, in his comparison of the notation of French music —exact and with little room left for embroidery, so that no theoretical requirements are entailed—with that of Italian music; he declares that Italian composers write certain passages "in a very simple and spare way in order to allow the player the liberty of varying them a number of times according to his capacity and judgment, so as to surprise his listeners each time with something newly devised."

We have numerous proofs for the fact that Vivaldi made himself at home with this practice, aside from the *come stà* and *arcate lunghe* directions specified on the exceptional occasions when he departs from it. First, there is the difference that exists between the *largos* and *adagios* that he writes in the customary way, that is, in a diagrammatic way with long time values, and those much less common ones that he takes the trouble to fill out with all the notes (Opus 4, the *largos* of the concertos Nos. 2, 3, and 5; Opus 11, No. 2; and others) as J. S. Bach did in the *Italian Concerto* and the *adagios* of the violin and harpsichord sonatas. It happens (here we have another piece of evidence) that Vivaldi, in using the same slow movement in two different concertos gives the diagrammatic version once, and the other time a more or less ornamented version. This is what occurs in the concertos Opus 4, Nos. 3 and 6, (Walsh's English edition), which have a single slow movement in common. The movement appears in a simple dia-grammatic outline headed *larghetto* in No. 6, and in No. 3 it is marked *grave* and soberly decked out. The differences are of this order:

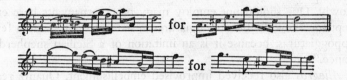

It was possible to go much farther. Vivaldi, interpreting his own music, certainly did not confine himself to these docile em-bellishments. Arnold Schering has published in the *Sammelbände der Internationalen Musikgesellschaft* for 1905–06 the ornamenta-tion of an *adagio* of Vivaldi, reconstructed probably by Pisendel or one of his followers. Like Tartini in the famous quotation in Cartier's *Art du violon*, the virtuoso in this hastily written manu-script fragment notates several possible interpretations without great care to the exact time values. A single measure will be enough for us to discern the liberties that he arrogates to himself.

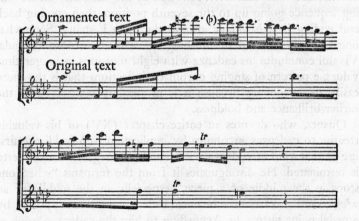

Ludwig Landshoff in his edition (Peters No. 4206) of a Dresden concerto manuscript (P. 228) has given other examples of em-bellishments added to a Vivaldi autograph by another hand, perhaps that of Pisendel, "during the lessons, under the very eyes of the master."

We know from Quantz that not all *adagios* sustained such vegetation, which occasionally ran wild. "A *siciliano* . . . ought to be played very simply, with scarcely any trills, and not too slowly. One should not employ many other ornaments here except for a few double appoggiaturas in sixteenth notes, and a few appoggiaturas, because it is an imitation of a Sicilian shepherds' dance."

Allegros also received improvised embellishment. Quantz recommends its moderate use. "One ought to avoid varying the beautiful singing thoughts of which one does not easily tire and, likewise, the brilliant passages which have a sufficiently pleasing melody themselves. One should vary only such ideas as make no great impression."

The edition of the above-mentioned concerto P. 228, dedicated to Pisendel, gives some valuable examples of ornamentation in an *allegro*. It reproduces also an original Vivaldi cadenza. That cadenza, inserted before the last tutti of the finale, covers thirty-nine measures. It begins with long and rapid scale passages of an accentuated tonal character, followed by modulations—an ascending sequence going up to the seventh position, then coming back and ending in a *bariolage* around the open E-string. Somewhat unexpectedly, instead of finishing off with a virtuoso formula, Vivaldi concludes his cadenza with eight measures in longer time values, a pattern of singing chromatic inflections that is the more easily made moving because it is in absolute contrast with the earlier brilliance and boldness.

Quantz, who devotes an entire chapter (XV) of his valuable treatise to cadenzas, attributes by implication to Vivaldi the first use of that kind of cadenza with which an *allegro* for a concerto is terminated. He distinguishes it from the fermatas "when one stops in the middle of a piece," especially in the middle of an *adagio*, and also from the terminal cadenzas that are supported by a pedal point *tasto solo*. According to him the cadenzas "such as we now have, where the bass stops," date "from between the year 1710 and 1716"—which he considers the period of Vivaldi's earliest concertos.

Unquestionably this attribution is correct in the sense that Vivaldi was the first to emancipate the terminal cadenza and give it a breadth that it had not yet attained in the concerto. But it is sufficient to recall what has been said earlier to see that in the theater Scarlatti and others had already experimented with it. In the concerto form itself, on the other hand, Vivaldi's predecessors appear very timid. Francesco Vatielli cites in a concerto for two violins by Corelli (1705) a long bravura passage entitled *Perfidia*, which presumes a certain virtuosity. (Brossard in his *Dictionnaire de musique* of 1703 defines *perfidia* as "a predilection to do always the same thing, to follow always the same scheme, to maintain the same rhythm . . . ," that is, the equivalent of the *ostinato*.) But this passage is still supported by the bass *tasto solo*, as are a number of cadenzas in sonatas from the period 1680–1700. Sometimes Vivaldi wrote such cadenzas without necessarily confining them to the last part of his *allegros*. Various concertos in the manuscripts of Dresden start with a capriciously paced solo; not all of these solos are supported by bass notes. This variety of opening cadenza in one instance reaches the length of seventeen measures, with the violin playing all alone for the first six.

But as early as 1712 in P. 165, the *Concerto fatto per la solennità della S. Lingua di S. Ant° in Pad°* [*Sant' Antonio in Padua*] we find a concluding cadenza that unfolds without any support for thirty whole measures. To be sure, it does not have the free pace of those that were to be written later which broke away from the barline and sometimes took unwarranted liberties with the construction of the work. Nevertheless, it does possess, what with its *brisures*, its sonorous double stops, and its ever-increasing load of embellishments, the demonstrative character that one expects of it; in it the virtuoso gives the public a résumé of his technical capabilities. The confirmation of that demonstrative character will be seen in the cadenza of the *Concerto in due cori con violino scordato* (*Concerto for Two Orchestras with Violin scordatura*, P. 368, F. I, 60), which lasts thirty-six measures and includes double stops demanding scrupulous execution, but which is not to be mentioned in the same breath with the demands of Locatelli's astounding *Capricci*.

Uffenbach has given us to understand that Vivaldi's playing could be of an unbridled fancy. But his work as it now stands bears hardly a trace of this. The level of virtuosity that he sets is that which he could expect from his usual interpreters. This is a more developed, more daring, and above all more brilliant technique than that of Corelli, but it is no less solidly based. What it contributed to violinistic skills was a permanent liberation, and we see in Vivaldi today the indispensable link between Corelli and Tartini, with Locatelli a glaring exception. From this point of view Vivaldi is essentially a classicist.

If we are to have a complete idea of Vivaldi's violinistic craft, it is necessary to study it also in its *cantabile* application. We see how often he makes good use of the instrument by contriving effects for it that are well known to singers; we learn how much he loves to contrast suave effects with vigorous outbursts or the legato of the soloist with the pizzicato of an ensemble—results of his education in the opera house. Information on this topic will be found in the section below devoted to the orchestra as treated by Vivaldi. One curious lacuna is the nonemployment of the G-string in such melodies. Vivaldi shifts often to the G-string in passage work, and he exploits it up to the sixth and seventh positions, but no more than did Corelli does he yet dare to entrust a sustained melody to it. Perhaps here again he is under the influence of the opera of his time, where sopranos, both natural and manufactured, captured the attention of the composer and the applause of the audience.

On the whole, Vivaldi's violin techniques provided the virtuosos of the eighteenth century with the essential part of their stock-in-trade. Knowing the elements that compose this technique, we ought to be able to conceive without too much difficulty what his manner of performance may have been. The dominant element seems really to have been rhythmic ardor—like that of a Kreisler in his best years—which the quality of the themes requires. The passage work, in time values shorter than sixteenth notes and usually of a full sonority with the nuance *forte*, consists of simple lines when compared to Locatelli, Tartini, and the French, and implies a long bow well on the string. The serenity of his slow movements as they are notated would support that point of view if the age had not allowed so many added *fiorature*, and if we did not know that the Olympian Corelli flung himself about like a madman while interpreting perfectly sedate *adagios*.

We do not have, to assist our conjecturing about Vivaldi's technique, either a textual source, such as Tartini's famous letter to Maddalena Lombardini to be found in Carlo Schmidl's *Dizionario* (1937–38), or even the existence of a line of descent to students in whom the continuity of a doctrine may be recognized. Undoubtedly Vivaldi schooled many people—all of the violinists of the Pietà for a period of thirty years (some of whom, such as Chiaretta, number among the best in all Italy) and most of the virtuosos, whether Venetian or not, who were able to sojourn in Venice during that time. His professional fame and the brilliance of his singular personality inclined all of them toward him.

However, among the properly authenticated pupils, besides Pisendel we know only Daniel Gottlieb Treu, a German also, although he Italianized himself by calling himself Fedele. We know from his autobiography that he received some lessons from the Red Priest in Venice, and that after he returned home to Germany, he busied himself with making known the concertos and operas of his master, particularly at Breslau.

Others who knew Vivaldi and to some extent sought his advice bear witness in their works to the fact that they made use of his music; but this does not put us in a position to state anything more precise. Among those assumed to be his students, I shall cite Giovanni Battista Somis, who had worked with him "in his youth," according to Francesco Regli (*Storia del violino in Piemonte*, 1863). I should also mention Carlo Tessarini, in 1729 violinist at San Marco and *maestro de' concerti* at the conservatorio of Santi Giovanni e Paolo of Venice, a counterpart to Vivaldi's position at the Pietà. Their contemporaries had no doubt as to the artistic consanguinity of Vivaldi and Tessarini.

Next comes Giuseppe Fedeli, son of a *maestro de' concerti* at San Marco, and then Giovanni Madonis and Giovanni Verocai, both Venetians. Quantz met Madonis in Venice in 1726, and he was the only violinist except Vivaldi to hold his attention. Vero-

cai, in the title of his collection of sonatas published in St. Peters-
burg in 1738, styles himself "M. Verocai, Venizien."

Nothing is known of Lodovico Candido, whose sonatas for
solo violin and *continuo* appeared in Venice in 1715, nor of Lodovico Ferronati, Giovanni Antonio Piani (Desplanes), and Francesco Ciampi, all three violinists who were in Venice and published there while the composer of *La Stravaganza* and *Le
Stagioni* was in his heyday.

As for Alessandro Marcello, it would be surprising if he,
patrician, rich, and free to choose as he was, had not elected one
of the celebrities of the city as his teacher. And a pupil of Vivaldi's
last years is unquestionably to be identified in the person of the
virtuoso Santa Tasca—"Madame Tasca, Venetian, one of the
musicians to the emperor [Francis I, Holy Roman Emperor]"—
who at a Concert Spirituel of September 8, 1750, at Paris "played
in the style of Vivaldi a concerto for violin of his composition,"
as reported by the *Mercure de France*.

Finally, in a discussion to appear below of the composers who
came under Vivaldi's influence, we shall find a group of German,
Austrian, and Czech musicians, mostly violinists, whose travels
led them to Venice and whose works are related to its methods
of composition and its characteristic orchestration. The depend-
ence of certain French masters—Jacques Aubert, J. M. Leclair
in his concertos—is no less manifest. Interpretation and composition were so intimately linked in that period that to write works
fashioned after Vivaldi's was to adhere to his school in the area of
performing techniques, whether or not the composer had actually
profited from his direct teaching. In the broadest sense, therefore,
Vivaldi had a multitude of disciples.

VIVALDI'S TREATMENT OF THE ORCHESTRA

I have dwelt at some length on the subject of Vivaldi as a
violinist. But more perhaps to be admired than the boldness and
ingenuity with which he treats the violin as a solo instrument is
the use he makes of the bowed instruments in combined performance, his way of arranging and proportioning their various

timbres, "orchestrating" with only the medium of the four-part string ensemble.

This talent as an orchestrator is dazzlingly apparent through all of Opus 3, starting with the first number of this, his maiden work in the concerto form. In this first concerto grosso the concertino is made up of four violins; far from being satisfied with quasi-mechanical opposition between the four soloists and the tutti, Vivaldi carries out the following combinations in less than fifty measures: At the outset the two first soloists are presented in the open, that is, without the bass, and without a preceding tutti. At the fifteenth measure the tutti breaks in, only to be moderated shortly by a cello solo that compels the rest of the strings to content themselves with punctuation in short time values. At the sixteenth measure the third violin stands alone, then the fourth violin comes in to reinforce it at the third. The return of the cello solo and the tutti, this time *piano*, is followed by *forte* passage work in the second violin over a bass *tasto solo*. Then comes a short tutti fanfare echoed by the third and fourth solo violins and a cello; scale passages for the first solo violin accompanied by the cello and the bass of the keyboard instrument; then a new tutti opened up from measure to measure by the embroidery of the four soloists taking turns. Further on there is a more delicately wrought passage of six real parts with the violins exchanging overlapping answers with one another as the bass performs a descending sequence in a different rhythm.

Considering of what little interest the themes and passage work are in themselves (only the opening theme is distinctive), one cannot choose but view this whole beginning as a play of sonorities above all, and as such admirably managed. In it there is real innovation that categorically contradicts those who would at all costs fix the Mannheim school as the source of the taste for timbres and the understanding of them. Opus 3 presents another example that is even more unimpeachable. In the twenty-two measure *larghetto* of the tenth concerto there is to be found not a single melodic pattern—nothing but superimposed chords arpeggiated in four different ways (the form of each arpeggio being specified by the composer), so that a shimmering kind of harmony with an uncommonly modern effect is generated.

The intention and the novelty of this passage escaped Julien Tiersot, who, in an analysis of the concerto in question in the June 7, 1929, issue of *Le Ménestrel*, characterized it as follows: "The repetitions of the principal tones in the orchestra mark the simple chords with steady pulsation; above, patterns of steady *staccato* notes for three violins rise up in tiers, and against them the first violin in sixteenth-note triplets [1] sets flowing a wide ar-

[1] No, the arpeggios of the first violin are, as Vivaldi indicates, in *biscrome*, that is, thirty-second notes. Alfred Einstein, in the pocket score that he edited for the Eulenburg collection, commits the same blunder as Tiersot, and I am also guilty of it in my *Antonio Vivaldi et la musique instrumentale*, p. 113.

peggio. Harmonic scaffolding results that is not without charm for the ear but in which invention is wanting—in short, sound, nothing more."

Precisely what is worthy of note in an age when, as a rule, the composer relied upon the performer to take charge of bringing into being in his own way what was expressed by a simple diagram, is an explicit request for a specific sonority, gauged minutely in both quality and quantity. Here the four parts for the solo violins, except for the first violin, each playing notes of the same time value, get four different indications with respect to bowing; and while the two viola parts proceed with their eighth notes *piano*, the cellos support them with the same rhythm but *sempre forte*.

In a concerto for four solo violins in the Turin library (P. 367, F. I, 59), a similar passage which is harmonically conceived is every bit as significant. Arnold Schering, writing in his *Geschichte des Instrumentalkonzerts* (1927), speaks in connection with another slow movement that I shall cite further on of "the spirit of *Lohengrin*"; that spirit can be found here in the upward climbing of the divided violins, and in the quivering of the triplets between trills at two different levels. This method of dividing the violins is hardly to be met with again, in any case, before Weber.

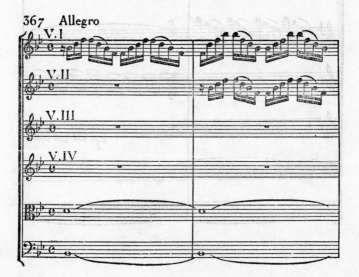

367   Allegro

(P. 367, F. I, 59)

Vivaldi has many other ways to lighten his palette. See, for example, how in the brilliant finale of the last concerto of Opus 10 (F. XII, 13, for flute, strings, and organ) he supports the inflections of the flute over a bass part reinforced only with an arpeggio in the first solo violin.

All this—and I am intentionally limiting myself—reveals Vivaldi as a colorist and even an impressionist very much ahead of his time. Does he not go so far as to employ "multilevelled" writing, so dear to our contemporary Georges Migot? In an episode from the concerto *La Primavera*, the goatherd's slumber, the solo violin plays *mezzo-forte*, the first and second violins accompany it *pianissimo sempre*, while the viola that represents the barking dog (*"il cano che grida"*) plays *fortissimo*.

Other effects, without being quite so novel, are just as new as regards the concert orchestra. For them Vivaldi, a dramatic composer even in the concerto, and the creator of the solo concerto precisely by reason of his temperament as a man of the theater, calls upon the opera. It is in the string writing that these borrowings are most pronounced and most characteristic. At the time when he published his first concertos it had been a good while since the dramatic composers had originally bethought themselves of the expressive worth of the orchestral quartet. Moreover, they had discovered certain ways to use it which guaranteed an effect on the public's nervous system. Just as earlier criticism scoffed at the tremolos, the muted passages, and the cello doublings of the voice in the Italian *verismo*, so two centuries before, Marcello lampooned such formulas of facile enticement. "The composer," he wrote, "should entertain the public by accompanying the arias with pizzicato and muted passages and with *trombe marine*." Elsewhere he prescribes in the same droll fashion some infallible means to bring off success—the use of ritornellos in unison, and the elimination of the bass from certain aria accompaniments. Such methods we find in Vivaldi's orchestral music, exploited at times by the hard-pressed entrepreneur thinking above all of saving time (as was necessary in the theater when he patched up old recitatives), and at times by an inspired innovator, capable of extracting expressive intensity and a variety of unsuspected colors from them.

UNISON SETTING

On the dramatic character that is ascribed in the eighteenth century to a unison setting, Quantz confirms the observations of Marcello: "The unison, which consists of a line resembling a standard bass line and which makes an especially good effect when there are many persons accompanying, ought to be performed in a lofty and majestic manner, with fire and with a vigor to the bowing and to the tone such as is not given to the notes of another sort of melody." One has but to open an Italian or German score of the period 1700–1720 to establish the justice of these remarks. And indeed they describe very well the tone of Vivaldi's unisons. I shall quote only one, which serves as the ritornello of the *largo* of Opus 3, No. 1:

This somber tutti, which astonishingly is often interpreted at concerts with an offensive want of vigor, is answered by a first solo of a gentle and singing character in sixteenth notes; but the tutti resumes its relentless rhythm, delineating the same chromatic descent, always in unison. A second solo, as delicate as the first, seems to intercede anew; for one last time the tutti opposes to the solo its brusque inexorability, its irremediable gloom. It is, in short, the contrast that Beethoven in his concerto in G and Franck in his *Variations symphoniques* will exploit more fully and more wittingly.

Elsewhere—always in slow movements—Vivaldi accompanies the solo with a string unison (*e.g.*, P. 419, F. I, 2; P. 59, F. I, 46). In that case, the effect sought for is not one of violence but of extreme simplicity. The most singular effect in this direction is perhaps in the *andante* of Opus 11, No. 3, where Vivaldi does not even endeavor to set forth two melodic voices; the violas move in just the way the cellos do, outlining a bass that is adorned as little as possible, just enough to supply a discreet support for the cantilena—one might write, for the *romanza*—of the solo violin.

PIZZICATO

The pizzicato of the string instruments is met with in dramatic scores from the very beginning of opera. In a passage in *Il Combattimento di Tancredi e Clorinda* (1626) Monteverdi indicates for the string parts, "Here one puts by the bow and plucks the strings with two fingers," and, a little further on, "Here one again takes up the bow." Nearer to Vivaldi, Biber, in a serenade from around 1670, prescribed that all the bowed instruments be played without bow "as on the lute [*wie auf der Lauten*]" with the violin held under the arm.

In Vivaldi's concertos, the printed collections present only two examples of pizzicato (Opus 11, No. 1, F. I, 89; Opus 9, No. 10, F. I, 49); however, the Dresden and Turin manuscripts are responsible for the appearance of exceptionally pungent uses of it (*e.g.*, P. 111, F. I, 91; P. 185, F. I, 77). In a Dresden sinfonia in G the *andante* includes the doubling of the parts for the first and second violins played with the bow by two identical parts for violins pizzicato; thus each note of the melody has at one and the same time a marked attack and a prolongation.

One of the most uncommon dispositions of parts is that of the *andante* of the concerto in *F* for three solo violins (P. 278, F. I, 34), in which one of the soloists plays a broad melody, capable of being ornamented—and it surely was—while the other instruments accompany it, one with thirty-second notes pizzicato, the second with *legato* arpeggios of sextolets in thirty-second notes.

MUTED PASSAGES

The opera orchestra of the seventeenth century made wide use of muted strings. An example is Lully's score of *Le Triomphe de l'Amour* (1681), where at the beginning of the *Ballet de la Nuict* he indicates "all the instruments ought to have mutes and play softly, particularly when the voices sing, and ought not to remove the mutes until directed." Marc Antoine Charpentier in *Médée* (1693), Reinhard Keiser in *Croesus* (1711) and *Fredegunda* (1715), and Handel on numerous occasions had recourse to this poetically soft tone color. Vivaldi was to require the same effects of it, in slow movements and in a more exceptional way in the *allegro* of Opus 10, No. 5 (F. VI, 1). In the *Concerto funebre* (P. 385, F. XII, 12) the solo violin without mute emerges from an entirely veiled ensemble; all the instruments, both strings and winds, are muted, *"non pero il violino principale."*

TREMOLO

Later we shall see a typical example of this.

ELIMINATION OF THE CELLOS

In his lampoon, which has already been cited, Marcello represents this practice as one habitually used in opera. "The arias [after long compulsory ritornellos by violins in unison] ought to follow without any bass. To hold the *musico* [castrato] on pitch the composer should accompany him with violins in unison; the violas may sound some bass notes but this is *ad libitum.*"

This is essentially a method of the theater. Its use in any concerto collections, outside of Vivaldi's, during the early history of the genre cannot be verified; on the other hand, however, it is frequent in dramatic scores—French, German, and Italian—

starting with Lully, who in *Roland* (1685) secured a very happy effect of lightening the texture of the third-act chaconne by leaving the viola and cello parts in abeyance for five or six measures or occasionally for as many as sixteen.

To musicians who assert ingeniously—and ingenuously—that Vivaldi wrote not six hundred concertos, but the same concerto six hundred times over, I would advise the reading of his slow movements simply from the standpoint of orchestration. In the concerti grossi prior to 1710, as in the sinfonie and the church sonatas for strings and winds, the slow movement was, as a rule, reserved for strings alone; the flutes, oboes, trumpets, and horns came in only in the *allegros* in an especially dynamic and rhythmical way. Vivaldi exercised his wits to give to a *largo* or *adagio*, highpoints of the concerto as regards expressive intensity, diversified orchestration calculated to revive interest, as at the opera when the *musico* or the prima donna prepared to move a captivated audience to the verge of tears.

Here are some of the combinations that Vivaldi employed:

1) The four-part string ensemble in addition to keyboard instruments to realize the figured bass.

This is the most crowded category, containing more than a hundred sinfonie and concertos. But the formula is not rigid. Sometimes a slow movement will be written from beginning to end for the whole ensemble; sometimes it is a question of the tutti section only, the solos being accompanied by *continuo* alone. Occasionally the soloist sings out above four string parts having long time values, which allow the soloist to stand out in full relief; again, the solo predominates above pizzicato writing even less obtrusive. At times, a tutti in fugal style for all the strings contrasts with the bareness of the solo supported simply by the *continuo;* at others, the tutti is in polyphonic style or that of vertical homophony, while the orchestral quartet of strings accompanies the solo completely in unison.

2) Accompaniment cut down to the cellos and the keyboard instrument.

Slow movements in this style number around a hundred. Here the ripieno violins and the violas are silent during the whole slow movement. This is fundamentally the most archaic pattern, the direct extension of the *adagio* of the sonata *da chiesa*. Bonporti, in his *Concerti Grossi* Opus 11 (1714–16), lightens the accompaniment of his slow movements in this fashion. In the theater, Marcello represents this method as superseded at the time when he issued his *Teatro alla moda* (1720): "The modern composer should never write arias with bass accompaniment only, saying to himself that, on the one hand, this is no longer the fashion and that, on the other hand, during the time spent on one of them he could compose a dozen arias with instruments [*stromenti*, that is, string instruments, the four-part ensemble]." In Vivaldi's works, this form of accompaniment is generally used in the *adagios* where the solo part needs great freedom of rhythmic pace, either by reason of its expressive intensity or because it is designed to receive copious ornamentation.

3) Accompaniment by the harpsichord with the cellos eliminated.

In this style, the extreme in denuding the orchestra of instruments, the strings hardly intervene at all; either the violas and cellos hold their peace, leaving the floor to the solo violin, the first and second ripieno violins, and the harpsichord; or the ripieno violins are themselves silent and only the *violini concertati* and cembalo are left.

4) Accompaniment by the whole orchestra, excluding the harpsichord.

Lully, in the prologue to *Proserpine* (1680), and Alessandro Scarlatti, at about the same period and regularly afterward, now and then suppressed the harpsichord part in their dramatic orchestration, retaining the cellos so that an entirely homogeneous string sonority is obtained. Vivaldi follows their example in a half-dozen slow movements of his concertos and sinfonie (*e.g.*, P. 288, F. II, 2) and once in a finale *allegro* (P. 125, F. I, 70).

5) Elimination of all bass instruments, clavier and cellos alike.

This is pre-eminently the "recipe" of the dramatic composers at which Marcello jeers and of which I gave a sufficient number of examples above. (Indeed still other examples could be found in instrumental music.)

It seems that this style deeply impressed Vivaldi. He resorted to it in nearly fifty slow movements—not, it must be added, in a uniform way; sometimes the violins accompany the soloist in light and airy harmonies with long time values, as in the *andante* of Opus 11, No. 2 (*Il Favorito*), or with tremolos of thirty-second notes *pianissimo* as in a Dresden *largo*, the very one with regard to which Arnold Schering speaks of the spirit of *Lohengrin*:

(P. 227)

Elsewhere (P. 173), the solo is accompanied by only one part for the violins, which are in unison, and one for the violas; accordingly the harmony is in only three parts but with an eighth-note rhythm that lightly propels it along.

More often the ripieno violins and the violas play the same part without any harmonic filling. The effect of bareness is all the more accentuated since that accompaniment does not try to be melodic nor does it proceed by imitation so as to give the illusion of a second voice; it is merely harmonic support reduced to a minimum (*e.g.*, P. 365, F. I, 99).

Vivaldi in certain cases suppresses the violas, and the soloist has nothing more for support than the violins in unison (*e.g.*, P. 379, F. I, 81; P. 306, F. VII, 2). Then the composer indicates that the violins play the bass, there being no bass—"*I violini suonano il basso senza bassi.*"

The instrument that has the bass function, whether it be the violin or the viola, is generally written in the F-clef and nearly always to be played an octave above the written notes. This bass role for the violas and violins was precisely described by Quantz in his chapter on the duties of accompanists (XVII). "When the solo part is accompanied only by the violins, each violinist ought to take careful notice whether he plays merely an inner voice, or one that at certain places changes off with the solo part, or whether he plays a 'little bass' [*Bassetchen* or *petite basse*]. If he plays an inner voice the strength of his tones must be much restrained; if his part alternates with the solo he can play more strongly, while he can play more strongly still if he plays a 'little bass.' " Likewise, the violette player (violist), "when, as frequently occurs in concertos, he must represent the bass and play the 'little bass,' ought to be able to do so with the requisite circumspection, so that the soloist may not be obliged to be more occupied with the part accompanying him than with his own." All this certainly stems from Vivaldi's innovation, although a similar layout may infrequently be found scattered in the works of other composers.

Without claiming to have exhausted all the orchestral combinations that Vivaldi tried out, which would require among other things the analysis of the great number of concertos for two or more soloists—two, three, or four violins, violin and cello, two violins and cello, one violin and two cellos, oboe and violin, and so on—I wish to describe further the concertos for two *cori*, and the echo concertos.

The latter are obviously of a theatrical origin, whereas composing for two *cori* relates rather to the music of the church. Without going back as far as the antiphonal chant of early Christianity, in the sacred music of the Renaissance there can be found an established technique of arranging the medium in two or more choirs, whether instrumental, vocal, or mixed. Venice always had a marked predilection for the *cori spezzati* (broken, separated). Around 1600 Giovanni Gabrieli furnishes some sumptuous examples of opposition between two instrumental groups in which strings and brass are intermixed. This type of composition had a vogue widespread enough for Praetorius to have felt that he ought to devote a copious chapter of his *Syntagma Musicum* (1615-19) to it. For a half-century Venetian presses published collections of such psalms, motets, and Masses by the dozen. Meanwhile, Rome had welcomed in a new style. The French viol-player, André Maugars, in his *Réponse faite à un curieux sur le sentiment de la musique en Italie* (1639), describes a concert given in the church of Santa Maria sopra Minerva, in which two principal choirs, each with the support of a large organ, answered back and forth from one side to the other of the high altar; eight more choirs of less importance (these had at their disposal only portable organs) were distributed the length of the nave. "Sometimes two choirs contended with each other and two different ones answered. Sometimes three, four, or five choirs sang together, then one, two, three, four, or five voices alone. And at the *Gloria Patri* all ten choirs resumed in concert." Charles de Brosses was to be present, a century later, at similar demonstrations.

It is no surprise that the genius of Vivaldi was tempted by the conflict of two instrumental masses with more distinct and forceful contrasts than those in the traditional concerto grosso, where only two or three instruments were opposed to the tutti. Four of his concertos, at least, call for two *cori*. In one (P. 309), each body is comprised of a solo violin, an organ, and the four-part string ensemble; in another (P. 226), each chorus includes three soloists—two flutes and a violin, the flutes occasionally having solo passages with an obbligato cello also; the third is a *Concerto a violino solo e 2 cori* (P. 164, F. I, 62), in which a single solo violin is superimposed on two string groups; finally, a *Concerto in due cori con violino scordato* (P. 368, F. I, 60) is laid out like the preceding, but with the violin *scordatura*, the G-string being raised to *B*-flat.

Had Vivaldi been led to this manner of composing for double choruses solely by the church, to which he had access from his youth, or by the theater as well, toward which his impetuous lyricism drew him ever more strongly? This question arises because, at the time when he first used it, certain dramatic composers had already resorted to it—for instance, Alessandro Scarlatti in the first act of *La Caduta dei Decemviri* (1697), in which the composer makes use of divided violins; or, again, Badia in *La Gara dei Beni* (1700) with, here and there, four small string orchestras.

As to echo effects, they had already been exploited in purely instrumental music for the easily achieved purpose of surprise. This use appears in Giulio Mussi's collection of *Canzoni* (1620; the *Amaltea* for two violins or cornetts in an echo-like arrangement), and Biagio Marini's *Sonata in ecco con tre violini* (1629). The organ, with its registers of greatly varied intensity, is an incitation to such contrasts; one finds them in the works of Banchieri, of Sweelinck, and his numerous imitators. Bach, Handel, Haydn, and Mozart transfer it to the orchestra and the quartet for purposes that are sometimes comic and sometimes serious.

The echo concertos in Vivaldi's output are obviously occasional works, designed for the amusement of a frivolous audience at some summer residence. Six such concertos are extant (P. 308, F. IV, 5; P. 58, F. IV, 3; P. 278, F. I, 34; P. 388, F. IV, 2; P. 238, F. IV, 6; P. 222). Of these six, the first five appear in the same collection of manuscripts, for the most part autographs, compiled for the sake of those whose leisure they had beguiled.

The first of the series clearly shows the stamp of a rather acrobatic musical diversion. It is entitled *Il Proteo o sia il mondo al rovescio* (*Proteus, or the World Turned Upside down*), and the composer specifies the manner of the performance thus: "The solos of the principal violin will be played an octave higher.

"The first *ripieno* will be fainter than the solo violin.

"The solo violin will be able to play the solos of the cello, which in reverse fashion can play the solos of the principal violin at the actual pitch."

A similar spirit is to be found in the *Concerto de' Cucchi* (*Concerto of the Cuckoos*) and in the *Coro delle Monache* (*Choir of Nuns*).

In the use that Vivaldi makes of the other string instruments, the viola does not call for special comment. Its role is modest, as it is in most other works of the time.

Much more varied and often more brilliant is the role of the cello. When it is employed as the bass, it doubles the harpsichord or the organ. Quantz gives us an idea of the extent to which it is bound to the bass line of the keyboard instrument. If the cellist is a very good musician, he is granted the right to embellish his part

as freely as he can without obstructing the soloist; but this embellishing is allowed only in the solos, because by improvising
during the tutti he would risk jumbling the sonority of the
ensemble. He is relied on to maintain the tempo and to stress the
interesting tones—not what we might call the "good degrees,"
but the notes over which there are dissonances, such as the second,
the diminished fifth, the augmented fifth, the augmented sixth,
and the seventh, or those that are changed from their normal
position, that is, raised by sharps or natural signs or lowered by
flats or natural signs. . . . Also, he should "arouse the attention
of the listener" by playing the three or four notes that precede a
final cadence somewhat more loudly.

Even while remaining an accompanist and, as such, often inter-
dependent with the keyboard, the cellist sometimes lays claim
to more rapid figurations. In several of the Dresden and Turin
concertos (*e.g.*, F. IV, 1–4) an obbligato cello competes with the
virtuosity of the violin. In one of the concertos of Opus 4, the
Walsh publication, the solos of the finale are accompanied by a
solo cello, to which the composer entrusts a very animated pattern in sixteenth notes. But Vivaldi also wrote concertos for solo
cello, of which two have been known for a fairly long time
(P. 24, F. III, 4; P. 176). Eighteen others are part of the acquisi-
tion of the Turin library, and seven more have recently been
discovered in Germany.

We have, as a matter of fact, arrived at a period when the
cello is leaving its humble position as accompanist. After Petronio
Franceschini, who died in Venice in 1630, after Domenico Ga-
brielli, called "*Minghino dal Violoncello*," certain masters such
as Giuseppe Jacchini, G. B. Bononcini, Antonio Vandini, and the
renowned Venetian Antonio Caldara were responsible for the
appearance of a solo literature. Vivaldi contributed to this
literature by his sonatas and by his series of concertos for solo
cello, which are the first and most considerable of the genre.
As with the violin, Vivaldi exploits especially the high and middle registers, without concerning himself too much with the
lower, apparently reserving it for the cello that accompanies.
If he ventures up to the high range, he tempers his boldness by
proceeding by conjunct motion in relatively comfortable posi-

tions. He requires that the instrument produce staccato runs that group together up to seventeen notes; *brisures* on several strings, arpeggios, and *bariolages* "*alla Bach*" (P. 176). But, above all, he composes slow movements for it that are confined to a rather limited tessitura—in general, the two upper strings, the D and the A—that have at the same time a purity of line, a suavity, and, in a number of instances, an emotional intensity that makes some of them anthologized pieces.

The *violone* (double-bass), which he employs at the outset of his career in the modern manner to play the lowest part, is gradually supplanted by the cello. The sonatas, Opus 1, and the first collection of concertos, Opus 3, include a part for *violone* or harpsichord, or for *violone* and harpsichord. In the later collections only the cello is singled out for mention. But a number of manuscripts now and then indicate *tutti li bassi*, and it is very likely that when double-basses are at hand they are used for support, the same services being asked of them as of the cello in its role as bass. Once, in fact, in a bassoon concerto (P. 47, F. VIII, 12) an accompaniment by *violone* solo is specified.

Vivaldi employs instruments of less current use, as well as the family of violins. He does not call for the *tromba marina*, though, as is sometimes asserted. The Dresden concerto (P. 16) that was referred to above as one of those that the Elector of Saxony heard in 1740 presupposed not marine trumpets but violins played in imitation of them—"*violini in tromba marina*" —that is, making wide use of natural harmonics and by some expedient (the mute placed beside the bridge?) evoking their characteristic buzzing.

On the other hand, he uses the viola d'amore effectively; for it he wrote at least eight concertos, in which it is sometimes accompanied by the four-part string ensemble and by winds with mutes. It is well known, though perhaps not unprofitable to repeat, that in contrast to the instruments of the orchestral quartet, which were capable of very diverse uses—solo, orchestral *ripieno*, or joined in equality for the performance of chamber music works—the viola d'amore was treated almost exclusively as soloist. Its very unusual tone color and its singular technique created for it the aura of an "attraction," of an oddity that a small number of virtuosos, mostly Czechs, exploited. Sometimes, by way of an exception, it was used in the theater or during a cantata to accompany a singer whose voice stood out best when contrasted with its silvery and yet veiled sonorities. That is what Ariosto did in the aria *Sia il destin* of his opera *Marte Placato* (1707). But it never takes the place of the ordinary violas in the four-part ensemble, where it would create a disparity of timbre and at the same time a disequilibrium. The groupings of old music in which the viola d'amore is associated with another exceptional instrument, the quinton, result in mixed sonorities with which the eighteenth century was not acquainted.

Vivaldi wrote for a six-stringed viola d'amore tuned (from low to high) *D, A, D, F*-sharp, *A, D,* or "put out of tune" according to the method then employed by lutanists and violinists. The style of writing he adopts has harmonic passages in which the ability to sound three or four tones simultaneously is easily exploited, alternating with rapid monophonic runs which are conceived in the spirit and the style of the violin.

Finally, the *Concerto funebre* for solo violin and orchestra (P. 385, F. XII, 12) includes three *"viole d'Inglese"* treated as a concertino and added to the normal string parts. Two of these "English viols" are written in the G-clef, one in the F-clef. In his oratorio, *Juditha*, Vivaldi also designed the accompaniment of an aria for *"concerto di viole all'Inglese,"* written on four staves. Exactly what are these instruments? In his *Violinschule* of 1756, Leopold Mozart refers to a viola d'amore slightly larger than the current type as the *Englische Violet*. But this term is never encountered in England, and Georg Kinsky expresses the very convincing idea that the adjective *englisch* is here only a substitute for *engelhaft*, that is, angelic, which may be easily explained by the seraphic character of the sonorities of the viola d'amore. There is good reason to think that by "English viols" Vivaldi meant that ensemble of ordinary viols of different forms and sizes, soprano, alto, tenor, and bass, making up a complete and homogeneous family, for which the British had a fondness. This ensemble furnished a trio or a quartet (frequently also a quintet, a sextet, or even a septet) of soft and penetrating sonorities, for which the greatest English composers from the Renaissance to the beginning of the eighteenth century had written master-pieces. Even after 1700, however much the success of the violin had spread, it had not yet ousted the "chest of viols" from the music rooms of London, nor the valuable repertory written for them by William Byrd, Orlando Gibbons, William Lawes, Coperario, John Jenkins, and Matthew Locke.

Although the bowed instruments constituted the essential ele-ment of Vivaldi's orchestration, he did not employ only them. He occasionally used the lute and the theorbo, the first already obsolete in Italy at the time that concerns us, and the second hardly less so. An aria of the oratorio *Juditha* is accompanied by four theorbos and harpsichord. Two trios in the Mauro Foà collection in Turin are written for lute, violin, and bass. Of the concertos properly so-called, there can be cited only a *Concerto con 2 violini, leuto, e basso* (P. 209, F. XII, 15) and two of the *Concerti con molti Istromenti* of 1740—No. 1 (P. 16), whose odd orchestration includes two theorbos as well as two mandolins, of which we shall speak below; and No. 3 (P. 266) "*con viola d'amor, e leuto, e con tutti gl'istromenti sordini.*" In none of these works are the parts for the lutes and theorbos, which act simply as accompanying instruments, determined specifically; a ground-work with figures, shared with these instruments by the cello, allows the performer to realize it according to his tastes and his means.

The mandolin, on the contrary, as a solo instrument has all its notes written for it, and Vivaldi requires of it some degree of virtuosity. Its use in the orchestra was not new. It is to be found in M. A. Bononcini's *Teraspo overo l'innocenza giustificata* (1704) alternating with the theorbo for the purpose of joining in concert with the singer. An aria from Ariosti's *Marte Placato* (1707) is supported solely by a mandolin and the *basso continuo*. In Conti's oratorio *Il Gioseffo* (1706), a mandolin tuned a tone above its normal tuning performs a ritornello as a solo over a unison of violins and violas.

Likewise, Vivaldi employs it in *Juditha* in the accompaniment of an aria, using it in conjunction with pizzicato violins. He introduces it also in the first concerto of the 1740 collection. He is the first to have composed concertos for one mandolin (P. 134, F. V, 1) and for two (P. 133, F. V, 2). Perhaps he intended them for Marquis Guido Bentivoglio, of whom he inquires in a letter of December 26, 1736, if "His Excellency still takes pleasure in playing the mandolin."

In any case, he made an honorable provision for this thin-voiced instrument. The theme of the concerto for two mandolins, like that of the first concerto of 1740, is of a noble and resolute demeanor. The rhythmic pattern is one of those that Albinoni and Vivaldi had long since made fashionable and that Bach did not disdain to borrow from them. The showy passage work consists of rapid scales, triplets, and, above all, tremolos, with higher notes shooting up from them like sparks. These are such formulas as the violins will be asked to execute in profusion in the Mannheim symphonies.

While generous to violinists and even bassoonists, Vivaldi would have left nothing for the harpsichord if Bach had not brilliantly filled in the lacuna with his transcriptions. Nor did he write more for organ solo; but we have at least two scores from him in which the organ joins in concerted performance with the violin (P. 311, F. XII, 19; P. 274), and one for two organs together with two violins (P. 309). But violin and organ express themselves in the very same language; while the left hand in the organ part is entrusted with the thorough-bass and the contingent harmonic filling, the right hand devotes itself to an exchange with the violin of answers of an almost disappointing equity, and the intentional symmetry of the writing does not permit a belief that the soloists would embellish their parts with improvised ornaments.

In most of Vivaldi's other instrumental compositions the harpsichord is present, whether or not it is explicitly mentioned in the score. In fact, it is possible that in a number of instances, and not only in the concertos for two *cori*, the orchestra includes two harpsichords. There are two figured harpsichord parts in a Dresden concerto for solo violin and strings (P. 351). In several others whose slow movements are designed for strings without accompaniment there is to be found at the beginning of that movement the indication "*senza cembali*." It is known that in performances of Corelli's concerti grossi two harpsichords were used, one supporting the concertino, the other the main body of the orchestra. In another connection Quantz specifies, according to the number of violins at hand, the proportions he considers best for the orchestra; he thinks the addition of a second harpsichord is necessary for a complement of twelve or more violins, which in his opinion also presupposes one theorbo.

Several concertos entrust the execution of the slow movements to soloists accompanied by harpsichord without the help of bowed instruments on the bass part. Realization of the harmony then depends on the harpsichordist's skill and inventive powers. The composer seldom specified the spirit in which he wanted the bass to be realized. However, the bass of the central *adagio* of the eighth concerto of *La Stravaganza*, Opus 4, bears the indication "*arpeggio con il cembalo*." In Opus 8, No. 3 (F. I, 24), *L'Autunno* merits similar instructions, "*il cembalo arpeggio*," for a slow movement of forty-five measures.

A close examination of Vivaldi's dramatic scores is necessary to learn what he could extract from the very unusual tone color of the harpsichord. *Ercole sul Termodonte* (1723), now in the Paris Conservatory library, attests that, quite aside from its traditional role as harmonic support or filling, Vivaldi requires coloristic effects from it—for instance, a kind of sparkling quality which is made more luminous by association with violins playing rapidly repeated, ascending arpeggios.

Of the 454 concertos that are at present recognized to be Vivaldi's, there are about 120 in which wind instruments are used. Brasses are relatively rare, despite the favor they had enjoyed in Venice since the Gabrieli. An account of a concert in Venice in 1608 can be found in Thomas Coryat's impressions of his travels. After expressing his admiration of the finished performance, unsurpassable in his opinion, the narrator continues:

Sometimes there sung sixteen or twenty men together, having their master or moderator to keep them in order; and when they sung, the instrumental musicians played also. Sometimes sixteen played together upon their instruments, ten sackbuts, four cornetts, and two viole da gamba of an extraordinary greatness; sometimes ten, six sackbuts, and four cornetts; sometimes two, a cornett and a treble viol. . . . Those that played upon the treble viols, sung and played together, and sometimes two singular fellows played together upon theorbos, to which they sung also. . . . At every time that every several music played, the organs, whereof there are seven fair pair in that room, standing all in a row together, played with them.

Outside Venice, Torelli's concertos indicate just as decided a taste for the brass sonorities. Around the same time or even before, Stradella wrote some sonatas for trumpet and strings.

If Vivaldi appears more cautious, it is on account of the circumstances for which his instrumental music was designed. Most of it was originally written for the Pietà. Now, some *maestre* could indeed achieve virtuosity on instruments little compatible with their theoretical frailty; these were women of exceptional prowess. In the records of 1742 mention is made of one Maestra Cattarina dal Cornetto. And probably violinists and harpsichordists became extemporaneously trumpet or trombone players as the need arose. Burney, having been present in 1770 at a concert of the Conservatorio dei Mendicanti, notes that the performers changed instruments very often. For horns, flutes, and oboes—winds of more general use—there were probably more regular instrumentalists.

The only concerto for two trumpets (P. 75, F. IX, 1) does not show anything new as regards the treatment of the solo instruments. They skillfully exploit known formulas with much less daring than J. S. Bach manifests in the second Brandenburg Concerto or the Christmas Oratorio.

The trombones, too, appear only once, and even this is not certain. A concerto in the Giordano collection (P. 319, F. XII, 18) includes *"primo e secondo trombon da caccia."* Perhaps these are the large hunting horns, with *trombon* being the augmentative of *tromba.*

In Vivaldi's work manifold evocations of fanfares are found, but stylized fanfares without brasses that are played by the violins used "in the manner of a trumpet"—concertos *"per violino in*

tromba" (*e.g.*, P. 138, F. I, 64; P. 117, F. I, 96; P. 179, F. I, 97).
Vivaldi in this usage exploited a very old vein. Farini's *Capriccio
Stravagante*, as far back as 1627, contained an episode in *D* for
four-part string ensemble, called *Trombetta*, with figurations
borrowed from the invariable vocabulary of trumpet fanfares. In
Uccellini's *Gran Battaglia* (1669), in J. P. Westhoff's *Guerra*
(1682), and in a manuscript sonata owned by the Bibliothèque
Nationale and attributed either to Lunati (*il Gobbo*) or to Nicola
Matteis, one meets with almost identical fanfares. Vivaldi took
the evocation of the fanfare as a starting point, but rapidly freed
himself from it; and his concertos go beyond a sterile exercise in
imitation.

As far as the introduction of horns into the symphonic orchestra is concerned, he may well be a precursor. Before Stamitz,
he used them by pairs in more than seven sinfonie and concertos.
As in many other ways, he borrowed useful suggestions from
the dramatic orchestra. Badia in his *Diana rappacificata* of 1700 had
accompanied an aria *alla caccia* with two horns, oboes, and
strings. In the overture to *Meleagro* (1706), M. A. Ziani, a Venetian, joins horns in concert with violins and violas, the triplets
of the horns being set in bold opposition to the duple figuration
of the strings. Handel, who wrote remarkably for horns in his
open-air music (the *Water Music*, for example), and entrusted
solos to them that deviated greatly from the stereotype of hunting fanfares, also made use of them in his opera *Radamisto* in
1720. But at pretty much the same time Vivaldi was treating them
symphonically and giving them a role supporting the cellos with
independent patterns. In the concertos, especially in P. 273, F. XII,
10, he occasionally assigned brilliant solo episodes to them; or
joined them to a bassoon or to two oboes in the concertino; or
even incorporated them into the tuttis, exploiting their resources
to the full like a true orchestrator.

He was undoubtedly responsible for the vogue which that instrument was having in sacred music at the time when Charles de
Brosses visited Italy. "In church music," he wrote from Milan on
July 16, 1739, "the great organ and the horns accompany the
voices."

It should be remarked that Vivaldi generally writes the horn parts without transposition. Once, however, in a Dresden concerto (P. 268), the horns are in F; and once, in the Amsterdam concerto (P. 444), in D.

Before the discovery of the Foà and Giordano bequests in Turin, only a few works of Vivaldi were known in which woodwinds were used: twenty-five in all, counting those printed— the six flute concertos, Opus 10; the two oboe concertos from Opus 7 (Book 1, No. 1; Book 2, No. 1); the oboe concerto in the collection *Harmonia Mundi* (No. 5, P. 264); Opus 8, Nos. 9 and 12, for solo violin or oboe; Opus 11, No. 6, which is simply a transcription of Opus 9, No. 3—to which are to be added eleven Dresden manuscripts, one in Upsala, and one in Schwerin. The Turin collections brought forward sixty-eight others, of which thirty-seven alone are for the bassoon. Consequently the aversion for this family of instruments attributed to the Italians appears more than doubtful. In his preface to the Vivaldi symphonies that he edited, Ludwig Landshoff, ignorant as yet of the Turin manuscripts, most properly lays stress on Vivaldi's predilection for strings, which, in a less happy fashion, he attributes to the failings of Italian woodwinds. To do this he puts his trust in a remark by Alessandro Scarlatti as reported by Quantz. But it is almost impossible to generalize from Scarlatti's opinion. One has only to think of the extremely advantageous place the flute occupies in the dramatic scores of the time. The oboe concertos of Valentini, Albinoni, and Marcello bear witness to the same effect. The oboe, in fact, is valued by more than one master as the equal of the violin. It is an oboist (very quickly fallen into oblivion) whose success, they say, darkened Corelli's last years. A half-century later the composer Mauro d'Alay asks in his will that on the feast of the Annunciation a renowned foreign musician should perform in the church of the Steccata in Parma—"a violinist or oboist or some other refined instrument."

Vivaldi seems to have shared this taste rather than Scarlatti's distrust. He was the first to publish concertos for flute (Opus 10, *ca.* 1730), and in these six concertos, as well as in the ten remaining manuscripts, he treats it in a new manner. Until then the flute and the oboe appeared in chamber music as *ad libitum* substitutes for the violin; dramatic music, however, used them in a more characteristic way, employing their tone color almost symbolically in scenes of a rustic nature. Vivaldi in the same way entrusts the imitation of birds twittering or of pastoral cantilenas to the flutes (*Il Cardellino*, Opus 10, No. 3, F. XII, 9). In this same *Goldfinch Concerto* he gives a model of *cantabile* writing for the flute in the slow movement. Perhaps only J. S. Bach, in the instrumental parts of his cantatas, achieves an equally finished result.

The tessitura exploited by Vivaldi goes from *a'* to *e'''*. Occasionally he prolongs a high pitched tone; more rarely still he descends downward as far as *f'*, the first space on the staff. The most common figurations, which were to remain in the flutist's repertory, are rapid scales, trills, and arpeggios boldly set going on the constituent notes of the tonic and dominant chords.

He writes readily for two flutes and the orchestral quartet of strings (*e.g.*, P. 76, F. VI, 2); or for a wind ensemble either alone or accompanied by strings (*e.g.*, P. 323, F. XII, 26; P. 81, F. XII, 30). He also knows how to use the flute in an assignment to an accompanying role; in a Dresden *larghetto* (P. 359, F. XII, 33) the solo violin plays a melody over an accompaniment entrusted to two flutes, a cello, and a bassoon. To the piccolo (*flautino*), for which he wrote three concertos, he offers passage work of great volubility and hazardous arpeggiations.

The oboe is treated in a variety of ways. It is occasionally the substitute for the solo violin in moderately difficult concertos, where the possibilities of neither instrument are fully exploited (Opus 8, Nos. 9 and 12). Even here a higher stage of virtuosity may be found than that evidenced around 1700 by the works of Keller, Rosiers, and Corbet, in which the oboe was employed in the absence of a trumpet. Elsewhere Vivaldi is content to have the oboe double the violins.

But there exist also many concertos written especially for the oboe whose passage work demands a high degree of virtuosity. The range exploited goes from *c'* to *d'''*. In this area Vivaldi was preceded chronologically by the German, Johann Michael Müller; the Estienne Roger catalogue of 1716 announces his *Opera prima*, *XII Concerts à un hautbois de concert, deux hautbois ou violons, une haute contre et basse continue*. Handel precedes him also;

the fourth of his *Concerti grossi*, Opus 3, performed in 1716 as the second overture to *Amadigi*, grants the oboe a place in the limelight.

Moreover, the oboe in Vivaldi's works, like the flute, is occasionally treated in a modern manner and incorporated into the orchestra for the purpose of supplying a touch of well-defined color; for example, in the *Concerto con due Corni de caccia, due oboe, fagotto, violino e violoncello obligato* . . . (P. 267), in which it serves as soloist only in the *grave*. As a soloist it can join in concerted passages with another solo instrument, be it the violin or the bassoon. Finally, several concertos are written for a pair of solo oboes (*e.g.*, P. 85, F. VII, 3).

Perhaps Vivaldi did not ask as much of the oboe as did J. S. Bach, who, as André Pirro says, treated it as "the outstanding soloist of the orchestra in the realm of pathos just as the violin is its lyric soloist" (*L'Esthétique de J.-S. Bach*, 1907). Vivaldi was satisfied to use it as a singing instrument suited both to melody and to the nimblest runs.

The bassoon profits from a rather surprising predilection on the part of Vivaldi. Outside of his work, scarcely anything for bassoon solo can be cited in this period save a movement in a Geminiani concerto, Opus 7, No. 6 (1748). It is true that some dramatic scores at times set the bassoon in strong relief. Handel in *Saul* (1738) makes use of its eerie character in the apparition scene, when the ghost of Samuel appears in the witch's cave. J. S. Bach early shows himself in his cantatas to be well versed in its virtuoso resources. The accompaniment of a duet in the cantata *Mein Gott, wie lang* (1716) includes a bassoon part with a swift running pattern in sixteenth and thirty-second notes extending over a two octave range.

But Vivaldi was really the first to assign the bassoon to concertos in which it alternates accompanied solos with passages of pure virtuosity. The Foà and Giordano collections contain no less than a dozen of these concertos. There must have been in the master's entourage an amateur or professional virtuoso endowed with a sound technique for whom Vivaldi took the trouble to frame a complete repertory. The range exploited in these concertos is two octaves and a half—C to g′ (the modern bassoon extends a whole tone lower and goes up to f″).

Apart from its use as a solo instrument, the bassoon (called sometimes *bassone*, sometimes *fagotto*) is also one of the instruments allocated to the bass part. In this use it does not necessarily simply double the cello. In the concertos for large orchestra (*e.g.*, P. 97, F. XII, 31) a solo bassoon occasionally accompanies a solo violin or two, or two flutes, or an oboe, often in a slow movement. The first movement of the cello concerto (P. 119, F. XII, 22) begins still more singularly, with a solo for the cello accompanied only by the bassoon. Such is Vivaldi's interest in its tone color that in a concerto for solo violin and strings (P. 351) he adds an oboe and a bassoon for the *adagio*.

An unusual instrument appears twice—the *salmò*, which occurs in the *Concerto funebre con Hautbois sordini e Salmoè e Viole all'Inglese* (P. 385, F. XII, 12), and in the first concerto of the 1740 Dresden collection (P. 16). In these two works the *salmò*, used in twos, performs a bass part written in the F-clef.

Its identification is rather puzzling. A qualified expert, Georg Kinsky, then curator of the Heyer Museum in Cologne, when consulted around 1930 by the author of a monograph on the concerto, Walther Krüger, replied to him, "I assume that *salmò* is equivalent to *scialmo*. . . . The scialmo is known, moreover, from the score of the oratorio *Eleazare* by Giuseppe Bonno in 1739, hence a contemporary of Vivaldi. In Bonno's work the instrument is treated like an oboe, a melodic instrument, whereas in Vivaldi's it is a bass that goes from *c* to *c"*. This tessitura corresponds to that of the basset horn (alto clarinet). . . . The matter therefore would be clear had not this concerto [of 1740] been written for the Pietà, and it is hard to believe that this instrument, cumbersome and difficult to play as it was, could have been in use in an orchestra made up of young women." And Georg Kinsky winds up by apologizing for not having supplied a more satisfactory answer. In this connection the distinguished Swiss flutist Raymond Meylan has been kind enough to point out to me that in the *Concerto funebre*, published in facsimile by Ticci's in Siena,* the *salmo* has for its range F to *b*-flat; that its part, written in the F-clef, is melodic

---

* This is one of two facsimiles of Vivaldi manuscripts issued by the Accademia Chigiana and published by Ticci in 1947, the other being an edition of the concerto P. 221.

most of the time; and that by transposing it an octave higher its tessitura corresponds to that of the clarinet of Johann Christoph Denner, invented shortly before 1700.

This problem ought not to be unsolvable. There is no difficulty as to the etymology of the word; the *salmò* is the French *chalumeau*, the German *Schalmey*, the *shawm* (or *schalms* or *chalmes*) of the English. From the beginning an instrument with a single beating reed, the *chalumeau* developed afterward into a family that comprised soprano, alto, tenor, and bass. It was used more especially in France, but it was in Nuremberg that Denner was to transform it into the clarinet by the addition of two keys.

The *chalumeau* had been used well before Bonno's *Eleazare* in a number of operas by Italian composers which were performed in Venice from 1700 onward. It was always a question of the soprano *chalumeau*. In Ariosti's *Marte Placato* (1707), bass *chalumeaux* are used in conjunction with the soprano. Vivaldi also used the soprano *salmò* in the oratorio *Juditha*, an aria of which is accompanied by strings and *salmoè* notated from *b*-flat′ to *b*-flat″.

Is it, in these different instances, a question of authentic *chalumeaux* or already of clarinets? Appearances of the clarinet, which was invented at the very end of the seventeenth century, have scarcely been mentioned by historians except by the nineteenth-century Belgian Chevalier de Burbure in 1720 at Anvers; by Victor Schoelcher (*The Life of Handel*, 1867) in Handel's *Tamerlano* of 1724; and by Carl Israel (*Frankfurter Concert-Chronik*, 1876) in 1739 at Frankfurt. But I find it completely differentiated from the *chalumeau* in the 1716 music catalogue of Estienne Roger, where the following are enumerated:

No. 348: Airs for two *chalumeaux*, two trumpets, two clarinets, with hunting horns or two oboes, Book I.

No. 349: *Ibid.*, Book II.

No. 358: Airs for two clarinets or two *chalumeaux* . . . composed by M. Dreux.

The oratorio by Vivaldi, *Juditha*, contains a chorus accompanied by two *claren* with the same range as the soprano *salmoè*. This also presents a problem; they could be high trumpets (sometimes called *clarini*), or *chalumeaux*, or genuine clarinets. Their writing does not differ from that for the *chalumeau*.

But Vivaldi employs the clarinet—and he is probably the first to treat it as a true orchestral instrument—plainly designated in two concertos in Turin: a *Concerto con 2 Hautbois 2 Clarinet, e Istrom^{ti}* (this last word designating the whole four-part string ensemble; P. 73, F. XII, 1) and a *Concerto con due Clarinet, Hautbois e Istrom^{ti}* (P. 74, F. XII, 2). Here the clarinets already have a range of the two octaves from *c'* to *c'''*. They are treated diatonically with the accidentals *B*-flat, *E*-flat, and *F*-sharp. Some rapid patterns abounding in triplets are entrusted to them, requiring an agility that nearly equals that demanded of the oboe but that often preserves the character of the old high trumpet (*clarino*) as well. The *largo* of P. 74 is daringly written for two clarinets and two oboes with no accompanying instruments.

THE INSTRUMENTAL FORMS: SINFONIA, CONCERTO GROSSO, SOLO CONCERTO

It is in the realm of formal construction that Vivaldi—I regret it for the sake of Luigi Dallapiccola's thesis—proves to be most extraordinarily inventive. To measure his contribution it is indispensable to understand first of all the situation at the time when he began to produce—a rather confused situation for several reasons. I have already noted the conflict that set two styles against each other—the old polyphonic style inherited from the Renaissance, which remained deeply rooted in more than one country and had yet the strength to be given a splendid efflorescence by J. S. Bach, and, opposing this style, but capable upon occasion of being combined with it in varied proportions, a "modern" style, worked out under the influence of opera and oriented toward accompanied monody.

The era was one of practical experimentation, rather than theory. New instrumental forms were sought, malleable and less clearly differentiated than might appear from classifications in handbooks; these forms, on the contrary, were connected by intermediary links, as much in matters of formal construction as of harmony, counterpoint, and orchestration. The terminology (I shall return to it) was just as imprecise. Finally, we who survey this music from a perspective of more than two hundred

years have an additional reason for confusion in the nearly universal lack of the limited but dependable guide that chronology
could provide. As for the publications, which are seldom dated,
a good many of them may be assigned to a year by cross-
checking. But the unpublished works, which are much more numerous, bear scarcely any other indication than the name of the
composer—not always accurate when one gets away from the
autograph manuscript. Such carelessness is understandable, since
most of the time it is a question of occasional works not at all
intended to outlast the occasion that had given rise to them.

The seventeenth century had been with regard to instrumental
composition pre-eminently the century of the sonata. The beginning of the eighteenth century marks the heyday of the concerto
grosso, of which Vivaldi found finished models in the works of his
immediate predecessors; and the first appearances of the solo
concerto, which it became his privilege to develop and consolidate
to the point of being deemed its "inventor." Parallel to, and occasionally merging with, the concerto there developed the sinfonia.
I shall continue in this book to use the Italian spelling—observing
in this an already established tradition—so that it may be more
easily distinguished from the Classical symphony of the second
half of the century.

THE SINFONIA

For the sake of the reader who has no special knowledge on
these questions of morphology, I think it would be useful here
to define sinfonia and concerto. The notions that can be found
on this matter in technical works are scattered enough so that
there may be some interest in gathering them together.

Chronologically it is the sinfonia that appears first. The word
sinfonia, used in many senses from the end of the sixteenth century to the beginning of the eighteenth, designates in a general
way a composition intended for an instrumental group, an orchestra. Certainly there may be found, above all in Venice in
the age of the Gabrieli, many "sacred symphonies for voices and
instruments"; but Praetorius' *Syntagma Musicum* as early as 1619
listed the sinfonia among the pieces "without words" [*sine textu*]
as *praeludia per se* in contradistinction to those that serve as the

introduction to songs or dances. Nevertheless, "the Italians sometimes make use of such compositions at the outset of a vocal
chorus in the manner of an organ preamble and also often within
sections for the concerted chorus." Sébastien de Brossard in his
Dictionnaire de Musique of 1703 preserved this definition: "Generally speaking, when two sounds harmonize well together they
make a *symphony*, and in that sense all music or any composition
that makes a good impression on the ear is a genuine *symphony*.
But usage restricts it to only the compositions created for instruments and more particularly those that are free, that is, where
the composer is not governed at all either by a fixed number or
by a fixed kind of measure . . . , such as preludes, fantasias,
ricercars, toccatas. . . ."

Ten years later, Mattheson in his *Neu-eröffnete Orchestre* takes
up Brossard's very expressions while pointing out, besides, that
the Italians have adopted such musical compositions to act as
preludes to operas and other dramatic works as well as to sacred
pieces. Finally, to conclude the list of theorists, J. J. Quantz in
1750 no longer views the sinfonia as other than an opera overture
in movements, customarily brought to a close by a "gay minuet."

If we desert definitions from books and look rather at the
musical texts, we find, starting with Monteverdi's *Orfeo* (1607),
many instrumental preludes or interludes labelled either ritornello
or toccata or, again, sinfonia, according to the composer's fancy,
since nothing specific differentiates them. They are always short
episodes, barely a few measures long, more noteworthy for the
opulence of the orchestration than for the refinement of the form.
But opera comes to accord more and more of a place to these
pieces, and the sinfonia, which under that name or that of overture will come to serve as an introduction to the dramatic action,
gradually becomes organized. This organization, during the second half of the seventeenth century, produces two well-defined
types:

1) the French overture, stabilized by Lully, which is made up
of a solemn introduction followed by a fugal *allegro* with occasionally a third part that goes back, if not to the same material
as the beginning, at least to its tempo;

2) the Italian overture, a later type, of which the plan *allegro-
adagio–allegro* is to be met with in its pure form very close to

1700 in the operas of Alessandro Scarlatti. As a matter of fact, several Venetian and Roman composers had already used this form. The sinfonia that precedes the second act of Landi's *Sant'A-lessio* (1632) shows this design.

But before these two types of overture were established, Venetian opera composers conceived overtures or dramatic sinfonie of a very pronounced character, which interest us in that several of their characteristics are to be found in the concertos of Vivaldi. Historians distinguish three stages of evolution in these Venetian sinfonie: 1) before 1660; 2) from 1660 to 1680; 3) from 1680 to 1700—after which Venice produced innumerable operas, but under the predominant influence of the Neapolitan school.

During the beginning of the first period, the overtures or sinfonie amount to some great solemn chords in a strict rhythmic style, which still evoke the atmosphere of the church. Soon short *allegro* fragments are introduced among the chords in strong contrast with their solemnity; and this contrast gives the overture the possibility of descriptive effects, which both now and henceforth are typical of the theater.

The second period is marked by the use of fugal writing side by side with the loudly-sounded chords of the older overture; only such writing is not used here for abstract purposes as a simple stylistic convention, but for a dramatic function, for the expressive potentialities that it carries within itself. Vivaldi often linked the vertical, harmonic style with polyphonic writing that lacks great strictness and is closer to the opera than to the academy—what the recent biographer of Albinoni, Remo Giazotto, in speaking of the writing of this master, defines as "cordial counterpoint" (in the sense of coming from the heart).

During the last period, a division occurred. While some composers confined themselves to a form inspired by the French overture, others make their way toward the tripartite model of the Neapolitan opera.

Through these changes a Venetian color persists, characterized by strength of tonal feeling—a marked predilection for affirmation of the tonic chord in both the themes and the harmony; by the brilliance of instrumental coloring and the taste for trumpet fanfares—of which Vivaldi gives ingenious equivalents in the four-part string ensemble; and by contrasts of tempos of a descriptive intent within a single movement. Corelli introduced the like of these things in his sonatas and concertos, and Vivaldi, borrowing them from Corelli, merely retrieved a Venetian invention.

Meanwhile, a new fact intervened in the development of the dramatic sinfonia. For a variety of reasons, the possibility was conceived of performing it outside the theater as an independent work, separated from the opera to which it served as introduction; and the "*sinfonia avanti l'opera*" became the concert sinfonia. The transplantation was all the easier because as a general rule the composers of the Neapolitan school, in writing their overtures, did not care to tie them in with the dramatic action, as had the Florentines and Venetians of earlier days; they wished merely—as in the badly run theaters of today—to give the public time to get comfortably settled and ready to see and hear. In his *Grove's Dictionary* article "The Symphony," Sir Hubert Parry observed on this subject that the musicians, who attached such small importance to the overture that it was sacrificed (all the more sacrificed because the listener reserved his attention for the vocal part, the arias sung by his favorite soloists), came to exercise more care when they had the opportunity of having it heard in concerts, which happened at the very time when the Neapolitan overture achieved its formal perfection. The slow and solemn opening that Alessandro Scarlatti still preserved in the sinfonia for *La Rosaura* (*ca.* 1690) becomes weak and disappears, leaving the overture as simply two *allegros* enclosing a slow movement. This scheme, which was to be that of the pre-Classical symphony, appears without ambiguity in the overture of *Dal mal il bene* (*ca.* 1696). The overtures of *La Caduta dei Decemviri* (1697), of *Il Prigionero fortunato* (1698), and of other operas strengthen the method and little by little complete the structure of the first *allegro*. The success of the new form was to be so swift that as early as 1699 Campra, wishing to insert a parody of Italian opera in his *Carnaval de Venise*, began it with a sinfonia in the Italian manner, *vivace–adagio–presto*.

Let us observe that others besides Scarlatti applied this plan in the theater in a number of scattered trials throughout the last third of the seventeenth century. In instrumental music the same outline is present not only in a sinfonia by Stradella, before 1682, but also in profusion in the *20 Sonate a 3, 4, 5, 6*, Opus 7, by the Venetian, Pietro Andrea Ziani (1678). Nearly all of them are in three movements as follows:

1) *Sonata*, without any further specification, but clearly of an *allegro* character in compound duple time;

2) *Seconda parte*, likewise without other annotation, but of a solemn character in 3/2;

3) *Terza parte*, again of an *allegro* character, in compound duple time.

(In the fifth sonata the central movement is expressly headed *largo*. When, as in a few of these sonatas, the first movement includes a slow introduction, the marking *allegro* appears following it.)

These sonatas for three, four, five and six instruments, which the catalogues of Roger of Amsterdam call "*sonates à fortes parties*" and Mattheson calls "*starke Sonaten*," may be seen along with the opera overture as possible forerunners of the symphony.

Paralleling the concert sinfonia there still continued to flourish between 1660 and 1700 a church sinfonia that was nothing but the sonata *da chiesa* for many instruments in four or five movements, starting with an *adagio* in a strict style. The Bologna school with Maurizio Cazzati, Giovanni Bononcini and, above all, Torelli, produced magnificent examples of it.

THE CONCERTO GROSSO

At the time of its full development around 1700, the concerto grosso was characterized essentially by the use of two instrumental groups unequal in size (and usually in quality) that were sometimes placed in opposition and at other times united with one another. The one, the concertino, is made up of a few select soloists, most frequently three—two violins and a cello, or two flutes, oboes, or trumpets and a bassoon—with a harpsichord realizing the bass; the other, the concerto grosso, is formed by the greater part of the orchestra, and its members are the *ripieni*. Romain Rolland needlessly complicates things when, in describing the orchestra of Handel's time, he writes, "The orchestra was divided into three parts: first, the concertino, comprising a first and second violin and a solo cello; second, the concerto grosso, comprising the chorus of the instruments; third, the ripienists, supporting the grosso" (*Haendel*, 1910). The third group is pure fancy. The ripienists or *ripieni* are by definition the musicians who comprise the concerto grosso. On solemn occasions parts usually played by two, three, or more in the concerto grosso were reinforced yet again by bringing in a complement of ripienists, the *strumenti di renforzo;* these last are incorporated in the whole and do not constitute an organically different group. The concerto grosso has its own harpsichord for accompaniment, but it happens that a single harpsichord may serve both the concertino and the concerto grosso. The grouping in this genre allows the public to enjoy a double contrast in the course of one performance—on the one hand, between the concerto grosso and the concertino; on the other, within the concertino itself between the soloists who make it up.

The distant origins of the concerto grosso lie in the music for several choruses, made up of voices and instruments or voices alone, that the close of the sixteenth century delighted in and that the Gabrieli in Venice had handled with singular magnificence. Very quickly this kind of composition made its way throughout Europe. As early as 1600, in a concert given at Avignon for the arrival of Marie de Medici, there appears the genuine plan of the concerto grosso. "There was," reports an anonymous account, *Le Labyrinthe royal de l'Hercule Gaulois,* which was brought to light in 1904 by Amédée Gastoué, "a chorus of music for voices and instruments, under the direction of M. l'Æschirol [Antoine Esquirol]. . . . They began graciously to sing a hymn for two choruses, the one having four select voices, the other full, reinforced chorus."

This plan passed from vocal music with or without instruments to purely instrumental music under the influences of the trio sonata, the opera sinfonia (particularly as seen in such works as Lully's, where a trio of winds often breaks in upon a string tutti), and, after that, the concert sinfonia. How this occurred is a long story, for which I cannot do better than refer the reader to Schering's *Geschichte des Instrumentalkonzerts,* which has so well laid down the broad outlines.

What matters to us is that this form had reached its maturity before Vivaldi's entrance upon the scene. It may be considered as having been entirely established by the time of Alessandro Stradella's death (1682); an authentic concerto grosso by him is in the libraries of Modena and Turin. Besides, Stradella in his operas makes use of an orchestra divided into concertino and concerto grosso. The composers to whom the devising of this form is generally attributed, Torelli and Corelli, only developed fully elements whose essential character was already present in Stradella's work.

In the concerti grossi of the great era of the genre—the end of the seventeenth century and the first decades of the eighteenth —two kinds or, more precisely, two styles coexist: the church style, *da chiesa*, and the chamber style, *da camera*. Both are used in the sonata from around 1650 on. Brossard's *Dictionnaire de Musique* distinguishes them as follows:

> The sonatas *da chiesa*, that is, appropriate to the church . . . usually begin with a solemn and majestic movement accommodated to the dignity and sanctity of the place, after which some gay and lively fugue is taken up. . . . They are what are properly called sonatas.
>
> The second type comprises the sonatas that are called *da camera*, that is appropriate to the chamber. They are, to be more exact, suites of little pieces composed in the same key or mode and suitable to be danced. This kind of sonata is usually begun with a prelude or a little sonata, which serves as a preparation for all the other movements; afterwards come the allemande, the pavane [and other dance movements]. . . . All this, composed in the same key or mode and played one after another, makes up a sonata *da camera*.

I have quoted nearly all of Brossard's article "*Suonata*" because it attests to the difficulty that a scholar of 1700, a music historian and an estimable composer, had in defining precisely the form with which the public was then most infatuated. Indeed, his definition of the chamber sonata could better be applied to the old suite of dances, than to the sonata that it claims to describe. In fact, music *da camera*—Georges Cucuel in his work on La Pouplinière (1913) gives an excellent translation of this as "*musique de cour* [courtly music]"—was not composed of a series of dances suitable to be used as such. Some pieces of choreographic origin appear in it, but these are stylized for the most part; they occasionally renounce square phraseology and repetitions. They were prefaced by preludes of free form and included instrumental arias closely based on the opera aria. If one wants to grasp the real spirit of music *da camera*, which has very little connection with present-day "chamber music," one may profitably reread Georg Muffat's preface to his 1701 collection of concertos (*Auserlesene Instrumental-Music*). "These concertos," he writes, "are suited neither to church symphonies (because of the *airs de ballet* that they contain) nor to dancing (because of the other intermingled conceptions, at times solemn and sorrowful, at times gay and sprightly, composed simply for the satisfaction of fastidious ears). They could well serve fittingly at entertainments or receptions of princes and great lords, as well as at the splendors of banquets and serenades and for the assemblies or concerts of experts and music lovers."

From the nonchoreographic nature of the concerto *da camera* comes the possibility of occasionally introducing it into the church. In return, the stateliness of the churchly style—stateliness that consents to being much attenuated in certain *allegros* and in the finales, which have rhythmic patterns of the gigue or minuet—is not opposed to the secular way in which a churchly concerto might be performed outside the holy place. Also, one finds collections that are entitled in a way that does not specify their usage; this was to be the almost universal custom when Vivaldi published his first collection of concertos, *L'Estro armonico*, in which, as will be seen below, the fusion of the two styles was nearly complete. It may even be conjectured that in collections such as G. M. Alberti's *Concerti per chiesa e per camera* (1713), where the two styles co-exist in but a weakly differentiated form, the title is rather an invitation to make use of them for both purposes.

THE SOLO CONCERTO

While the differences between the concerto grosso *da chiesa* and the concerto grosso *da camera* continued to diminish, another sort of contrast was being established between these two forms and a newcomer, the solo concerto. I shall not retrace its origins any more than I have done for the concerto grosso.

Keeping to the last stage of its history, there can be seen in the course of the seventeenth century more or less developed solos—generally assigned to the violin—that break in upon the tutti of a sinfonia. Solos occasionally stand out also from the sonatas *à fortes parties* published in great numbers around 1670, often showing the spirit which was to be that of the concerto. Brilliant passages and even cadenzas for the solo violin are to be found in the trio sonatas of the same period, which it was permissible to play with double or even triple desks, thus making them concertos or sinfonie. Even the solo sonatas for violin with *continuo*, such as those by Balzer, Biber, Westhoff, Uccellini, Bassani, and others, in a way augur the solo concerto by displays of adroit technique, and, less often, by a lyricism that breaks forth in the slow movements. Such lyricism was later to unfold fully in Vivaldi's *adagios*.

Finally and pre-eminently, the opera—Venetian as well as Viennese (an offshoot of the Venetian) and Neapolitan—gave a development and an unaccustomed brillance to the ritornellos of the violin solo and raised them to a much higher level of technique than that of the concertos of Torelli, who was Vivaldi's most conspicuous precursor in this new genre.

It is with Torelli's Opus 8, appearing in 1709, the year of the composer's death, that the solo concerto may be considered fully constituted in its formal traits. But the expressive intensity of which this kind of concerto is capable is only to manifest itself with Vivaldi. In spite of the external resemblances, the two men's conceptions differ profoundly. If in the works of Torelli brilliant passage work is entrusted to the soloist, this is for the purpose of guaranteeing a maximum of clarity to the performance. This can be deduced, among other evidences, from the preface of his Opus 8, where, recommending the use of ripienists in order to give fullness to the concerto grosso, he asks on the other hand that the violins of the concertino never be doubled in order, he says, "to avoid confusion." Vivaldi's purpose is entirely different; an inspired performer, he designed solos for himself that would concentrate the impassioned attention of the listeners on him as on a beloved singer at the opera, and this in the contemplative *adagios* still more than in the showy sections of the *allegros*.

He glorified a personal feeling, a new lyricism, the vogue for which was as widespread as it was sudden. Soon the solo concerto as he treated it—with a groundwork of luminous simplicity, with a captivating fervor, with a homophonic style of writing similar to that of the opera, and with pleasure in virtuoso feats—this concerto was to appear as the modern form, the form par excellence of the concerto *da camera*. The concerto grosso, with its two or three soloists making up the concertino, its less expansive virtuosity, and its more severe writing, came to be considered an archaism, although such masters as Bach and Handel were to return to it. It became associated in the public's mind with the church concerto, and both were relegated to the things of the past.

Consequently, the definitions became changed. In 1752, Quantz, the most precise of the theorists and the most trustworthy on matters of instrumental music, arrived at formulations that henceforth set concerto grosso in opposition to concerto *da camera*. (This supersedes the concerto grosso–solo concerto opposition and that of the *da camera* and *da chiesa* concerto.) And Quantz sees no other form of concertos to be described than these.

To sum up, at the beginning of Vivaldi's career four types of concertos existed:

Concerto grosso: a) church concerto; b) chamber concerto.
Solo concerto: a) church concerto; b) chamber concerto.

However, the old kind of polyphonic writing, to which the churchly style remained connected, progressively lost ground before the homophonic writing propagated by the opera. At the same time, the concerto grosso, inclined by its very nature toward polyphonic writing, gave way to the solo concerto, which was determinedly homophonic and which thereby tended more and more toward the chamber style. When Vivaldi died (1741), the identification of which I have spoken above was an accomplished fact. For Quantz's contemporaries the concerto grosso equaled the church concerto, and the solo concerto equaled the chamber concerto.

All this would remain clear for the most part were it not for two things. First, an absurd terminology unnecessarily confused matters, and, second, the music of that time placed compositions of a clearly distinct form side by side with hybrids of all sorts.

Of the unsettled state and contradictions in the vocabulary much has already been written. I shall note only the most flagrant in endeavoring to shed some light on points that have impeded more than one researcher. At the very start the meaning of the word *concertant* contributes to the confusion because, in French and German, as in Italian, it is connected with two different ideas —with that of the *concert* form (from *conserere*, to unite); and with that of the *concerto* form (from *concertare*, to contend). In the first case, the concertant instruments and parts are those that join together harmoniously in order to make up a "concert"; in the second, they are those that are set in opposition to the full orchestra in order to "concert" with it (more properly, and according to the etymology, "against it," one might say) or among themselves (more properly, "against one another").

The emergence of the trio sonata, for two violins and *continuo*, at the beginning of the seventeenth century brings the notion of *concertare* back to that of a polite dialogue—no longer a struggle —between the two violins, which alternate melodies and passage work at the same range and level of technique for both instruments. This is also what occurs between the soloists of the concertino in concerti grossi of the pure type, of which Corelli's Opus 6 furnishes us with the most beautiful examples.

But Torelli in his Opus 8 returned—as yet only moderately— to the ideas of contention and of pre-eminence for certain instruments, when he specified that the first six concertos of this collection are for "*due violini che concertano soli*" and the last six for "*un violino che concerta solo*," set alone in opposition to the orchestra, thus occupying the foreground by itself.

When, at around the period 1720–1730, the solo concerto had almost completely ousted the concerto grosso, the solo part often carried the indication "*violino concertino*"; it is impossible to decide if this is because it alone is "to concert," or because it makes up by itself the old group of the "concertino." To increase, if possible, the confusion, some composers—for instance, Torelli and Francesco Manfredini—were struck by the idea of entitling simple duets for violin and cello *concertini per camera*, even though they have no connection with the form of the concerto.

In titles of printed works or manuscripts the words *concerto*, *sinfonia*, and *sonata* are used in perpetual, mutual exchange. The use that J. S. Bach himself makes of the word *sinfonia* is odd. He applied it to the piece with which the second partita for harpsichord opens. Some have tried to explain that by *sinfonia* Bach meant music for several voices; well, nearly the whole piece is written for only two parts. Burney, a musicographer by trade, christens as a *symphony* an intermezzo for viola d'amore (a concerto?) performed by Attilio Ariosti in 1716 between two acts of Handel's *Amadigi;* while Handel, composing a genuine solo concerto around 1710, entitled it *Sonata a cinque.* Telemann, when dedicating a more or less authentic solo concerto to his friend Pisendel, expresses himself on the autograph manuscript as follows: "*Concerto grosso per il Signore Pisendel.*" In the twentieth century it happens that composers entitle as "Sonata for Orchestra" or "Concerto for Orchestra" works that have nothing about them of the concerto or the sonata. With them it is simply a question of naïveté or thoughtlessness. In Bartók's work, the Concerto for Orchestra requires from each instrument the virtuosity and conspicuousness usually demanded of soloists. Among the works of others, such titles indicate a prejudice for archaism or simply the desire for easy originality.

If we put aside the attempt to draw any precise idea of form from titles and pass on to an examination of the works themselves, we shall come across formal and stylistic anomalies fit to raise serious obstructions at least so long as we do not perceive that the composers of that happy time were unaware of most of the restraints with which the Classical composers confined themselves soon after. Differentiation by genre is hardly more possible in the musical texts than in the wording of the titles.

The concert sinfonia is in principle designed for full orchestra. Now, if it pleased the composer to leave a solo instrument—a violin, a flute, an oboe—in the open for a moment, he was not violating any prohibition of principle. If in a church concerto he thought well of finding a place for a movement of secular dance, more or less stylized, he did it without hesitation, just as he would interpolate a polyphonic piece in a chamber suite.

A single composition could, when played, undergo changes in the number of instruments used which made it, according to circumstances, a sonata, a concerto, a sinfonia. The reinforcing—doubling, tripling, and greater duplication—of trios and quartets was common practice well before the trio-symphonies of Mannheim "intended to be played as a trio or by a larger orchestra."

With equal freedom, the composers placed side by side, in the same collection, and under the same title, works of dissimilar spirit. Of Alessandro Scarlatti's *VI Concertos in seven parts*, published in London by Benjamin Cooke, four are in reality concert sinfonie without soloists; one (No. 3) is a solo concerto; and another (No. 6) is a concerto grosso.

Even in Corelli's Opus 6, which it is agreed may be considered as the most representative monument to the concerto grosso style, the last concertos are oriented toward the solo concerto—timidly, yes, but perceptibly; the *allegro* and the minuet of the tenth, the *allegro* and the gigue of the twelfth, no longer have the three soloists play together in concerted fashion, but permit the first violin to be in the limelight while its partners content themselves with accompanying. In this series the chamber and the churchly styles interpenetrate one another. The first eight concertos are in a general way designed for the church; but fast movements are admitted in which dance rhythms are glimpsed.

THE CONCERTO AS CONCEIVED BY VIVALDI

It would be of no use to stress further the unstable situation that prevailed around 1700, as much with respect to instrumental forms as to the vocabulary that described them. I think enough has been said about it, first, to put the reader on guard against adopting a rigid classification into which the works could only be fitted by Procrustean treatment; and second, to make obvious both the freedom from which Vivaldi profited when he set out as a composer, and his marvelous instinct in progressively discarding what was anarchical in such freedom to the end that he might affirm—we could almost say establish—the tripartite plan, so logically balanced, on which the new instrumental style was going to be nourished.

His first collection of concertos, *L'Estro armonico*, Opus 3 (*ca.* 1712), illustrates as well as possible what has just been said on the subject of the imprecision of the instrumental forms of that time. Most historians, including Schering, distinguish four solo concertos (Nos. 3, 6, 9, and 12) and eight concerti grossi among its twelve concertos. Perhaps the truth is not so simple.

There is no doubt about the solo concertos, but what about the others? Two (Nos. 5 and 8) are written for two solo violins with the orchestra; two (Nos. 2 and 11) for two violins and solo cello; two (Nos. 1 and 4) for four solo violins; two (Nos. 7 and 10) for four violins and solo cello.

Now of these eight concertos, three (Nos. 2, 4, and 7) preserve in their form some features of the church concerto; they have four movements, the first being a rather developed *adagio*, and the third a slow movement reduced to a few measures which constitutes a transition between the two *allegros*. The others, whether written for two or four violins, already have the tripartite shape of the chamber concerto: *allegro–largo–allegro*. From the point of view of orchestration, the soloists of the four-violin concertos, or those with two violins and a cello, do indeed make up a concertino. It is not the same with Nos. 5 and 8, in which the two violins are treated in a soloistic spirit, far removed from that of the concerto grosso. Their virtuosity is more venturesome than that displayed in the concertos for solo violin; they give themselves up to the job of arpeggios and *brisures* that are just as difficult, and they ascend further into the upper range of the instrument.

Even in places where the concertino exists, it appears rather like a succession of soloists with marked predominance given to the first violin; there is no essential resemblance to the concertos *"con due violini che concertano soli"* of Torelli's Opus 8, in which the two violins remain on a footing of strict equality. The theater, more than the church, makes its influence felt here. In Opus 3, No. 1, for four violins, each of the soloists comes in by turn and each of them makes himself heard out in the open; occasionally, however, the first and second violins or the third and fourth sometimes progress in thirds. The *largo* of this concerto sets up an opposition, as in the opera then in fashion, between the singing ornamentation of the solos and the inflexible unison of the tutti. In No. 10, likewise for four violins, with obbligato cello, the violins are again conspicuous by turns, playing extended passage work, which is longer and more brilliant in the case of the first solo violin. In No. 11, whose fugue would not mar the most strict concerto *da chiesa*, the delightful siciliano is only a cantilena for a single voice; and in the finale, which starts in imitative style, the first violin quickly comes to prominence. Its last passage has the demeanor of a virtuoso cadenza; we are all the way into the modern style.

In general the composer may be clearly seen to have been drawn toward a dramatic opposition of tutti and soloists, toward a lyrical outpouring in the slow movements contrasting as sharply as possible with the square phrasing of the initial *allegro* and the cheerfulness of the finale. All this moves further and further away from the frame of the concerto grosso. For that matter, in Opus 3, the concerto that is most loyal to the old ideal, No. 7, seems to be less a spontaneous outpouring than a tribute to the master of the genre, Corelli, the nature and treatment of his themes being invoked throughout the first movement.

Aside from this particular instance, *L'Estro armonico* indeed ushers in the new spirit. To a considerable extent it frees itself from the constraints of the churchly style, with its injunction of humility stemming from collective performance; the soloist escapes from the concertino to monopolize interest. It tends to express the individualistic inclinations that unfold in the concerto of the so-called Classical period and that belong really within the purview of romanticism. Answering the inquiry conducted by Jacques Gabriel Prod'homme on the occasion of what was called the Battle of the Concerto, Saint-Saëns wrote in the *Zeitschrift der International Musikgesellschaft* (1905): "As to what constitutes a concerto, that genre held to be inferior to the superior level where the performer is allowed to show his personality . . . the concerto solo is the part that ought to be conceived and executed as a dramatic personage." It is this kind of concerto that Vivaldi was the first to realize.

In all his output subsequent to Opus 3, the outline in three movements, fast–slow–fast, is the rule. But his imagination prompts him to many an exception. Some unusual concertos return to the profile of the concerto grosso; others have two consecutive slow movements between their two *allegros*, or finish off with two *allegros*, or change their tempo with the same freedom as does a symphonic poem.

The most singular experiment from the standpoint of form is probably a concerto in *e* for cello (P. 119, F. XII, 22). It has three movements, which would be, taking into consideration their incipits, *adagio*, *allegro*, *allegro*. But the first two movements follow a strange plan in which an expressly indicated tempo, always the same, is assumed by each of the two interlocutors, soloist and tutti, throughout the section. In the *adagio* the solos correspond to the opening introduction, and the tuttis are *allegro molto*. The division into parts is drawn up as follows (the solos are accompanied only by a bassoon):

> *Adagio* solo, 11 measures; *allegro* tutti, 12 measures
> *Adagio* solo, 13 measures; *allegro* tutti, 13 measures
> *Adagio* solo, 14 measures; *allegro* tutti, 11 measures
> *Adagio* solo, 4 measures; *allegro* tutti, 4 measures
> *Adagio* solo, 7 measures; *allegro* tutti, 4 measures
> *Adagio* solo, 3 measures; *allegro* tutti, 13 measures

The second movement presents the reverse arrangement—*allegro* solos for the cello and bass broken up with *adagio* tuttis.

In the matter of tonality, Vivaldi established himself as the resolute champion of what Maurice Emmanuel has nicknamed the "tyrant tonic," that is, Classical tonal organization confined to two modes, major and minor. Except for one or two examples inspired by folk material, these two modes were enough for Vivaldi, some of whose themes are indeed nothing but the tonic chord arpeggiated. The key of C has his preference. Of some 480 concertos and sinfonie that have come down to us, eighty are written in that key. The order of frequency of the keys he uses is as follows: D, 61 times; F, 51; B-flat, 47; g, 41; G, 40; A, 29; d, 28; a, 25; e, 17; E-flat, 16; c, 16; E, 11; b, 11; f, 2; f-sharp, 1.

The use of some of these keys was rather daring for the period. Tartini, a generation younger, did not venture to write a single concerto in c or E-flat, or, with greater reason, in f or f-sharp. Perhaps only Locatelli proves more rash than Vivaldi by writing a recitative for the violin in e-flat (Opus 7, 1741, concerto No. 6, *Il Pianto d'Arianna*).

This stubborn predilection on the part of a violinist for the key of C is an astounding thing. Not only his contemporaries, but almost all virtuoso-composers are more fond—as much for reasons of technical convenience as for sonority—of the keys more strongly supported by the open strings. Of Tartini's 125 concertos, 27 are in *D*, 23 in *A*, and only 14 in *C*.

Another feature peculiar to Vivaldi is the frequent adoption of a minor key as the opening key. This is the case with more than a third of his symphonic output. For Corelli's work the proportion is a sixth—2 concertos in minor out of 12; for Tartini's a seventh—16 concertos out of 125.

Coming now to the relation of tonalities between the first *allegro* and the slow movement, we do not find the same strictness as in the works of composers of the Classical period. A good third of the concertos and sinfonie have their three movements in the same key, after the example of the old suite. Somewhat less often the slow movement is in the relative major or minor; less often still in the dominant or the subdominant. But it also happens that it has only a distant relation with the first movement; where one concerto in *D* has its *largo* in *F*, others likewise in *D* have a *largo* in *e*. The key is occasionally determined by unexpected reasons, in which artistic considerations play little part.

The most typical pattern in this connection is that of the concerto Opus 10, No. 5 (F. VI, 1), for flute, in *F*, with a *largo* in *g*. The autograph manuscript discloses that the composer had at first begun a slow movement in *F* in compound duple time, giving it up after eight measures. He then composed a *cantabile largo* in *f* of twelve measures. But upon reflection this key seemed risky for the flute (perhaps he wrote it for a poorly trained amateur). He then enjoined the copyist to transpose it one tone higher; "*scrivete un tono piu alto tutto e scrivete tutto in g.*"

Rather than seeking a logical connection of keys among various movements, Vivaldi uses for the slow movement the key that will afford the greatest expressive resources. This is the moment when he means to move his audience deeply. He succeeds in this through orchestration; we have seen how he lightens or even suspends the accompaniment of the tutti to allow the soloist to sing freely in a tone of tender intimacy or to burst out in feeling accents. He attains this especially by making a wide use of the minor mode, stamping it with an elegiac meaning that was not inevitably attached to it at that period. Two slow movements out of every three are in minor; the proportion is exactly reversed in his *allegros*. Under these conditions the Classical tonic-dominant or tonic-relative key relationship is often sacrificed. One illustration of this is seen in the fact that Vivaldi flaunts a marked preference for the key of *e* in expressive passages. Used only 17 times as a main key, it is used 43 times as the key of the slow movement; and it is surprising to survey the very different relations with the first movements. Ten times it is the key of the first movement; 4 times it shares the same tonic with a first movement in *E*; 11 times it is the relative minor of a first movement in *G*; 3 times the dominant of one in *a*, and 3 times the subdominant of one in *b*; 10 times its tonic is the distance of a third from that of a movement in *C*; twice its tonic is a major second from that of a movement in *D*.

It should be observed that Quantz, so deeply impressed with Vivaldi's influence, points out that the keys of *e* and *c* express "audacity, rage, and despair"; and he sanctions the composer's writing his *adagios* in tonalities remote from the initial key.

The finales are for the most part in the opening key, and, save for rare exceptions, in major in conformance with the reigning aesthetic which demanded that the listener be left with a light and pleasant impression. Some concertos, however, begin in major and end in minor. Nearly always the reason for this is to be found in the haste with which the composer was obliged to finish the job, and this explains those cases, still more remarkable (I have given some examples of them in the biographical part of this book, p. 30 above), in which Vivaldi, breaking with a custom that had the force of law, completely forsakes the initial key in the last movement.

The first movement in a solo concerto, in Vivaldi's work, is in an almost unvarying way a moderate *allegro*—sometimes headed *andante* or *molto andante*—which aims at grandeur rather than at emotion. Vivaldi corroborates this for us when he specifies, in order to indicate an exception clearly, "*allegro* ma *cantabile*."

Beginning with Opus 3, the tutti–solo alternation that is characteristic of the genre takes on a different meaning from that which it assumed in the works of Albinoni and Torelli. For them the temporary obliteration of the orchestra to the advantage of the soloist chiefly aimed to give the principal part greater independence, distinctness, and volubility. Vivaldi sought for an essentially dramatic conflict between the virtuoso and the orchestra.

The composers of the Venetian opera had long since been exploiting the contrast between orchestral ritornellos and solo song, alternating them according to a plan that very nearly heralds that of the concerto *allegro*. Arnold Schering observes that in their works the ritornello, instead of returning in the same key, as in the early Florentine opera, is useful in modulation. He gives the aria of the stammering Demo in Cavalli's *Giasone* (1649) as an example:

> Ritornello (or tutti) in *e*
>   Solo
> Ritornello in *a*
>   Solo
> Ritornello in C
>   Solo (or more properly, accompanied duet)
> Ritornello in *e*

all things considered, it is the outline of the Vivaldi *allegro*.

E. T. A. Hoffmann, in his *Kreisleriana*, has amusingly defined the role of the concerto tutti at the beginning of the nineteenth century. "The tuttis of a concerto are, in short, only a necessary evil. They exist merely to contrive a rest for the soloist, during which he can calm down and get ready to launch out again." This is absolutely correct if applied to the empty bravura concertos that abounded at the very time when Beethoven was producing his masterpieces, and hardly caricature if the concertos of Chopin and Liszt are thought of. But this definition is not right in any way for those of Vivaldi.

In his works the tutti represents the most vigorous and nearly always the most interesting and characteristic element in the musical discourse. To it, as a rule, is given the exposition of themes around which the soloist unfolds periods that are, on the whole, essentially ornamental. It is also the tutti that outlines the harmonic groundplan of the piece by settling itself on the degrees from which the modulations of the soloist depart. This is the general plan, subject, as will soon be apparent, to numerous exceptions.

A tutti by Vivaldi is ordinarily made up of several dissociable melodic or rhythmic motives, each of which is capable upon occasion of being presented again apart from the others in the course of the *allegro*. This is instanced in one of the Dresden concertos (in *d*) which begins as follows:

270 Allegro

(P. 270)

This opening tutti has eighteen measures which contain four motives—marked A, B, C, and D. The second tutti is made up of the motives A–B–and D, in the dominant; the third uses A–A–B (the first A in the relative major, the second in the original key); the fourth and last brings in only C and D.

It is the make-up of this kind of tutti that Quantz explains in Chapter XVIII of his *Versuch:* "A serious concerto for one solo instrument and a large accompanying body requires in the first movement: 1) a majestic ritornello that is fully worked out in all the voices. . . . A proportionate length must be observed in the ritornello; it ought to consist of at least two main parts. The second should contain the most beautiful and majestic ideas since it is repeated at the end of the movement as a conclusion." In fact, the opening tuttis seldom are limited to the presentation of two motives. Most of them include from three to six.

In the progress of the work the tutti has not only the roles of introduction and conclusion. "The best ideas of the ritornello," writes Quantz, "may be broken up and placed between or inserted within the solos." (In Opus 3, No. 6, the first solo at its entrance goes back and literally repeats the beginning of the tutti.) He adds that the solos ought to be broken in upon "by short, animated, and splendid sections of the tutti, so that the ardor of the movement will be maintained from beginning to end." Vivaldi proceeds in this way when, aside from large tuttis, he has the tuttis and the solos clash with one another, throwing back and forth rejoinders of one or two measures each. This sort of jousting between orchestra and soloist prefigures the spirit of the Classical concerto, foreseen, if ineptly described, by C. R. Brijon as early as 1763: "A concerto became a dialogue among several interlocutors, with one set against the others. . . . The concerto is the coupling of the symphony and the solo. The tutti with which it begins sets forth the propositions that it is a question of discussing in the course of the piece; the contradictions that arise from it then create a musical battle between the solo and the tutti, a battle that ends in a reconciliation of feelings and of ideas" (*Réflexions sur la musique . . .*).

Finally, if the composer has provided for it and if the accompanist at the harpsichord is expert enough to do it in an impromptu fashion, the tutti can be included in the accompaniment of the solos by inserting its motives literally or by hints. The unity of the work is reinforced by just so much. I again quote Quantz: "If the solo passages permit, or if one can devise them in such a way that the accompanist can play during them something already heard in the ritornellos, this will create a very good effect."

The will to subject the whole of a movement to a single controlling thought asserts itself splendidly in a concerto in *B*-flat in the Dresden library (P. 349, F. I, 95). Of the three motives of the tutti, marked as A, B, and C, in the following illustration—the fourth motive is only the *da capo* of the first—only one, the first motive, A, moves throughout the *allegro*. It serves as the bass under B and C, first in the dominant, then in the tonic. The beginning of the solo reflects it. The second tutti combines it with C, and the third with B; the fourth takes up its rhythmic pattern again, which keeps up under the 17 measures of the ensuing solo;

during these 17 measures the pattern of the four eighth notes of the beginning pass from one to another of the instruments of the orchestral quartet of strings. The last tutti is made up of C, on which it is seen that A also stamps its impress.

349   Allegro (tutti)

(P. 349, F. I, 95)

The fullness of the first tutti is very variable. As for the writing, it is generally harmonic, though it may also, as in the above example, follow the old imitative style. Vivaldi also makes use of the dramatic device of the unison, nearly always in a strongly rhythmic way, as a striking contrast to the pliant inflections of the solo.

Nothing is less systematic than Vivaldi's conception of the solo. In general he grants it less importance than he does the tutti, especially from the standpoint of the thematic elements. Often, in fact, it is the lot of the orchestra to set forth all the themes, and for the solo to come in after the manner of the episode in a fugue, more brilliant and less rich in substance. Usually the solo consists of decorative figurations lightly accompanied by the harpsichord or organ, which realizes the bass with a string reinforcement of the bass line and occasionally some touches of the four-part string ensemble. Passage work, in Opus 3 of a somewhat staid virtuosity, is developed and made more venturesome in other printed collections, and still more in some of the unpublished works at Dresden and Turin. It must be admitted that it makes up the most dated part of Vivaldi's work. The novelty of the *brisures* and the arpeggios can last only for a time, and development by rosalia, of which Vivaldi took advantage when he was in a hurry to finish, soon exhausts its charm, especially if, as is the case in most of the modern editions, we fail to enliven the accompaniment by recalling melodic elements borrowed from the tutti, as advocated by Quantz.

Before censuring Vivaldi's expansion of material by symmetrical sequential patterns, it is well not to forget that they were the tradition in the works of the contemporary violinists—Corelli and his fellow-countrymen, as well as such Austro-Germans as Biber, Walther, and Westhoff—whose virtuoso passage work spontaneously took this form.

But so simplistic a way of modulating is very far from being the only one that Vivaldi had at his disposal. Beginning with Opus 4, he gives dazzling proof of this. Perhaps the title of that work, *La Stravaganza*, refers more to its harmonic daring than to its difficulties of instrumental technique. The slow movements of the fifth, seventh, and eighth concertos abound in modulations, the savor of which has not yet been lost. I shall limit myself to one quotation where, at the end of the first measure and the beginning of the second, an enharmonic treatment is met with that was not to have many counterparts in that period:

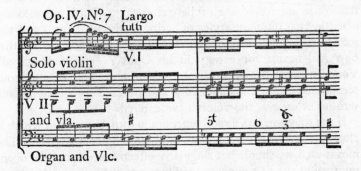

The connections between the first tutti and the first solo are in reality very flexible, though attempts have been made to codify them in a rigid way. A good part of the specifications that Vincent d'Indy's *Cours de Composition* gives on this subject, in defining the *allegro* of the Vivaldi concerto, ought to be rejected:

1. A simple thematic pattern treated more like a fugue subject than like a genuine theme.

2. Three distinct subdivisions, of which the last is only the all but literal repetition of the first, the one in the middle being more indeterminate.

. . . One thing alone distinguishes it [the concerto] essentially from any other form—the unalterable exposition of the theme by the tutti at the beginning and the end of the piece.

It will be seen below that the second and third paragraphs of this quotation, while not always true, are very nearly so. As for the first, it is enough to go through Opus 3 to verify a quite different freedom of construction—occasionally, in fact (Nos. 2 and 5), the first solo is a light, purely decorative section without resemblance to the main theme. Elsewhere (No. 12), without framing a theme, the solo already has a melodic character and presents itself as a genuine correlative of the tutti. Or (No. 6) it appears unreservedly melodic, appropriating, as has been said already, the opening of the tutti, thereafter diverging and dissolving in modulatory passage work. It can also (No. 8) comprise a genuine theme entirely different from that of the tutti.

Whatever may be the solution adopted, the result sought—and obtained—is a marked opposition between the tutti and the solo. When the first solo is decorative, its mobility contrasts with the massive solemnity of the orchestral opening. Tutti and solo are often in two different styles of writing—the tutti fugal and the solo homophonic. Biagio Marini had already made use of that powerful device for variety in his Opus 1 (1617). Above all, Venetian opera provided Vivaldi with the example of numerous scenes that begin contrapuntally and proceed into homophonic writing as soon as the voices have entered.

If the solo borrows a motive from the tutti, the way in which it alters the motive gives it a more intimate and persuasive tone. The means used are simple but singularly effective; compare the opening tutti of the first concerto of Opus 6 to the solo, nearly identical—distinguished by one note transposed an octave higher and one appoggiatura—and it will be seen that the motive changes without any trouble from a tone of brutal recrimination to one of gentle entreaty.

As to the first solos that, though thematic, do not borrow from the tutti, they admittedly often do not have enough emphasis to give birth, through opposition, to the conflict that in the Classical period was to be the essence of the development. Most of the time they are as short as they are ephemeral, quickly dissipating in decorative garlands and not appearing again; whereas the orchestral ritornello emerges either wholly or in fragments throughout the *allegro*, for which it provides a skeletal structure. But some solos have "breath," one such being that of the concerto in *d* whose tutti I have quoted a little above. Here is the entrance of the solo violin:

(P. 270)

It is quite unquestionable that in this long, seventeen-measure phrase the notes that I have "accented" ought to sing, and that the whole design is a noble and expressive utterance. The composer indicates neither nuances nor bowing, but an interpretation approximating that which I propose can easily be imagined—the opening calm and somewhat playful, the fifth through the eighth measures *scherzando*, and the end growing gradually more animated to the point of vehemence. I add that Vivaldi refrained from turning the expressive possibilities of this theme to good account. A scarcely perceptible allusion to it will be seen at the end of the last solo. Therefore, bithematic construction cannot be spoken of here. It exists, however, in some of Vivaldi's concertos, though it was a matter of small concern at that period.

If Maurice Emmanuel is to be believed, "from a purely doctrinal viewpoint bithematic construction met with resistance in the minds of certain composers, and not the lesser ones, since J. S. Bach himself considered it the proceeding of an amateur, of a dilettante" (as quoted by Lionel de la Laurencie, *L'école française de violon*, 1922–24). Vivaldi uses it, nevertheless, in a rudimentary fashion in Opus 3, No. 8, in which an almost elegiac solo answers the impetuous *élan* of the tutti. Later, this contrast stands out in manuscript concertos of a more complicated structure (*e.g.*, P. 185, F. I, 77).

In solos other than the first, solos that are sometimes a re-exposition of it, Vivaldi is often satisfied with an ornamental formula, more or less brilliant and difficult in performance—runs and arpeggiated passage work, repeated on several consecutive degrees of the scale according to the easy sequential procedure that had been widely used in Venetian opera beginning with Cavalli. These intermediary solos are accompanied even more lightly than the first solo; the composer at one stroke both saves time and gives more freedom to the virtuoso in case he should choose to enrich this passage work with supplementary ornamentation. But nothing prevents the composer, if he is in good form, from elevating the style to lyricism; in the eighth concerto of Opus 8, where the first solo is half-ornamental, half-thematic, the second, starting out with decorative patterns, soon takes on an intense, dramatic expression that has no kinship with the inflexibility of sequential progressions in the manner of Corelli.

The last solo may offer exceptional interest when, as in the case of Opus 3, No. 2, the theme of the opening tutti is again stated by it before the conclusion or when a virtuoso cadenza, written or improvised, is anticipated. Sometimes this last solo is combined with the most salient elements of the first tutti. One of the most beautiful examples of this is in Opus 8, No. 11. The third and last solo is a long passage that at the outset seems to give notice of only a show of brilliant technique. But after some measures of rapid figurations, the principal theme of the piece comes in below them, returning at that point in the first violins; then it is taken up in imitation two measures later by the second violins, to which the violas and then the cellos are added at intervals of two measures. This re-entrance of the theme—"an inspired solution to the problem of the recapitulation," says Hans Engel—foreshadows a similar moment in Mendelssohn's violin concerto, before the cadenza.

Op. VIII, No. 11, 1st movement (28th m. before end)

Solo violin

Ripieno violins and violas

Vlc. and Organ

V. I

V. II

violas

(F. I, 30)

It is only fair to remark that Albinoni with less breadth and ingenuity several times combined the recapitulation of the tutti theme with ornamental embellishment from the soloists.

The intermediary solos that aim primarily at diverting the listener are not necessarily without links to the melodic motives of the piece. Without being able to speak of "thematic working-over" in the Beethovenian sense of the term, Vivaldi's expositions and developments, when they have not been obviously hurried over, attain homogeneity by very diverse means—by the symmetry that he establishes between two decorative solos; or by the likeness of the rhythms and the melodic patterns on which they are embellished; or, again, by the echo-like repetition of a motive from the tutti, which he then leads to a different ending.

The tonal plan of an *allegro* is always clear and logical; it possesses an already Classical balance. The road traversed can be measured if a concerto by Vivaldi is compared to one of the sonatas *à fortes parties* of the period 1670–1690, in which the tutti-solo dialogue clearly emerges but with the respective dimensions of the two elements and their tonal relationships still a matter of chance. In Vivaldi's work, thanks above all to the tonal relations that forcefully arise from the main tutti, the order tonic-dominant–tonic, or tonic–relative key–tonic, or tonic–subdominant–tonic is firmly established, especially since the tutti of secondary importance will often return and rest on the main key.

The *allegro* is occasionally prefaced by a slow introduction in strict style, or, more frequently, in the vehement style of the opera overture or recitative. The introduction seldom admits of a solo. Even if an alternation of the tutti and solo appears, the make-up of the *allegro* that follows is not modified by it.

In the opposite direction, other *allegros* not only do without an introduction, but even renounce the stateliness of the majestic opening tutti. Torelli had given some examples of *allegros* in which the soloist starts off the whole movement accompanied only by the cellos and the harpsichord (Opus 8, No. 8).

Vivaldi goes further. As has already been observed, it may happen in his work that the solo violin begins not with a melodic theme, after the manner of Torelli, but with a genuine flight of virtuosity over a thorough-bass accompaniment or without accompaniment. Thus it is with a Dresden concerto in *F* (P. 271). Indeed this work in its entirety is a fine example of the freedom with which Vivaldi combines, when it seems to him proper, the characteristics of the solo concerto with those of the old concerto grosso, and the secular style with the churchly style.

For most of the concerto composers before Vivaldi the middle slow movement played a transitional role between the first *allegro*, the essential component of the concerto, and the finale, which was to conclude it with cheerfulness. Sometimes the middle movement was a short modulating fragment in sustained harmonies or in imitative style, and sometimes it was a kind a cadenza for the solo instrument over a bass *tasto solo*.

The influence of dramatic music, however, began to modify this. Cavalli, at Venice, had adumbrated the first models of the *da capo* aria, which the Neapolitans were to use and eventually abuse. It was at Venice that Taglietti in 1702 carried over this type of aria into instrumental literature with his Opus 6, *Pensieri*

musicali a Violino e Violoncello col B. C. all'uso d'arie cantabili,
quali finite si ritorna a capo e si finisce al mezzo cioè al segno.
Again at Venice, Albinoni in his Opus 5 (1707) transferred such
arias into the concerto, but he did so infrequently and with
timidity. Torelli went further in his last collection, but such
tranferences were incidental. We are still far from the expressive
intensity of certain purely instrumental ritornellos that occur
in Venetian operas and oratorios.

Vivaldi was the first to bring the pathos of the most impassioned Venetian opera arias into the slow movement, which
became the culminating point of the concerto. Henceforth the
adagio was to be less a structural abstraction than a great
lyrical outpouring; in it the soloist gives himself up to his own
feeling with a force that the orchestra is no longer able to restrain.
And the tutti is effaced—the accompaniment being limited to
the harpsichord alone or to the organ—or remains on the scene
for ritornellos that frame the solo. Occasionally some sustained
notes by the violins and the violas persist as discreet background
before which the virtuoso is able to express himself without
hindrance, to cry out pathetically, unless he chooses to oppose the
tranquillity of a serene and smooth cantilena to the agitation of
the first *allegro*.

A number of Vivaldi's *adagios* carry the indication "*a piaci-*
mento," which tells enough of the new spirit in which they were
conceived. The emotion with which the composer means to
charge them is evidenced further by dynamic nuances, such as
pianissimo sempre, and by the orchestration, of which I have
given a rapid survey.

Quantz sets forth at length the theory of this new *adagio*, and
it would not be supposing too much to state that the model that
he describes is the one which he discovered in Vivaldi's work
around 1714, and to which he never ceased to adhere in his long
career as virtuoso and composer. To him the slow movement appeared so important that, having devoted an entire chapter to the
manner in which the *adagio* should be played, he returned to the
concerto *adagio* in Chapter XVIII. I shall reprint the essential
part of his text, the rules by which the composer should be bound
in the slow movement.

1) He should try for all possible brevity both in the ritornellos and in the solo sections. 2) The ritornellos should be melodious, harmonious, and expressive. 3) The solo part should have a melody that admits of some additional ornamentation but that will be satisfying without it. 4) The melody of the solo part should alternate with sections of the tutti. 5) This melody should be composed in as moving and expressive a way as if there were words belonging to it. 6) Now and then some passages from the ritornello must be made use of. 7) One should not wander off into too many different keys, for this generally is an obstacle to brevity. 8) The accompaniment to the solo ought to be more plain than figural, so that the solo part will not be prevented from embellishing itself, but rather will have complete freedom to introduce many or few ornaments in a judicious and reasonable manner. 9) Lastly, one should try to characterize the *adagio* by a designation that will clearly express what emotion it contains, so that one can thereby easily determine the tempo that is required.

Such are indeed the broad outlines of the Vivaldi slow movement, but his imagination was not content with a stereotyped pattern. There as elsewhere he conceived a number of different types, as regards the plan, the orchestration, and the emotional content.

In Opus 3 alone, setting aside the short *adagios* of transition that are to be found in the four-violin concertos which are allied to the old church concerto, and the curious harmonic *larghetto* of No. 10, the following structures are to be met with:

1) A single song-like phrase by the soloist, without ritornello—a continuous melody, without repetitions or any periodicity;

2) a solo phrase framed by two tutti either of the same character (No. 12), or with a more marked rhythm than the solo (No. 11);

3) two sections with repetitions (No. 2);

4) a dialogue for the orchestra and the soloists, at first alternating measure by measure, the tutti in chords that are hammered out, the solo with a flexible *legato* pattern (No. 3);

5) finally (No. 9), a plan borrowed directly from the theater. After a four-measure tutti of big vertical chords in even quarter notes, as is found in the works of Albinoni, a very singing solo theme enters, only to be abruptly interrupted after two measures by the return of the opening tutti shortened to two measures. The soloist then takes up his own cantilena from the beginning

again and proceeds with it without other interruption. The tutti reappears only for the purpose of conclusion, in five measures of chords marking the beats, similar to those of the beginning.

It is an exact transfer of the vocal form that Hugo Riemann in his *Handbuch der Musikgeschichte* (1922) names the "*Devisenarie*," that is, an aria with an initial motto; the motto is the first proposition of the soloist, which is interrupted by the orchestra and then repeated, this second time being carried through to the end. Here is an example of it, drawn from Domenico Scarlatti's *Irene* (1704):

Io parto.   Io parto, io parto sen_za   co - re

This procedure, appearing as early as 1640 in Roman oratorios and in 1642 in Monteverdi's *Coronation of Poppea*, was used throughout at least a century by Italian and German composers. At Venice, Legrenzi, Vivaldi's master, constructed twenty-six arias in this way in his only opera, *Eteocle e Polinice*.

Outside of Opus 3, we shall find many other plans—in Opus 10, No. 3 (F. XII, 9), a siciliano without ritornellos, in two sections, each repeated; elsewhere, fairly frequently, the simple song form A–B–A, with or without tutti. Also we meet with a monothematic form with repetitions, as it appears for instance in Opus 8, No. 12 (F. I, 31)—the theme repeated twice in the first section and taken up again in the dominant at the beginning of the second, then returning to the tonic. Or, still more reduced, monothematic pieces are found in which only a single idea is presented, cadencing with different endings on the tonic, the dominant and again the tonic. The species of solo, nearly always supported by a simple *basso continuo* or a very light orchestra, is one which lends itself best to the virtuoso's improvised ornamentation.

Some slow movements present an operatic practice that Vivaldi had already exploited in *allegros*—a tutti set in imitative style in opposition to a bare solo line treated homophonically (*e.g.*, P. 430, F. I, 75). Others, of a quasi-improvisatory character, are profusely ornamented; they unfold above an accompaniment in long time values which is set forth at the outset by the tutti and which maintains its stability during the whole piece (*e.g.*, Opus 11, No. 2). Still others are broken up by short incursions of the tutti. In others, which are in a Venetian tradition, a few *allegro* or *presto* measures appear for one or two repetitions (*e.g.*, P. 316, F. I, 21). Finally, I shall point out the not very frequent use of a *basso ostinato* of four or five measures repeated all the way through a movement that may be termed an *andante* or a chaconne (*e.g.*, P. 368, F. I, 60).

The finale of the concerto, according to the aesthetic of the first half of the eighteenth century, is defined by Quantz in this way: "The last *allegro* of a concerto should differ greatly from the first both in the nature and kind of its ideas, and in its meter. As much as the first should be serious, so the last should be, on the contrary, light and playful. . . . The accompaniment should not be too full or overburdened with parts. It should rather consist of notes that the accompanying part can perform without much work or trouble, because the last movement is generally played very rapidly." Quantz also points out that the respective durations of the different movements should be about five minutes for the first *allegro*, and five to six for the *adagio*, against only three to four for the finale.

Vivaldi's finales correspond in general to these particulars. They are conceived in a rapid tempo; only one (P. 225) is of a moderate quickness, "*allegro ma poco, poco*." Nearly always it is a question of ending the work rather lightly, so as to leave the listener with such a feeling of euphoria that he can pass without shock from the concert hall to the pace of everyday life, or can approach the remainder of the program with fresh attentiveness. After all, the music lovers of the eighteenth century absorbed sinfonie, sonatas, and concertos in doses that would astonish the public of today. At the court of Frederick the Great the custom was for several concertos to be performed at a sitting. Dittersdorf reports in his autobiography that at the household of the Prince of Hildburghausen, to which he belonged at around 1755, a certain Reinhard played six of them in an evening, and that he himself performed the following day a dozen of Benda's concertos at a stretch.

However, the adoption of a uniform plan is not to be expected from Vivaldi any more than is a uniform mood. Due allowance being made, the finales present the same diversity of character and proportion as do the initial *allegros*, with even more freedom in the disposition of the solos and the tutti.

Opus 3 already includes several different types, in which a step toward the pattern of the rondo may be discerned. The tutti or one of its component motives represents the refrain. This refrain is, however, not yet obliged to come back in the same form; rather it is permitted contractions and amplifications. The solos are less closely comparable to couplets, because, like those of the opening *allegros*, they take instead the form of caprices or decorative passage work. One notable exception occurs in the finale of No. 7, for four violins and obbligato cello; in this movement the solos enter before the tutti and first set forth the refrain. How this rather heavy dance rhythm is made airy may be seen in the way in which Vivaldi changes the alternation of the solos and the tuttis, proceeding sometimes by eight measures and sometimes by small groups of from one to four measures.

Going on from Opus 3, as early as Opus 4 (*La Stravaganza*), which is subsequent to it by hardly three or four years, we witness a considerable extention of the finale. The solos assume amplitude, often exceeding forty measures in length; but the tuttis, especially, become organized and attain the size of an exposition in a symphonic movement.

Vivaldi has recourse in his finales to many other structures, dictated sometimes by haste. As a rule, he does not by any means attach the same importance to his finales as to the two preceding movements; an examination of the manuscripts testifies eloquently to this. Sometimes, however, he takes an interest in them and shapes them with exemplary care; thus it is with the finale of Opus 6, No. 1, which has a tutti whose first motive, in unison, with an implacable uneven rhythm, is, throughout, opposed to the gentleness of the solo. Even in more or less superficial finales, we come across unexpected finds; for example, in Opus 7, Book 2, No. 2, after a tutti that seems to complete it, there is an un-looked-for return of the solo rising for one last passage more brilliant than the others, followed by—the true close this time—a unison of four measures.

There are finales that call on the resources of the fugal style. Some that are monothematic go on with the use of the theme in the solo, like a certain curious finale in the Giordano collection, the popular origin of which is not to be questioned:

Others assign the more or less strict imitative style to the tutti, the solos being conceived in the new spirit, with accompanied melody. Others still are allied thematically to the first movement of the concerto (Opus 4, No. 8; Opus 12, No. 1; and others), following in this a precedent established by Albinoni and Torelli.

There are few dance movements; several finales start with themes that are in keeping with the minuet, but they soon forsake this character. True minuets appear only in some rather exceptional concertos, intended for instruments other than the violin—the oboe (P. 41, F. VII, 6), bassoon (P. 90, F. VIII, 9), and cello (P. 282, F. III, 7).

In full agreement with Quantz's doctrine, the texture in the finale is often lightened, being reduced to three parts by the elimination of one or two inner parts. It is true—Marcello points it out ironically—that writing for four voices is frequently only bad writing for three: "If the modern composer wants to compose in four parts, two of them must proceed in unison or in octaves." It is also true, as the appearance of the autographs prove, that in many finales in three voices, Vivaldi had in mind above all to save time. However, a concerto ripieno is to be found in which the first two movements are in three voices and the finale in four (P. 378, F. I, 78).

I point out, finally, as regards performance, that the custom of improvised ornaments in the finale, of which we have further evidence from other sources, is confirmed by the words *come stà* (as is) set by Vivaldi over a very simple passage in P. 377 (F. I, 76) to which he wants nothing to be added.

VIVALDI THE SYMPHONIST

The origins of the Classical symphony have remained in obscurity for a long time. The decisiveness of those whose explanations make either Joseph Haydn or Johann Stamitz the "creator" of the new genre settles nothing; it merely displaces the mystery. Georges Cucuel in his *La Pouplinière* . . . (1913) has spoken of it excellently as follows: "Nothing is more absurd than to represent the symphony as emerging from one man's genius like Minerva fully armed from the head of Jupiter. This is to impute a dangerous paternity to Haydn, Sammartini, or Mysliweczek, to cite the principal names put forward. However, such a conception still presided over the celebrated prefaces of ten years ago by which Hugo Riemann disclosed to the learned world the Mannheim symphonists—Johann Stamitz, Richter, Filtz, and Holzbauer."

Recent works have brought solutions to the problem that are less absolute and, by so much, the more satisfactory. Above I recalled the long gestation of the sinfonia up to the time when, at the dawn of the eighteenth century, it attained its first relatively stable form, that of a composition in three movements, fast-slow-fast, which reveal more than a hint of the lineaments of the Classical symphony. At this stage of development, which covers about fifty years, it presents a number of traits that Michel Brenet's *Dictionnaire . . . de la Musique* (1936, the article "Symphonie") has listed with regard to Agrell and Sammartini. "From that time the symphonic style encompasses the following: the plan of the first movement—on one, two, or several themes, in the form of an overture, sonata, or the like; the order of movements—three in number, then four (an opening *allegro*, a slow movement, and a third movement in the form of a minuet, a rondo, or an *allegro;* then a fourth movement comes to follow the minuet); the orchestral layout—instrumental parts treated in an orchestral way, not like a solo composition or a concerto; nuances of performances—treated likewise. All this is found outside Mannheim, where the German musicologists have tried to set the cradle of the orchestral symphony, and before Mannheim, because it was only from 1741 to 1757 that the Czech composer Johann Stamitz, who directed the chamber musicians of the Palatine elector, introduced such symphonies with his orchestra."

All this is found also, before Agrell, before G. B. Sammartini and, pending a fuller inquiry, before anyone you care to name, in the works of Vivaldi—found there in an exact and solid enough way to give him the figure of a precursor. It is probably he who most effectively blended the elements furnished by the church sonata, the concerto, and the dramatic overture so as to bring the concert sinfonia into an existence independent of the church and of the theater. Admittedly he did this at the same time as Albinoni and several others, but he did it with a wholly different prescience as to the requirements of the new genre. (Four symphonies of Albinoni are preserved at Darmstadt which have a minuet inserted between the *andante* and the finale, and in this approaching nearer to the Classical plan than those of Vivaldi do. But they are later, dating from around 1735.)

Surprisingly, an awareness of Vivaldi as a symphonist hardly existed until recently, although his role in the formulation of the concerto has long been recognized. In the eighteenth century scarcely anyone save La Borde (*Essai sur la musique*, 1780) can be found to point out that "he left beautiful concertos and large symphonies" unless one takes into account a letter by Charles de Brosses. Two fragments of that letter, when put together with what he wrote of Vivaldi in other connections, take on value as evidence. "That one of the four asylums to which I went most frequently and where I enjoyed myself most was the asylum of the Pietà. It is also the first as regards the perfecting of symphonies. . . . They have here a type of music that we do not know in France and that appears to me to be more appropriate than any other for the Jardin de Bourbonne. These are the large concertos in which there is no solo violin."

These pieces of information for a long time had no echo. The first publication in which justice was done to Vivaldi in this matter was the edition by Ludwig Landshoff in 1935 of three sinfonie manuscripts from Dresden.* He added an introduction that gives a true idea of their newness for their time.

If, pushing further the study outlined by Landshoff, we consider the mass of Vivaldi's symphonic production, it is impossible not to be struck by its abundance, by the firmness of the conception, and by a maturity sufficient to justify our attributing to Vivaldi a determining role in the formulation of the genre.

The libraries to which I have had access contain eighteen of his symphonies, not including the five whose incipits only are

---

* The sinfonie edited by Landshoff and published by Peters of Leipzig are the following: Sinfonie in C (*dell' opera 2ª Sant'Angelo*) and G (1716); and also a Sinfonia in G, played before Prince Frederick Christian of Saxony in 1740.

extant in the Breitkopf catalogue. But some fifty compositions must be added, for the most part preserved at Turin in the Foà and Giordano collections under the title of concerto *a quattro* or concerto ripieno, which are authentic string symphonies.

Here again the chronology is nearly obliterated. Nevertheless, we know that Vivaldi's first sinfonie, related to the opera overture, date from the beginning of his career as a dramatic composer, that is from the period 1710–1720. Two of those that Landshoff published are from 1716. Another, in the library of the Conservatory of Naples, is from 1727, and is a copy of an original that could date several years earlier. Others, from their style and even their calligraphy, are assuredly contemporary with the first concerto collections, which were put out between 1712 and 1725.

Now, Alessandro Scarlatti's twelve sinfonie (1715) were still of an archaic design, with their five movements, including two transitional *adagios* (*allegro–adagio*–fugue–*adagio*–march or dance). Among the three hundred sinfonie of the Fonds Blancheton of the Paris Conservatory library there are chamber sinfonie in three movements that are often very close to Vivaldi's; but none of these seem to have been written before 1725 at the earliest. (These were made known to us by the studies of Lionel de la Laurencie and Georges de Saint-Foix.) J. S. Bach's sinfonia in *F*, the only one of the works of the great Cantor the contents of which correspond to the title, is a late reworking of the first Brandenburg Concerto of 1721, which around 1730 had already been converted to serve as the introduction to a cantata. As for Agrell, Telemann, and G. B. Sammartini, their first known productions in this genre are dated at intervals from 1725, 1730, and 1734, respectively. Hence the precursor, if there is a precursor, would indeed be Vivaldi.

His sinfonie, as is expected, have numerous points of resemblance to his concertos. Occasionally the titles proclaim this: in a manuscript of the Foà collection a "concerto *a quattro*" also carries, half-erased, the title "sinfonia" (P. 127, F. XI, 13); and a sinfonia of Dresden is labeled "sinfonia-concerto" at Turin (F. XI, 29).

But there is other evidence—internal evidence—of the interdependence of the two genres or, better, of their common origin. Obviously musical material is often suitable alike to one or the other genre, and a final push can at the last moment transmute a concerto into a sinfonia or vice versa. We know this from such a concerto at Turin (F. I, 68), in which the composer has no set purpose at all. Here the first movement, *allegro*, is symphonic; the second, a short slow movement (eleven measures) is again so, but another *adagio* follows it in which extended passage work in sixteenth notes for the violin solo disengages itself; and the finale alternates solo and tutti in the fashion of certain Neapolitan overtures.

Another more significant example is from a concerto in *g* for a four-part string ensemble, on a theme that may have inspired the theme of one of J. S. Bach's Inventions.

(P. 394)

The autograph manuscript is entitled *Concerto originale del Vivaldi*. In its first drafting it is indeed a concerto for two solo violins and the orchestral strings, the solo parts being written on the same stave as the first and second ripieni violins. The tuttis are in the strict style, the homophonic solos are in a lighter spirit. But the composer changes his mind and proceeds after the event to a general leveling. Everywhere that the tutti was indicated he has crossed it out and replaced it with an *F* (*forte*); in the same way the solo is canceled and replaced by *P* (*piano*). The result is a sinfonia with some fixed intentions indicated in regard to dynamics, which remind one of the old tradition of the alternately *f* and *p* repetitions in the suites derived from dance forms.

We have seen that Vivaldi's symphonies are called either sinfonia or concerto (concerto ripieno or concerto *a quattro*). Works designated by these two names are not absolutely equivalent;

on the other hand, there is no airtight partition between them. As with all these forms, the vocabulary is ambiguous, and the composer had little reason to be concerned about fixed categories, the less since no one had as yet laid down definitions. For contemporaries the sinfonia was in a general way just an opera overture. This is so much the case that ten years after Vivaldi's death J. J. Quantz, in his conscientious survey of instrumental forms, speaks of the French and German overture and then specifies that the Italian symphonies "have the same purpose," that is, are identical with it; the whole paragraph devoted to the symphony affirms that he knows no other variation of it. He deplores, from the viewpoint of dramatic continuity, that it does not always have "some connection with the content of the opera" and that its tripartite scheme requires that it be concluded with a "gay minuet," whatever may be the mood that immediately thereafter animates the first scene of the drama. According to him the composer might limit himself to the opening movement, *allegro*, "if the first scene involved heroic or other strong passions." He could stop after the first two movements, *allegro* and *adagio*, "if sad or amorous passions occurred in it. . . . And if it had no marked passions or if they were to be found later on in the opera or at its close, then he might end with the third movement of the sinfonia. By so doing, he would have an opportunity to arrange each movement in accordance with the immediate purpose. However, the sinfonia would remain useful for other purposes."

The common origin of the first concert sinfonie and the opera overtures has never been better described. As for their separation at this time from the sustained style of the old church sinfonie, Benedetto Marcello, mocking as always, discusses that in his *Teatro alla moda*. "The sinfonia is to consist of a *tempo francese* or *prestissimo* in sixteenth notes in major, which is to be followed, as a rule, by a *piano* movement in the same key but in minor; the finale should be a minuet or a gavotte or a gigue, again in major; fugues, suspensions, imitation, and the like, are to be avoided as worthless old stuff that is completely out of fashion."

These two sources quite well set the boundaries of the Vivaldi sinfonie. Of the eighteen examples that still exist, several are properly authenticated dramatic overtures. One of those at Dresden comes from *Arsilda Regina di Ponto* (1716); another is entitled *Sinfonia del Sgr. Vivaldi dell'opera 2a S. Angelo,* and must date from the same period. Most of the other sinfonie, properly so called, present the same characteristics as these, and an examination of the Turin scores will undoubtedly allow more than one of them to be linked to some rediscovered opera.

We shall not study them at great length, because their kinship with the concerto is so close. It is enough for us to see what differentiates them. We shall pass most quickly over their orchestration. In fact here we do not find the multiplicity of tone colors in which Vivaldi delights in certain concertos, such as those of the last Giordano collection (P. 73, F. XII, 1; P. 74, F. XII, 2; P. 319, F. XII, 18). They were written to order for certain financially well-endowed princely orchestras, while the opera scores had to be suitable for theaters whose impresarios often proved to be most miserly. Consequently, most of the sinfonie— more than two-thirds—are limited to the string ensemble and the harpsichord with its thorough-bass. As for the five that call for wind instruments (flute or two flutes; two oboes; two oboes and a bassoon; two oboes, two horns, and a bassoon), these are not treated in a different way. Only the function of the horns is notable, for they are used in a truly symphonic way—not uninterruptedly as mere doubling of the bass, but at just the right moment to supply dynamic reinforcement, color, or a particular rhythmic pattern. In the section above devoted to the orchestra, it was demonstrated at length that it is in the four-part string ensemble that genuine "orchestration" must be sought, which is the realm where Vivaldi is without a rival.

The groundwork is that of the concerto type, and consequently that of the Neapolitan overture—three movements, fast-slow-fast, with some dissimilarities, however, in the slow movement, which we shall take note of in their place. Only two sinfonie, one published as F. I, 68, have, in addition, a slow introduction. One, finally, is of an irregular structure, with two consecutive slow movements enclosed between two *allegros* (F. I, 7).

The proportions among the different movements are not exactly the same as in the concerto. The work as a whole is usually less well-developed, the reduction occurring in the fast movements and especially in the finale, which is always in 3/8 and which seldom lasts more than two minutes. The *presto* that concludes the aforesaid sinfonia *dell'opera 2a S. Angelo* played at an appropriate tempo lasts less than thirty seconds.

Still more than the thematic aspect of the concertos, that of the sinfonie *allegros* has a character of vigorous tonal affirmation evocative of the old Venetian *intonazioni*. Nearly always the opening motive—one can hardly speak of a "theme"—is reduced to a rhythm that is built up on the tones of the tonic chord or scale. From this modest point of departure Vivaldi excels in deducing a whole development that has an unrelenting drive spurred on by persistent patterns, as forceful as they are sober, repeated right through clear modulations.

The scheme of these *allegros* deviates a bit from the two to which most concerto first movements submit. In one of the sinfonie in the d'Aiguillon collection (preserved at Agen) the element of contrast that is generally asked of the tutti-solo opposition and that the Classical symphonic style will extract from the use of two clearly differentiated themes is procured by the insertion of a "center" in minor that has a melodic character and a notably slower tempo. Elsewhere, momentary recourse to the contrapuntal style produces the same result of contrast.

The instrumental writing differs from that of the concertos. It is markedly orchestral writing, designed for ripienists. It keeps within a more moderate tessitura, making use of each instrument in its more sonorous register; its scale passages have easy fingerings and simple and effective bowings, and devices (for example, the sixteenth-note tremolos with higher notes outlining a melody) that could already be taken for genuine Stamitz. This writing, homophonic most of the time, aims above all at brilliance. The violin parts proceed at the interval of a third or they cross, when they are not at the unison; but such is their liveliness and so sharp is the composer's instinct that the scores, which might seem dull to the eye because of their simplicity, are never dull when they are actually played.

The slow movement of the Neapolitan overture was generally short, and was sometimes reduced to a few measures for the purpose of providing the audience with a little respite between the two *allegros*. Many symphonists of the Milan school adhered to this conception; G. B. Sammartini is satisfied in one instance with a *grave* of six measures.

Vivaldi's sinfonie, on the other hand, with a few exceptions, no longer give the central movement a transitional role, but rather make it an independent piece, which can be the most interesting and elaborate of the whole work, and one in which the composer tests new orchestral colors. So it is in that Dresden sinfonia in *G*, already cited, in which the violins are divided so as to play the same phrase in unison, some with pizzicato, some *coll'arco*.

Nevertheless, the slow movements of the sinfonie rarely convey the fervent pathos which marks so many of the concerto *adagios*. Their melodies are more calm, their tempos less serious—*andante* (that is, "going") rather than *adagio* or *grave*. The fact is that in the theater, which was the first destination of these sinfonie, the expression of violent passions is reserved for the singers.

In conformance with the aesthetic of the time, the finale is the shortest part and the least seriously fashioned, usually one of those "gay minuets" whose presence Quantz found inappropriate in the overture to a serious opera. Vivaldi usually puts it in 3/8 rhythm. Other finales, all of them light and rapid, are in a binary rhythm. The customary structure is in two symmetrical divisions with repetitions. Some do not extend beyond repeated sections of eight measures each, which might move us to ask if they were not sometimes repeated more than once and embellished with ornaments improvised by the solo violin; their length again identifies them with the proportions of the sonatas closing with minuets and variations thereon, which abound in the Italian, French, English, and German repertories of the period 1730–1760 and later.

A number of works entitled concerti ripieni or concerti *a quattro* correspond in every respect to the sinfonie proper that have just been described. They are or might have been dramatic overtures. Others testify to different origins and tendencies. The dissimilarities that exist are not brought out with any regularity; as always, Vivaldi's imagination has created imperceptible gradations between the extremes.

This second category of concerti ripieni can, nevertheless, be roughly connected with the old church sinfonie. They no longer were written with the four-movement groundplan, but with the tripartite scheme of the overtures. And by using a more elaborate kind of writing, one that resorted more easily to imitative style than to vertical harmony and dispensed with the frivolity of a minuet finale, they were made as appropriate to the church as to secular concert halls. Capable of being used in either setting, they do not exaggerate austerity; thanks precisely to their moderate character, they could be set side by side with more buoyant sinfonie. By a natural and beneficial osmosis they imparted to the latter a little of their gravity and prevented them from becoming too anemic by going rather too far toward the public's taste for the brilliant formulas that were to grow more and more devoid of musical value as they began to be mass-produced by the new style.

By virtue of this, the concerti ripieni were probably composed to supply easily executed material for the young musicians of the Pietà, and Vivaldi, who was undoubtedly the first to write them, played a large part in the preliminary steps toward the Classical symphony. To them the Classical symphony owed the persistence of a kind of polyphony that acted at that time as a principle of enrichment, a role diametrically opposed to its sterilizing effect at the end of the Renaissance. With musical speech in danger of being reduced to a simple accompanied melody more or less crammed with virtuoso passages, the resort to an unburdened and modernized counterpoint capable of coming to terms with vertical harmony served to ward off the decline of the orchestra. Writing for several voices became a stimulus to composers toward exploration in the domain of orchestration as well as of form. Such writing is therefore one of the principal springs of the development of the symphony.

An idea of these serious sinfonie and of how they may be combined in varied proportions with those allied to the overture may be obtained by perusing a manuscript collection entitled *Concerti del Sigr. Vivaldi* at the library of the Paris Conservatory. This collection is in separate parts for first and second violins, viola, and harpsichord (a part common to the harpsichord and the bass instruments of the string ensemble), and it contains a dozen concerti *a quattro* or concerti ripieni, of which ten are replicas of originals preserved at Turin and two—Nos. 2 (P. 113) and 5 (P. 27)—are found only in Paris.

No. 1 (P. 361, F. XI, 21) is completely in strict style, Nos. 4 (P. 279, F. XI, 14) and 11 (P. 114) are completely in the homophonic style, and the others are composite. Some—for example, Nos. 3 (P. 422, F. XI, 20) and 9 (P. 363, F. XI, 12)—have their three movements in the same key; in the others (*e.g.*, No. 7, P. 230, F. XI, 22) the slow movement is in the relative key or the subdominant.

The opening allegro. In the first movement the homophonic style preponderates, with a vigorous theme employed which admirably suits the symphony and lends itself to brilliant orchestration even as confined to the four-part string ensemble. And the first movement of No. 1, although its contrapuntal writing over a *basso ostinato* is of pure Venetian tradition, does not, for all that, renounce the modern violin figurations, the sparkling tremolos that give so much bite to purely harmonic passages. Here again we observe how little influence the barline has on the rhythm. The pattern of the ground bass, which is consecutively repeated eight times, comprises not a flat number of measures but two and a half; if only the strong beats are accented with some strength, the impression is that of a measure in five time.

(P. 361, F. XI, 21)

Side by side with this specimen of polyphonic writing, there are examples of homophonic writing that reach extremes in the matter of paring down the score. For instance, the first movement of No. 10 (P. 175, F. XI, 30) has a twenty-two measure unison passage of rather empty grandiloquence. It is very hard not to attribute this thinning of the texture to haste rather than to artistic purpose, because the *adagio* that follows is likewise unstudied and the work comes to an end with a very brief and slapdash *allegro* in two voices, with all the violins in unison and the cellos doubling the violas.

Some opening *allegros* are still allied to the dances of the old suite. In general, both the opening and closing fast movements are more developed than they are in the sinfonie proper. One finale at Turin (P. 371, F, XI, 27) reaches 103 measures in length.

The slow movement. The collection of the Paris Conservatory clearly demonstrates the variety of conceptions to which this central movement was susceptible, as much regarding its breadth as its tempo and expression. While in the sinfonie the prevailing slow movement is an *andante*—that is, a piece in somewhat animated pace, fit to express sportiveness rather than sorrow or vehement emotions—this tempo appears here only two times out of the dozen. Everywhere else it is an *adagio* or a *largo* that occupies the central place, nearly always in a polyphonic style. Only No. 4 has a simple melody with accompaniment. Some others (*e.g.*, No. 8, P. 280, F. XI, 19) are of a harmonic character, with chains of modulating chords that are punctuated by organ points in the manner of Torelli.

(P. 292, F. XI, 2)

Unlike the *allegros*, the slow movements are relatively short; but they have great intensity, to which an eloquent use of chromaticism contributes, as it does in these few measures that make up the middle movement of one of the Turin concertos. (No tempo is indicated.)

Most of the time chromaticism in Vivaldi's works and in those of all his contemporaries conveys pathos. It is linked to the idea of sorrow or misfortune. André Pirro has shown the power of this association throughout the works of J. S. Bach, who is himself only carrying on a tradition firmly established in Italy and in Germany, exemplified in pieces by Heinrich Schütz, S. A. Scherer, and others. A particular instance where a strictly Venetian influence is manifest occurs in the *bassi ostinati* with descending chromatic line, such as Cavalli, Legrenzi, and Draghi had a fondness for.

The finale. The finales in the concerti ripieni have more varied groundplans than do those of the sinfonie proper. Few minuets similar to that of No. 4 of the Conservatory collection are to be found. In the same collection, No. 5 is concluded by a *"ciacona,"* and No. 12 (P. 231, F. XI, 1) by a rondo of sorts with a rather special structure; although the first two movements of No. 12 are completely symphonic, the finale is made up of a six-fold alternation of solos and tutti, the solos in minor, the tutti in major. This is not a unique example of the balance between major and minor, which gives so much charm to a melody when it is set forth, as it occasionally is, within a single measure.

The most characteristic, if not the most numerous, of these concerti ripieni finales are treated in the strict style. This is probably due to the fact that, since the concerti ripieni were designed for solemn religious ceremonies, the strict style was used to offset any excessive lightheartedness that the lively tempo might cause by its more sustained thematic treatment and regard both for a more chastened kind of writing and for a more elevated kind of expression.

From this quick examination of Vivaldi's symphonies, we may conclude that he already had at hand—because he had either created them himself or taken them over from other sources, among which dramatic music is the first and foremost—most of the elements that the masters of the following generation had at their disposal. All the would-be new effects that the historians pick out in the works of Gassmann, Hasse, and Gossec—themes based on the tonic chord, leaps of an octave, *brisures, bariolages*— are in his music along with the *Vögelchen* and the *Seufzer* of Richter and Johann Stamitz.

Furthermore, the sense for symphonic writing and for symphonic sonority, matters of more importance than the detailed devices, bursts forth in the *allegros* of his concerti ripieni, as it does in the magnificent tuttis of his solo concertos. The latter works are, from the point of view of form, also a step toward the symphony. Julien Tiersot, though entirely ignorant of the sinfonie and the concerti ripieni, was able to write in the *Ménestrel* (1929), "It is as a prototype of the Classical symphony that the concertos of Vivaldi deserve our attention first of all."

In fact, if only by his steadfast adherence to the three-movement framework, fast-slow-fast, in some hundreds of concertos, Vivaldi contributed not a little to the establishment of the balance to which the symphony was to remain henceforth attached and which the subsequent addition of the minuet-scherzo would not change in any profound way. The scheme of his opening *allegros* heralds no less plainly that of the *allegros* of C. P. E. Bach and his successors. And it has just been seen that his symphonies and, perhaps still more, his concerti ripieni, hold in their form and spirit the essentials of the Classical symphony.

THE DESCRIPTIVE MUSIC

A particular type of formal construction remains to be discussed, one that Vivaldi handled with great daring, great originality, and—with due deference here again to those who make him out to be a man of only one stereotyped scheme repeated six hundred times—great variety. I speak of his descriptive music. If his fame was established by *L'Estro armonico*, it owed still more to *Le Stagioni* (*The Seasons*), the four concertos with which his eighth opus begins.

Nothing is more natural than for his dramatic temperament to have inclined him toward description in purely instrumental forms. And the taste of the time also brought him to it. An aesthetic was arising that would go on from its acceptance of the imitation of nature as a criterion to bestow a heightened brilliance on "program music." This music, which some of Vivaldi's contemporaries were unveiling as an innovation, actually had a long history at the time when he started to write it. Among immediate predecessors and contemporaries, the only difficulty is one of selection. There were harpsichordists such as Kuhnau, Poglietti, and the whole French school culminating magnificently in François Couperin. And there were violinists from three nations who shared the heritage of Carlo Farini—in Italy, Marco Uccellini with the *Gran Battaglia;* among the French, François Duval with the *Rossignols* that close two of the suites in his first book (1704), and Jean Fery Rebel and his *Cloches;* and among the Austro-Germans, Walther, Westhoff, and Biber. (The latter rises sometimes to soulful evocation, as in the fifteen Mystery Sonatas, or indulges in portrayal and even caricature with amusing and minute details. In the serenade, for example, the violins, held under the arm and played pizzicato, imitate the lute; and the bowed basses counterfeit the side-drum by putting a sheet of paper between the strings and the finger board, or by slapping the strings with the right hand, like our jazz double-bass players.)

Vivaldi may have known some of these attempts from their being carried abroad by the fame of migrant virtuosos. Other sources of program music that were easy to come by were in opera and its surrogate, oratorio, and in ballet, as often as the orchestra without the conjunction of the singers was used to create atmosphere, to underscore the character of the setting, or even to depict natural or supernatural events whose description the voice is unable to take on. Antonio Draghi's ballet, *Albero del ramo d'oro*, opens with a sinfonia that imitates the noise of wind in a forest (*"come di strepito di vento in un bosco."*). In an opera by him, *Il libro con setto sigilli*, a sinfonia for three trombones and a bassoon has the mission of portraying terror. The storms in Colasse's *Thétis et Pélée* (1689) and Marais' *Alcyone* (1706) are celebrated.

But the theater of Venice was the richest of all in episodes of this class. In Cavalli's work, the *Sinfonia navale* in *Didone* (1641), the murmuring of the brook in *Ercole* (1662), the *Sinfonia infernale* in *Le Nozze di Teti e di Peleo*, and the like, were admired. After him and for the remainder of the century, opera houses offered their public a profusion of visitations by ghosts and demons, enormous cataclysms, the magical *sommeil* in enchanted gardens—all the repertory of large stage effects of which the Venetians never managed to tire.

Such depictions are bound to be discovered in abundance in Vivaldi's scores when research on the collection in the Turin library develops. As we might have anticipated, his own genius, when allied with so strong a local tradition, stimulated him to transfer this pictorial genre into instrumental music, through which, whether intentionally or not, he had already infused so many features of dramatic music. He makes this transfer fairly often even outside *The Seasons*. Like Biber and François Couperin,

184   VIVALDI

he ranges from suggestion to realistic painting, from the vagueness of great feelings to imitating the cry of an animal.

He composes *Il Piacere* (Opus 8, No. 6, F. I, 27), the title of which does not much involve him. But the titles *L'Inquietudine* (P. 208, F. I, 1), *Il Riposo* (P. 248, F. I, 4), and *Il Sospetto* (P. 419, F. I, 2) foretell the summoning up of states of mind that he realizes by effectively symbolic procedures—attenuated chords for repose, lively asymmetrical figurations for unrest.

The *Concerto funebre* expresses grief mingled with fright. Its beginning makes one think of the appearance of the masked devil in the fourth tableau of Stravinsky's *Petrushka:*

385 Largo

(P. 385, F. XII, 12)

The *Concerto o sia il Cornetto a Posta* (P. 112) keeps most closely to pictorial detail. It exploits the traditional motive of the postilion, an octave leap, used in the same way by Bach in his *Capriccio* on the departure of his beloved brother. This octave leap reappears in Vivaldi's *Caccia* (Opus 8, No. 10), representing this time the fanfare of the hunters.

With the two concertos, Opus 8, No. 5 (F. I, 26) and Opus 10, No. 1 (F. XII, 28), both entitled *La Tempesta di mare*, we reach genuine "program music." The first is much the more interesting. Although the ingredients traditionally worked together in this genre are all present in it, their use is new in that they are arranged according to the regular plan of the concerto form. The tutti—persistent tremolos and descending scales in sixteenth-notes *detaché*—is allotted the evocation of the background sound in the storm. The solos are made up of a series of broken chords, which may represent the monotonous shock of the waves as they ceaselessly form and reform, and of rapid ascending *legato* runs, which could signify the clamor of the wind, or, just as suitably, the sailors' terror. In the *largo* Arnold

Schering chooses to see "a kind of *lamento* of the castaways." It is, in any event, a piece that aims at pathos, in which the violin sounds a recitative of anguish in a high tessitura with brusque modulations and ascending chromatic scale passages of an unusual turn. The orchestra breaks in with dark chords from time to time and again comes in to close, after the last organ point of the soloist, on an unexpected *pianissimo* that is all the more striking in that it is played at the unison (the unison, as we know, ordinarily specializes in effects of brute force). The finale is above all a virtuoso piece. Description recedes to the background; the vivacity of the passage work—up to thirty-second and sixty-fourth notes in a *presto* tempo—suffice to convey the composer's purpose. The other *Tempesta di mare* (from Opus 10), where the solo instrument is a flute, is in the same spirit but with less breadth and clarity.

Two concertos have night for their subject (*La Notte:* P. 401, F. VIII, 1, and Opus 10, No. 2, F. XII, 5). To be especially pointed out in the second is a *presto, Fantasmi* (*Phantoms;* this recalls Venetian opera) in which the effect of the fantastic is achieved by the use of unusual modulations, ascending minor scales without alteration of either the leading tone or submediant, and rapid passage work at the third or unison.

Bird songs, one of the commonplaces of descriptive music of all times, furnishes the subject for two concertos—that of the *Cuckoo Concerto* and of *Il Cardellino* (*The Goldfinch*). Both of these little creatures also appear episodically in the aviary of *The Seasons.*

The *Cuckoo Concerto* (P. 219), of which there seems to have been only a single edition—the English one—enjoyed, nevertheless, an extended vogue. All the British historians cite it with an air of ironical condescension. For instance, Burney in his *History* writes as follows: "His *Cuckoo Concerto*, during my youth, was the wonder and delight of all frequenters of country concerts; and Woodcock, one of the Hereford waits, was sent for far and wide to perform it. If acute and rapid tones are evils, Vivaldi has much of the sin to answer for." But Ginguené in the *Encyclopédie* writes simply, "His *Cuckoo Concerto* was long performed in all the concerts with admiration."

The virtuosity that this work requires no longer has the power to surprise; rather, its musical quality disappoints us. With the same theme Pasquini had found inflections of a poetic revery that it would be vain to look for here. The best part is the *largo*, which forsakes all toying with realism; it is satisfied to sing in a broad and beautiful phrase, the ornamentation of which is written out in its entirety, *alla* Bach. (Actually one may legitimately wonder if it is not J. S. Bach who fully realizes his melodies *alla* Vivaldi; the *Cuckoo Concerto* appeared in the list of the firm of Walsh and Hare around 1720, and the publication probably crowned long years of success.)

Il Cardellino, the third concerto of Opus 10 (F. XII, 9), for flute and strings, is a delightful study in orchestration. There are no formal problems, and the three movements, *allegro*, *cantabile* (*largo*), and *allegro*, are of moderate dimensions. The flute, which is, of course, vested with the imitation of the bird song, does not pride itself on accuracy. It is not a correct document like Messiaen's notations or, even as early as 1832, like Gardiner's in his *Music of Nature*. The descriptive label is of benefit chiefly in giving great freedom of behavior to the soloist. He first comes in with short calls over a unison tutti, then without any accompaniment he seems to improvise a cadenza. His second appearance is nearly as free; after a curtailed repetition of the tutti he enters again alone, soon to be joined by light figuration in the violins, which leave him in the limelight. At each return he propounds new embellishments, a certain unity being attained by similarities in rhythm and by the repetition of the tutti.

The transparence of the writing is notable. The accompaniment is sometimes reduced to violins without cellos, to first violins and violas, to first violins and cellos *tasto solo*, to cellos scarcely intimating the strong beats, or even to violas alone.

As in the *Cuckoo Concerto*, the slow movement renounces ornithology. This *cantabile* movement, in the rhythm of a siciliano, is one of the most pure and charming that Vivaldi ever wrote, and it is also, due to the suitability of the solo instrument to the musical quality of the piece, an evidence of the wondrous instinct of the composer in the matter of orchestral coloring. It is not impossible that the success of this section may have ordained the association of the siciliano rhythm with the timbre of the flute which endures up to our time, as may be seen in Fauré's *Pelléas* suite.

The few works with "program" that we have just discussed are far from offering the interest that is attached to the first four concertos of Opus 8, *The Seasons* (F. I, 22–25). For the latter, their breadth, the clearness of the conception, the obvious pleasure with which the composer wrought them, the favorable reception that has been theirs from the first, their reverberations since then—all these unite to make them one of the masterpieces of descriptive repertory. If historians specializing in the study of "program music" (see Frederick Niecks, *Programme Music in the Last Four Centuries*, 1907; Otto Klauwell, *Geschichte der Programmusik*, 1910) are not of this mind, it is assuredly on account of some wholly external oddities which are more easily explained if one goes to the trouble of placing the passages in the context in which they are encountered.

The succession of the seasons had for a long time supplied musicians with the subject for ballets (that of Lully, for example, in 1661) and for spectacles. Perhaps in his youth Vivaldi heard echoes of a spectacle given in Rome in 1698 entitled *The Dispute of the Seasons* (*La Contesa delle Stagioni*), which has Time, Spring, Summer, Fall and Winter as characters. If I am not mistaken, he was the first to attack this subject symphonically, with no means of expression other than the instruments of the traditional orchestra.

Actually poetry is not entirely absent from his undertaking. Four explanatory sonnets, engraved at the beginning of the solo violin part without the author's name—the composer may have dashed them off or have asked one of his customary librettists for them—partly refer forward to the music itself by means of guide letters, the progress of the work in each part indicating all the details of the scene that the music is supposed to depict.

Each of them is headed *Explicatory sonnet upon the concerto entitled Spring* (or *Summer, Fall,* or *Winter*).

Spring

Spring has come, and the birds greet it with happy songs, and at the same time the streams run softly murmuring to the breathing of the gentle breezes.

Then, the sky being cloaked in black, thunder and lightning come and have their say; after the storm has quieted, the little birds turn again to their harmonious song.

Here in a pleasant flowery meadow, the leaves sweetly rustling, the goatherd sleeps, his faithful dog at his side.

Nymphs and shepherds dance to the festive sound of the pastoral *musette* under the bright sky that they love.

Summer

In the season made harsh by the burning sun the men and the herds languish; even the evergreens are hot. The cuckoo unlocks his voice and soon the songs of the turtledove and the goldfinch are heard.

Soft breezes breathe, but unexpectedly the north wind from its quarter seeks out a quarrel, and the shepherd weeps because he is overwhelmed by fear of the gusts and of his fate.

Fear of the flashing lightning and of the fierce thunder denies his tired body any rest while his furious troop is on the move.

How justifiable is his fear! The sky lights up, the awe-inspiring thunder brings down the fruit and the proud grain.

Fall

With songs and dances the peasants celebrate the happiness of a fine harvest, and after being greatly kindled by bacchic spirits, their rejoicing ends with sleep.

Thus everyone quits both his singing and his dancing. The air is pleasant and moderate, and the season invites everyone to the agree-ableness of a sweet sleep.

At the break of day the hunter goes to the hunt with guns, dogs, and horns; he puts the wild beast to flight and tracks him down.

Tired and terrified by the loud noise of the guns and dogs, the beast, now in danger of being wounded, longs for escape, but is over-come and dies.

Winter

To tremble frozen in the icy snow; to be buffeted by the wild wind; to stamp one's frozen feet; to have excessive cold set one's teeth to chattering;

To pass to a fireside of quiet and contentment, while outside the downpour bathes all; to walk carefully on ice, going slowly in fear of falling;

To slip and fall sharply to the ground, start out again on the ice, and run until the ice breaks apart;

To hear the south wind, the north wind, and all the other winds unloosed in battle: such is winter, these are joys it brings.

To what extent was the composer tied down to these texts? This is the question that one is naturally tempted to put to oneself. But it is not certain that, in this form, it would be well put. The dedication of Opus 8 to Count Morzin specifies as a matter of fact that this nobleman had heard *The Seasons* with favor long before their publication, but that here they are done over, as it were, by the appending of the sonnets and by the detailed explanation of all the turns. To this end, not only are fragments of the poems set against the musical text from place to place; but the most significant tableaux have, besides, different subtitles conforming to differences in the instrumental parts. I have already noted the episode in *La Primavera* where the solo violin part carries the indication "*Il capraro che dorme* [the sleeping goatherd]" and the viola part, "*Il cane che grida* [the barking dog]."

How far this is from the attitude held today by composers of descriptive music! Their first care is apology, or, even more likely, denial. They never intended to describe; at most they intended to suggest certain states of mind as they would appear when transferred to the lofty realms of pure music. You are given, for instance, a work whose content arises from the remote evocation of a locomotive, though you claim to identify in it the shudder of the train as it pulls away, the increasingly noisy rattling, and the thousand familiar sounds rendered with a hallucinating mastery, right down to the end of the run where the brakes are applied for the last time. Already Beethoven had written of the Pastoral Symphony, "More expression of feelings than depiction," while having a quail and a cuckoo sing forth with a pretty good likeness.

In the eighteenth century the situation is reversed. The musician claims to present the listener with as exact a portrayal as possible—as "natural" a portrayal, say the French aestheticians—and we have seen how Vivaldi, to intensify the drawing power of *The Seasons*, supplements them with four clarifying sonnets.

But—and in this Vivaldi surpasses Poglietti, Biber, and Kuhnau—these synopses and the compositions that they explain are arranged in their broad outlines according to the plan of the sinfonia or the concerto: slumber between a storm and some rustic dances, tranquillity in a chimney corner between two wintry storms—these are just the central *largo* preceded and followed by the two fast movements. Thus description is superimposed on the unfolding of a standard composition.

Within each movement we have about the same situation. The tuttis play their traditional role as the foundation of structure and the element of symmetry and stability; at the same time, they express the dominant mood of the piece—the carefree gaiety of spring, the oppressive languor of summer, and so on. The solos are at once the modulating sections, the virtuoso passages that we are familiar with, and the pictorial details—the bird songs, the murmuring of springs, the barking of a dog, the reeling walk of a drunk, and a winter walker's tumble on glare ice.

When the solo violin and its two associates converse on an equal footing, interchanging passage work of equal virtuosity, it must not be inferred that Vivaldi is returning in Opus 8 to the concerto grosso formula. The incipient trio of soloists or concertino that follows the first tutti of *La Primavera* (*Spring*) is incidental; everywhere else, with rare exceptions, the solo violin toweringly dominates the orchestral mass. When the newspaper reports say, "Monsieur Guignon (or Vachon or Canavas) played the concerto *La Primavera* by Vivaldi," a phrase that is encountered not once but twenty times in the journals of the mid-eighteenth century, they confirm the fact that the work was beyond all doubt a solo concerto.

I shall be sparing with musical examples because the choice is too difficult, for every page presents instrumental dispositions that are worthy of notice. I want, nevertheless, to point out this murmuring of the springs, an exquisite anticipation of the accompaniment of "Soave sia il vento," the most beautiful trio in *Così fan tutte*.

Solo Violin and V I *Scorrono i fonti*

I shall also give an example from the *largo* (*Il capraro che dorme*), to which I have already alluded. It superimposes three elements, corresponding to three different dynamic levels. The background of the picture is a soft rustling of leaves (the violins in thirds with a dotted sixteenth and thirty-second note pattern, *pp*); above this the cantilena of the solo violin expresses the quietude of the sleeper or his dream; while down below the violas represent the barking dog ("*il cano che grida*") by an *ostinato* pattern "always loud and rasping."

Il Capraro che dorme

As Hans Engel (*Das Instrumentalkonzert*, 1932) points out, there is some similarity between this *largo* and the *andante* of Beethoven's Pastoral Symphony; the latter approximates at one and the same time an objective description of the brook and an evocation of a protagonist, while Vivaldi gives us simultaneously the rustling of the leaves and the repose of the herdsman (here Dr. Engel ignores the noisy four-footed supernumerary). The serenity of this movement is worth noticing, managed as it is without change in the layout of the rhythmic patterns that are the accompaniment for thirty-nine measures.

From the peasant dance that serves as the finale I would quote, if the procedure employed had not been known long since, the passage in the second solo where the solo imitates the musette or hurdy-gurdy by a well-marked melody over the sounding of an open string as a pedal point.

In the second concerto, *L'Estate* (*Summer*), the first tutti constitutes the most notable find. Full sonorities and a weighted rhythm that is imposed on the whole orchestra set up a torrid atmosphere, which after a while is rent by the mechanical call of the cuckoo, the stylization of which is no surprise. The goldfinch that appears a little further on expresses himself like the one in Opus 10. Between these two the gentle lamentation of the turtledove is inserted. We fall back into a more conventional realm with restless figurations intended to depict the gentle breezes, the north wind, or, in the finale, the summer thunderstorm. There is, on the other hand, a rather modern feeling of melancholy in the dejected plaint of the little shepherd.

In the concerto *L'Autunno* (*Autumn*) the first tutti forcefully establishes a scene of country songs and dances. The initial solo takes up the theme as an echo and gives body to it with strong double-stops. The chorus gives a shorter answer to it. Meanwhile—the prefatory sonnet informs us—the peasants have a bacchanal. The drunkenness that comes over them is revealed by the disarray of the runs in the solo violin. Then, after a debauch of modulations, roulades, trills, and *brisures*—a drunken peasant run riot—there comes a tutti that displays for a second time the motive of the peasants' chorus, transposed and soon enlivened by syncopations. One last run is heard, a last prank of the drunk, who immediately thereafter falls into a deep sleep. A lull—and suddenly the refrain of the jolly drinkers breaks in as if to wake their sleeping comrade with a start.

The *adagio* is again a *sommeil*—this time a collective one. The cello part bears the subtitle *Ubriachi dormienti* (*Sleeping Drunks*). But nothing in the music depicts drunkenness any more, and this is so much the case that, limiting himself to transposing this *adagio* and labeling it *largo*, Vivaldi returned to it again to make it the middle movement (*Il Sonno*) of Opus 10, No. 2.

In the hunt finale the tutti trumpets forth a fanfare theme. The solos sometimes represent the call of horns (double-stops on the rhythm of the central motive of the tutti), and sometimes the distress and fright of the animal, who is pursued, encircled, and finally reduced to surrender—rapid, panting triplets, and runs in thirty-second notes that ascend at first and then tumble down with a desperate speed as if to indicate the victim's collapse.

The fourth and last concerto, *L'Inverno* (*Winter*), may be somewhat inferior to the preceding ones. The verbal summary, which is less successful than the others, determines a fragmented composition, a mosaic of rather monotonous small effects. The repeated trills for the violins are those of the comic interlude of the *trembleurs* in the old French operas; the rapid passage work designed to depict the storm has already served the same end. There is nothing unexpected except the figurations that seek to evoke the cautious step of the pedestrian on the frozen ground, his falls, and the shattering of the ice. Furthermore, the fine balance between the tutti and the solos is endangered; the contrasts are established only between some curtailed elements. Thus the two *allegros* take on the appearance of small symphonic tableaux in a free form with the violin especially favored. The *largo* (according to the sonnet, the joys of the chimney corner when a storm is raging outside) has a calm melody of beautiful lines, one that might just as easily be given a place in a nondescriptive work.

Just as it is, this series of *The Seasons* put its mark on Vivaldi's career and on the musical life of his century. Its success in Italy outdid that of *L'Estro armonico*. In France the Concert Spirituel in Paris presented *The Seasons* beginning February 7, 1728. It is possible that they were performed in full on that day, because the *Mercure de France* wrote with its customary imprecision, "Next, Vivaldi's concerto of the four seasons, which is an excellent symphonic piece, was played." But for the concerts of April 4th and 5th in the same year the soloist was Jean Pierre Guignon, who interpreted *La Primavera* and *L'Estate*. After this, popular favor settled on *La Primavera* alone. Guignon gave it again on February 21, 1729. On November 25, 1730, at Marly, the king asked him expressly for it: "The king asked next that Vivaldi's *Primavera*, which is an excellent symphonic piece [the editor did not pride himself on variety], be played, and as the musicians of the king were not as a rule at this concert, the prince de Dombes, the count d'Eu and several other lords of the court were willing to accompany Monsieur Guignon so as not to deprive His Majesty of hearing this beautiful symphonic piece, which was performed to perfection" (*Mercure de France*, December, 1730).

New performances of *La Primavera* with Guignon as soloist came on January 16 and February 2, 1736. On November 1, 1741, it was the turn of the young Gaviniès, who was thirteen years of age. He kept this concerto in his repertory for a long time, for Roualle de Boisgelou at the beginning of the next century has direct recollection of it. "It was always rapturously applauded," he wrote in his manuscript *Catalogue de la musique pratique* (1813), "when it was given with all the charm of Gaviniès' pleasant playing." Then came Domenico Ferrari, Vachon, Canavas, Capron, and le Duc. This list, probably very incomplete even insofar as it relates to the Concert Spirituel, does not take account of the private gatherings that such patrons of the arts as La Pouplinière organized with the co-operation of the best-known virtuosos. As long as the cult of things Italian was fashionable, it may be considered as certain that *La Primavera* remained one of its chief attractions.

French publishers, too, took a lively interest in Opus 8, which included *Le Stagioni,* and in *La Primavera* in particular. This concerto achieved the distinction of having numerous and varied transcriptions. When Nicolas Chédeville in 1793 asked for a license to publish several Italian works that he wanted "to adapt, to transpose, and to arrange in a way easy to be performed on the musette, the hurdy-gurdy, or the flute with the accompaniment of violins and a bass," *La Primavera* appeared at the top of his list. In 1748 he had the Privelège of 1739 renewed for this work alone. Corrette exploited the same original in another way; he derived a large sacred composition from it. This is his *Laudate Dominum de Coelis, Pseaume 148, Motet à Grand Choeur arrangé dans le Concerto du Printemps de Vivaldi,* which was sung on November 22, 1765, for the Mass of Saint Cecilia at Les Mathurins. Going to another extreme, Jean Jacques Rousseau, who did not have a sense of polyphony, arranged this same concerto for solo flute in 1755.

Vivaldi as a descriptive musician could not have gained such popularity without exerting some influence on composers of his time. He served as a sanction and model for Locatelli when he wrote his *Pianto d'Arianna* (Opus 7, No. 6, 1741) just as he did for Geminiani in *The Enchanted Forest, an instrumental composition expressive of . . . the poem of Tasso of that title* (London, 1750).

He most certainly inspired many of the musical paintings of nature and of country life that mark the road between his Opus 8 and Beethoven's Pastoral Symphony—Graupner's *Four Seasons* (1733), instrumental suites only the title of which is extant (but this title and the closeness of the dates are significant); or, better still, Gregor Joseph Werner's peculiar work *Neuer und sehr curios musicalischer Instrumental-Calender, Parthien-weiss mit 2 Violinen und Bass in die zwölf Jahrs-Monath eingetheilet . . .*

(Augsburg, 1748). In this work are found all the scenes depicted in *The Seasons*—the storm, the hunt, the *sommeil*, the pastoral, and all the bird songs—with the addition of some new accessories and the set purpose of having everything, even down to the most minute details, governed by a symbolism that was as ingenious as it was tyrannical. Thus Werner makes it a strict rule to indicate, month after month, the respective lengths of the day and night by twelve minuets, each in two sections, the first having as many measures as there are hours of daylight, the second corresponding in the same way to the number of nighttime hours—that is, for January two repeated sections of nine and fifteen measures, for February eleven and thirteen measures, for March twelve and twelve, for April thirteen and eleven, and so on. The year 1748, the date at which this almanac was published, is expressed by a fugue whose subject is built on the intervals of the unison, the seventh, the fourth, and the octave. The rest is in keeping.

Werner was the *Capellmeister* for the Counts Esterházy, who were neighbors of Count Morzin, recipient of the dedication of Vivaldi's Opus 8. The connection of the two works, at least with regard to the program, for they are very different in spirit, appears from this to be all the more plausible. And it would be no more surprising if Joseph Haydn, succeeding Werner in his post in the Esterházy household after having worked for Count Morzin, had taken the idea of the oratorio *Die Jahreszeiten* from Vivaldi through the agency of Werner. Hans Engel has, moreover, found typical uses of procedures that we know from Vivaldi in some ten symphonies by Haydn, of which he gives a description in his remarkable study on Mozart's early symphonies, "Über Mozarts Jugendsinfonien," *Neues Mozart-Jahrbuch*, V, 1952.

There is kinship again, musical this time, between certain episodes of *La Primavera* and *L'Autunno* and the charming Boccherini quintet Opus 13, No. 6 (1771), of which the first movement is entitled *L'Ucceliera* and the second *I Pastori e i cacciatori*.

Finally, the last link between *Le Stagioni* and the Pastoral Symphony, Justin Heinrich Knecht's *Le Portrait musical de la Nature*, published at Speyer in 1784, attests an exact knowledge, if not of Vivaldi's music, at least of the sonnets that set forth the program.

The place of the sonnets is taken by a summary drawn up in French. Here is the beginning:

The Musical Portrait of Nature, a large symphony, which expresses by means of sounds:
1. A beautiful countryside where the sun shines, the sweet breezes hover, the streams run through the vale, the birds chirp, a rushing stream falls murmuring from above, the shepherd whistles, the lambs skip, and the shepherdess makes her sweet voice heard.
2. The sky begins to become sudden and dark [*sic*], all the vicinity can scarcely breathe, and they take fright [*sic*], the black clouds mount. . . .

After which—I summarize—the storm bursts and then abates, and "nature overcome with joy raises its voice to heaven. . . ."

This last stroke comes nearer to Beethoven than to Vivaldi, and Knecht's musical language no longer has much in common with that of 1720-1730. What is clearly perceived is the source of the plan that Beethoven fixed for himself and the pictorial details and the contrasts that he thought it good to preserve.

The Seasons draws its full interest in our eyes from the echo that it excited among historians and philosophers of the eighteenth century; for in some way it crystallized the theories of a time when aesthetics was dominated by a solicitude for the "natural," when all of the arts, even music, were obliged to apply themselves to depicting some precise object.

It was in France that praise was most full and abundant, whether or not Vivaldi and his music were expressly brought into the matter. Charles Henri Blainville wrote as follows in his *Esprit de l'art musical* (1754):

Study nature. You see what variety and contrasts it offers to you. There it is an arid desert bounded by steep crags, the abode of silence and of dread. Here it is a pleasant plain of tufted slopes and a verdant meadow bedecked with flowers, where everything breathes gaiety.
Or else you depict the effects of a storm or tempest—subterranean sound, the whistling of the winds, the heaving of the waves of the sea, the noise of the waters mingling with the noise of the thunder; let everything portray the confusion and havoc that this short-lived strife causes. But the sun reappears, the wind drops, the air becomes quiet

and serene, the birds revert to proclaiming by their sweet twitterings the peace of the elements. . . .

If Blainville here forgoes naming Vivaldi, who is, nevertheless, perceptibly close at hand, the fact is that a little above he does refer to his example. He proposed to distinguish three kinds of music—the *genere harmonico* (the old polyphonic style), the *genere sonabile* (the new style, instrumental in nature, which according to the rather muddled definition that he gives of it would fit the Italians), and finally the *genere cantabile* (the French branch of the new art, less acrobatic and more melodious). After conceding that music of the second type can entertain us even if it depicts nothing, he hastens to add, "The pieces of the *sonabile* type that have a tinge of the other two, that have a distinguishing character and a particular object, are very satisfying to hear. Such is Vivaldi's *Primavera*, of which the opening by itself appears to set forth a serene and quiet sky. Everything in nature seems to revive. The birds flutter in the air, everything re-echoes their twittering; the shepherds come running and dance with the shepherdesses to the sound of their musettes—everything breathes the pastoral pleasures that this smiling season proclaims. In the other seasons, the composer with as felicitous conceptions shows himself to be a skillful painter; at least he is the best we have up to now in this genre."

Jacques Lacombe, the author of *Le Spectacle des Beaux-Arts* (1758), does not accept any music other than that genre. The preface, or *Avertissement*, of his book states this most clearly. "The spectacle that the fine arts present to us is none other than that of beautiful nature. The visual arts convey it to the eye, music to the ear, poetry to the imagination. It is always nature that is perceived in their pleasing products." In the body of his work, having praised the descriptive passages in Mondonville's motets and operas, he adds, "We have good imitations of storms, thunder, and the like, from several musicians. It is only a question of following this plan and not permitting oneself any vague or undefined compositions. It is necessary to get down to detail in art and always have in view a model to copy. There is no expression at all without depiction." Lacombe does not stop halfway. He reaches the point of proposing, like a competition jury for the *Prix de Rome*, some subjects for treatment, some "plans for musical compositions—the dawn, pleasure gardens, fireworks, a dispute." Then he goes on, "Would it be impossible to portray the four parts of the world, the four parts of the day, or the seasons of the year in music through accessory images? . . . I shall close this subject with an outline of the picture of the seasons." Whereupon we find ourselves confronted with an unskillful and commonplace translation of the sonnets of Opus 8. Vivaldi is not cited, but we are in 1758 and the audience of the Concerts Spirituels could not fail to make the obvious connection.

Almost identical discourses are found in *Les Œuvres mêlées de Madame Sara Goudar, angloise* (1777) and in a less dogmatic form in Du Chargey's *Entretien d'un musicien françois avec un gentilhomme russe* (1773), which holds forth with even more satisfaction on the details of depiction like Vivaldi's.

The only sour note in this chorus of admiration is sounded by an anonymous author who precisely in the name of the contemporary French ideal takes Vivaldi's descriptions to task for their lack of accuracy. If one performed, he writes in one of *Les Lettres sur la musique française en réponse à celle de Jean-Jacques Rousseau* (1754), "before a foreigner or any unprejudiced person a French symphony and an Italian one and asked him what the two composers wished to portray, he could easily tell what the subject of the French had been, whether it was grief, happiness, or love; and I would bet that he would find in the Italian only varied prettiness. I would challenge this new and impartial listener, for example, to divine anything other than a storm in the storm piece from *Alcyone*, and in Vivaldi's *Primavera* he would find only shepherd dances which are common to all seasons, and where consequently spring is no more represented than summer or fall."

Is it necessary to remark that this criticism seems to us today to be beside the point, just as do the preceding analogies? The element of "likeness" is indeed the last one we take account of in the assessment of a work, even if the composer has laid down a program for himself and taken us into his confidence. If we are given good music, the accuracy of the imitation will come as a bonus.

But Vivaldi's audience called for this accuracy, and he achieved it more than adequately, without having injured the music by it. He gave a light twist to what could have been heavy and tiresome. He deserves even more praise for having been successful in this pleasant exercise while stylizing it and integrating it in a musical structure as balanced as that of the nondescriptive concertos. Let us be grateful to him especially for what he contributed at one stroke in the way of new orchestral colors and, beyond the limits of the technical, in the form of poetical inspiration. Through this he managed to give new life to a genre doubly in danger—on the one hand, from the public's complaisance and on the other, from the philosopher's theories—of being confined to the most insipid kind of realism.

THE OPERAS AND SACRED WORKS

The discovery of the manuscripts in the Foà and Giordano collections bequeathed in 1927–1930 to the Biblioteca Nazionale in Turin had among other results that of bringing attention back to a part of Vivaldi's work which till then had been completely forgotten—his operas and his sacred and secular vocal music. One of his dramatic scores, *Arsilda, Regina di Ponto* was indeed previously known to be in the Dresden library, but apparently no one had taken the trouble to study it. It was known, too, that the Paris Conservatory possessed seven arias from *Ercole sul Termodonte* catalogued under a rough approximation of that title, *La Créole*. (I once pointed them out to Alfredo Casella, who transcribed several of them.) Finally, there was an awareness of existing motets, cantatas, and operas dispersed among the libraries of Paris, London, Munich, Dresden, Rostock, and other cities where they slept peacefully.

There is nothing very surprising in such indifference. People at all times feel reluctant to recognize in one artist the gift to create in two different domains. In the case of Vivaldi, at the height of his career attempts were made to have him limit himself to his specialty of composing concertos. Charles de Brosses in 1740 records the following statement by Tartini: "I have been urged to work for the Venetian theaters, and I have never been willing to do it, well knowing that a gullet is not the neck of a violin. Vivaldi, who wanted to practice both genres, always failed to go over in the one, whereas in the other he succeeded very well."

Without being so categorical, Quantz holds the Red Priest's operatic activity responsible for the admittedly obvious decline in quality that exists in certain concertos from the last years. He does this in the course of a comparison that he makes between Tartini and Vivaldi. (He names neither of them, but the portraits that he draws leave no room for doubt.) "Two famous Lombard violinists, who some thirty-odd years ago [he is writing in 1752] began in close succession to be known, acquired great fame for their accomplishments. The first was lively and richly inventive, and he filled nearly half the world with his concertos. . . . whence he attained general acclaim as had Corelli with his twelve solos [Opus 5]. But composing daily and too much and especially turning out vocal music for opera, he fell at the end into frivolousness and eccentricity both in composing and playing. This is the reason why his last concertos did not earn as much applause as the first."

With time opinions became more unqualified. Gerber, in his dictionary (1792), which devotes a laudatory and rather detailed notice to Vivaldi, disposes of the dramatic composer in two lines. "In Venice he was held in higher esteem as a violinist than as an opera composer, and that was just." A good musician of recent times, the Venetian, G. G. Bernardi, writing in 1908, is even more positive: "Vivaldi, a celebrated violinist and instrumental composer, a mediocre opera composer. . . ."

Was this actually the view of his contemporaries? If so, how is one to explain a dramatic output maintained from 1713, with *Ottone in Villa*, up until around 1740? And what accounts for the fact that one theater alone, the Teatro Sant'Angelo, ordered eighteen operas, often revisions of earlier works, from a *"mediocre operista"* and that Rome made a success of three others in 1723–24? (At that time, according to Quantz, the sudden vogue of the Lombard rhythm was caused by this music, which drew the favorable attention of the Pope himself.) And what of *Ipermestra* in 1727, which restored the encumbered finances of the Florentine theater (so said the abbé Conti); and what of the Munich staging of *La costanza trionfante* after its Venetian success; and what of the delight that Charles Albert of Bavaria, when making a short stay in Verona, apparently took in applauding *Catone?*

To judge by the numerous arias drawn from his operas that we find in the music libraries of Europe, the favor that greeted him was not extinguished with the end of the opera season; it went far beyond the precincts of the theaters. Witness, among many others, that volume in the Paris Bibliothèque Nationale entitled *Raccolta d'Arie Italiane scelte nelle composizioni degli autori più celebri in Roma 1739,* which contains one hundred arias by eighteen composers, including Handel, Hasse, Porpora, and Bononcini. Well, Vivaldi is represented by eight arias, which puts him among the privileged few. When the Abbé Conti announces to his Parisian correspondent that he is going to address a bundle of Italian music to her, he continues, "Next week I shall send you some of Porpora's arias. . . . I shall look also for arias by Vivaldi; you would be enchanted by their liveliness and their variety."

This was not the opinion of amateurs alone. In contrast to some experts who deny Vivaldi the gift of composing for the voice, others grant it to him unreservedly. Mattheson, in *Der vollkommene Capellmeister* (1739) took a stand with his accustomed vigor. "Although he was not a singer at all, Vivaldi knew so well how to forgo in his vocal music the large intervals of the violin, that his arias impress the specialists in that species of composition as being a thorn in their flesh." This is pretty much what Burney was to reiterate; he makes one think that he judged in fact from examples. "D. Antonio Vivaldi merits a place among the candidates for fame in this species of composition: several are inserted in the collection mentioned above [the famous collection of Dr. Henry Aldrich of Christ Church, Oxford]; but these, and all that I have seen elsewhere, are very common and quiet, notwithstanding he was so riotous in composing for violins. But he had been too long used to write for the voice to treat it like an instrument." A French music lover, Du Chargey, in 1773 compared his church works with those of his compatriot Lalande. "Lalande often moved listeners to tears by his motets. Vivaldi, as expressive as Lalande, often moved his fellow Italians by his." These opinions, together with no less significant ones from authoritative writers of a time closer to ours, persuade us not to agree to condemn Vivaldi's operas, motets, and cantatas sight unseen.

Before looking at them more closely, let us first of all draw up a summary inventory of the vocal music and particularly of the operas and oratorios. I shall call to mind that the season designated by the name of Carnival, or winter season, extended from December 26th to March 30th, the spring season from the day following Easter to June 30th, the fall season from September 1st to November 30th. Some doubts, some variances between the dates indicated below and those supplied by other historians may arise from the fact that some of the sources used the old chronology according to which the Venetian year began not on January 1, but on March 1. The dates of January and February and in general those of the winter season may differ by a year, depending upon whether they are fixed *more veneto* or according to the Gregorian calendar. In the following list the librettists are named within brackets right after the titles.

1713: *Ottone in Villa* [Domenico Lalli], given first in Vienna. Revived in 1715 and 1729. Ms. score at Turin.

Fall, 1714: *Orlando finto pazzo* [Grazio Braccioli], Venice, Teatro Sant'Angelo. Ms. score at Turin.

1714: *Moyses Deus Pharaonis* [. . .], an oratorio sung at the Pietà.

Carnival, 1715: *Nerone fatto Cesare* [Matteo Noris], music by several composers, containing twelve arias by Vivaldi. Venice, Sant'Angelo.

Carnival, 1716: *L'incoronazione di Dario* [Morselli], Venice, Sant'Angelo. Dated by some historians as of the winter of 1717. Ms. score at Turin.

Carnival, 1716: *La costanza trionfante degli amore e degli odi* [Antonio Marchi], Venice, Teatro San Moise. Revived in 1718 (Munich), 1731 (Venice, Sant'Angelo), 1742 (Bologna, Teatro Formagliari).

Fall, 1716: *Arsilda regina di Ponto* [Domenico Lalli], Venice,

Sant'Angelo. Occasionally dated as of the spring of 1716. Ms. scores at Turin and at Dresden.

1716: *Juditha triumphans devicta Holofernis barbarie* [Jacopo Cassetti], an oratorio sung at the Pietà. Ms. score at Turin.

Fall, 1717: *Tieteberga* [Antonio Maria Lucchini], Venice, San Moise. It is possible that in this same year Vivaldi collaborated in composing the opera *Il vinto trionfante del vincitore*, composed by several composers on a libretto by Antonio Marchi and given at the Teatro Sant'Angelo in the fall. In fact, a Dresden manuscript contains a *Sinfonia del Opera 2a di Sant. Angelo del Sigr Vivaldi 1717*, which has not been identified up to the present; it is bound with a *Sinfonia 1a* imprecisely dated 1717, which comes from *Arsilda* (1716). The hypothesis has been put forward that the *Sinfonia del Opera 2a* may come from *La costanza* or *Tieteberga*, operas from 1716 and 1717 whose scores are lost; but both of them were produced at the Teatro San Moise, not at the Sant'Angelo.

Carnival, 1718: *Artabono re de' Parti* [Marchi], Venice, San Moise. This is *La costanza trionfante* of 1716 with some changes. A new version, touched up by Galeazzi, was given in 1731 at the Sant'Angelo under the title *L'odio vinto dalla costanza* and possibly repeated there in 1738.

Spring, 1718: *Scanderbegh* [Antonio Salvi], Florence, for the reopening of the Teatro della Pergola (June 22).

Fall, 1718: *Armida al campo d'Egitto* [Giovanni Palazzi], Venice, San Moise. Twice revived in Venice, at the Teatro Santa Margherita in 1731 and at the Sant'Angelo in 1738. Ms. score (the overture and Acts I and III only) at Turin.

Carnival, 1720: *La Candace o siano Li veri amici* [Francesco Silvani and Domenico Lalli], Mantua, Teatro Arciducale.

Fall, 1720: *La verità in cimento* [Giovanni Palazzi], Venice, Sant'Angelo. Ms. score at Turin.

1720: *Gli inganni per vendetta* [. . .], Vicenza, Teatro delle Grazie.

Fall, 1721: *Filippo re di Macedonia* [Domenico Lalli], Venice, Sant'Angelo. The third act alone may have been by Vivaldi; the others by Benvenuti or Giuseppe Boniventi.

1721: *Silvia* [. . .], Milan, Teatro Ducale.

January, 1723: *Ercole sul Termodonte* [Giacomo Francesco Bussani], Rome, Teatro Capranica. Seven arias from this opera are in manuscript score in the library of the Paris Conservatory. The copyist artlessly misinterprets *Ercole* as *La Créole*.

Carnival, 1724: *Il Giustino* [Nicolo Berengani], Rome, Teatro Capranica. Ms. score at Turin.

Carnival, 1724: *La virtù trionfante dell'amore e dell'odio ovvero Tigrane* [Francesco Silvani], Rome, Teatro Capranica. The second act only is by Vivaldi; the first is by Benedetto Micheli, the third by N. Romaldi. Ms. score at Turin.

Fall, 1725: *L'inganno trionfante in amore* [Noris, retouched by G. M. Ruggeri], Venice, Sant'Angelo.

Carnival, 1726: *La fede tradita e vendicata* [Abbé Silvani], Venice, Sant'Angelo. The music of this opera was used again in 1750 in *Ernelinda*, which was performed at the Teatro San Cassiano in Venice and whose score is appropriated from Vivaldi, Galuppi, and Gasparini.

Carnival, 1726: *Farnace* [Antonio Maria Lucchini], Venice, Sant'Angelo. Revived in 1727. Ms. score at Turin with a second version of Act I and II for the 1727 revival.

Fall, 1726: *Dorilla in Tempe* [Antonio Maria Lucchini], Venice, Sant'Angelo. Ms. score at Turin, made use of for a revival of 1734.

Carnival, 1727: *Ipermestra* [Antonio Salvi], Florence, Teatro della Pergola.

May, 1727: *Siroe re di Persia* [Metastasio], Reggio. A *Siroe* by Vivaldi was performed at Ancona in 1738, but its libretto may have been by Giovanni Boldini. Metastasio's libretto was used in 1767 for a *Siroe* staged at the grand ducal theater of Braunschweig; the music was appropriated from Handel, Hasse, Vinci, Wagenseil, and Vivaldi.

Fall, 1727: *Orlando* [Braccioli], Venice, Sant'Angelo. This opera has nothing in common with *Orlando finto pazzo* (1714). Ms. score at Turin, under the title of *Orlando furioso*.

Carnival, 1728: *Rosilena ed Oronta* [Giovanni Palazzi], Venice, Sant'Angelo.

Carnival, 1729: *L'Atenaide* [Apostolo Zeno], Florence, Teatro della Pergola. Ms. score at Turin.

Carnival, 1731: *L'odio vinto dalla costanza.* See above, *Artabano re de' Parti* (1718).

1731: *Semiramide* [. . .], Verona. Repeated at Mantua, 1732.

January, 1732: *La fida ninfa* [Scipione Maffei], Verona. Ms. score at Turin.

Fall, 1733: *Montezuma* [Girolamo Giusti], Venice, Sant'Angelo.

1733: *Sarce* [. . .], Ancona. Mentioned only by Mendel's *Musi-kalisches Conversations-Lexicon;* perhaps it is a question of confusion with the *Siroe* given in Ancona in 1738 (see above, *Siroe re di Persia,* 1727).

Carnival, 1734: *L'Olimpiade* [Metastasio], Venice, Sant'Angelo. Ms. score at Turin.

Spring, 1735: *Griselda* [Apostolo Zeno, with modifications by Goldoni], Venice, San Samuele. Ms. score at Turin.

1735: *Tamerlano* [Count Agostino Piovene], Verona. Revived at Florence, 1748. Ms. score at Turin, under the title *Bajazet,* with music by several composers among whom Vivaldi has the most important place.

Carnival, 1735: *Adelaide* [. . .], Verona, Teatro dell' Accademia Filarmonica. On the libretto Vivaldi flaunts a title new to us, "*Maestro di cappella di S. A. S. il Duca di Lorena.*"

Fall, 1735: *Aristide* [Calindo Grolo, anagram for Carlo Goldoni], Venice, San Samuele. Vivaldi is identified as the composer of this "*dramma eroico-comico*" by the anagram Lotavio Vandini.

January, 1736: *Ginevra principessa di Scozia* [Antonio Salvi], Florence.

Spring, 1737: *Partenope* [. . .], Venice, Sant'Angelo. It is mentioned only in the manuscript supplement to Giovanni Carlo Bonlini's repertory (1730); the characters are the same as those of *Rosmira* (1738), so perhaps it is the same work.

Spring, 1738: *Catone in Utica* [Metastasio], Verona. Ms. score at Turin (the first act missing).

Carnival, 1738: *Rosmira* [Stampiglia], Venice, Sant'Angelo. Ms. score at Turin, under the title *Rosmira fedele.* According to Fernando Liuzzi, writing in 1934, this is a pastiche of fragments from works by Hasse, Antonio Mazzoni, Girolamo Micheli, Paganelli, Pergolesi, and others, gathered together by Vivaldi.

Carnival, 1738: *L'Oracolo in Messenia* [Apostolo Zeno], Venice, Sant'Angelo.

Fall, 1739: *Feraspe* [Francesco Silvani], Venice, Sant'Angelo.

We do not possess any precise information on the date and place of performance of the following:

Il Teuzzone [Apostolo Zeno], the score of which is at Turin.

Tito Manlio [Matteo Noris], two scores of which are at Turin; one, an autograph, carries the superscription *"Musica del Vivaldi fatta in 5 giorni."*

A *Demetrio* and an *Alessandro nell'Indie*, which are mentioned by Vivaldi in a letter of December 29, 1736, to Marquis Bentivoglio; they have disappeared without a trace. So has a *Mitridate*, except for an aria from it that is found in the Casanatense library of Rome in a collection (Ms. 2222) in which arias of operas performed in that city and in Naples from 1721 to 1724 are brought together.

Mopso, although sometimes counted among the operas, is actually a cantata. A work by Leone Allacci (1755) lists it in the following terms: *"Il Mopso*, a piscatorial eclogue for five voices, sung by the young women of the charitable asylum of the Pietà of Venice. . . . [For information on its performance in 1739, see above, p. 50.] Poetry by Egidio Nonnanuci, that is, Giovanni Cendoni, Venetian. Music by Don Antonio Vivaldi."

Finally, we have observed that some Vivaldi arias, probably taken from already performed operas, were occasionally introduced during his lifetime into other composers' stage works. In 1727 at Breslau several arias were interpolated in this way in Pollaroli's *Ariodante*. The following year in the same city others were included when *Merope* was put together, a work in which ten German and Italian composers collaborated, some more knowingly, some less. Vivaldi made use of the same system in *Rosmira* ten years later.

This long enumeration has its own eloquence. At Venice, as elsewhere, it was open to any musician, whoever he was, to compose four dozen operas; but I do not see how the opera houses could have staged them and repeated them with such great perseverance against the fancy of the public. (This by way of answering Tartini's remark on Vivaldi's consistent lack of success as a dramatic composer.)

A prince or patron receiving at his home could to some extent impose on his guests, bound as they were by worldly propriety, a spectacle that did not please them. But at Venice the theaters were public, paid for and frequented by listeners in whom a disciplined attitude or a passive acquiescence was not to be anticipated. On this subject we have precise testimony from Herr von Uffenbach, that occasional pupil of Vivaldi whom we have already met. I recapitulate his curious travel observances, paraphrasing Eberhard Preussner, who first brought them to light again.

Arriving in Venice in 1715, Uffenbach thought first of all of seeing an opera. The immediate difficulty was choosing one, for at the time two opera houses and three troops of comedians were giving performances. His first visit was to the biggest and most famous of the theaters, the Santi Giovanni e Paolo, where a work was being performed for the first time. This "Persian tale" was probably Carlo Pollaroli's *Marsia deluso* [*Marsyas Disappointed*], which was in fact performed at the Santi Giovanni e Paolo with the two famous singers mentioned later by Uffenbach, the castrato Senesino and Diamantina Scarabelli.

In the opera house the excitement of the Carnival season reigned. The audience was extremely unruly. Uffenbach got a seat in the parterre. He found himself among the people of rank, who were seated below the loges. Having a seat at all was a recent development, for a little while before the people in the parterre would have listened standing. But the fact of having paid well for a seat did not protect him from certain inconveniences. It seems that with the masks worn by almost all the audience there came a disruption in customary morality and manners.

The inexperienced tourist could hardly believe his eyes when the gentlemen in the loges started to spit on the people in the parterre and to bombard them with a variety of objects—pipes, and apple and orange peels—which the parterre took as if it were a completely natural occurrence. The most beautiful masks were the most often aimed at. Uffenbach was not spared, although he was not wearing a mask. Someone from the loge above "spits a revolting gob [*ein entsetzliches Maul*]" on the libretto that he holds. He would gladly have had it out with the rascals, but there was nothing to be done but follow the example of the gentry who take it. The only possible revenge was to sit next time in the loge and exercise oneself "in throwing and spitting [*im werfen und speien*]." The behavior in the loges was, in general, startling. They ate, they smoked, they played cards.

And what was occurring on stage? The settings and the lighting were remarkable. The stage machinery was constantly in action. The most impressive set was one representing the temple of Saturn; it had three storys, with stairways, balconies, statues, and columns. The latter were of glass lit from within, and when they were moved—undoubtedly turning about on their axes—they glittered brilliantly. Another scene involved mass effects, putting on stage a multitude of people and animals—mechanical camels and elephants, and live horses (nearly the only ones in Venice, where they did not, could not, use horses).

Absorbed though he was in the spectacle, Uffenbach did determine that the orchestra was excellent and its make-up well balanced. The singers, apart from a single bass and the women, were all castratos, among them the incomparable Senesino. Diamantina was impressive despite the fact that her voice was aging.

On February 4 the traveler went again to see an opera. According to his diary, "I went with several acquaintances to the Teatro Sant'Angelo, which was smaller but also not so costly as the one I have described above. Its impresario [*der Entrepreneur*] was the famous Vivaldi, who had also composed the opera, which was very fine and pleasing to see [probably it was *Orlando finto pazzo*]. The machinery was not so elaborate as in the other theater; the orchestra was not so strong, but was no less worthy of being listened to. In fear of being mistreated and spat upon as in the big opera house, we took a loge (it was not very costly) and revenged ourselves in the local fashion upon the parterre just as had been done to us the previous time, which struck me as almost impossible. . . . The singers were incomparable and yielded nothing to those of the big opera house, especially certain of the women; of these, the so-called Fabri [Anna Maria Fabbri, who sang the part of Orrigille] excelled as much in musicianship as in charm. Moreover, she was very beautiful; at least she appeared so on the stage."

On February 19 Uffenbach heard another Vivaldi opera, *Agrippina* (that is, *Nerone fatto Cesare* under another name). This time he is outspoken in his unfavorable judgment of the story, the settings, and the costumes—a hodgepodge of French, Spanish, and Persian styles. He is so disgusted that he mentions only one performer, Fabri, who played the young Nero. Perhaps lack of funds was responsible; a composer who puts on one of his own works probably thinks first of the music and only after that of the staging.

On an unspecified date between February 28th and March 3rd, Uffenbach again saw *Nerone fatto Cesare* at the same theater. The production and the costumes again displeased him, but he was quite enchanted by the excellent singing. By March 4th he had gone to still another performance of a Vivaldi opera, because he was now interested in the composer as a person. (At this time he was making his efforts to meet Vivaldi himself.)

The information that Uffenbach gives conveys much to us. When added to what we already know about the huge consumption of operas in Venice and of the haste with which they were worked up, it helps us to form a more accurate picture of an atmosphere which in no way resembles that of the opera in our time. We know that so spasmodic a production, one so capriciously surrendered to the exigencies of time and financing, could not avoid having weak points. The main thing is to determine if what remains after more or less severe pruning deserves to be considered.

A recent Vivaldi biographer, Mario Rinaldi, has devoted a portion of his voluminous work to comparing his merits as the composer of instrumental music and as the composer of opera. He arrives at this conclusion: "Between his concertos and his operas there is an abyss." And to the lack of originality in the operas, their "annoying regularity," their obvious purpose of "doing only what is necessary and nothing more," he opposes the constant desire to do things over that is perceived in the concertos, "gallant urgings to excite a genuine revolutionary movement."

Not only do I fail to see the "abyss," but I am struck by all that Vivaldi's instrumental music and his dramatic music—I would even add his sacred music, a matter I shall return to—have in common; struck, but not surprised. His career as a dramatic composer began with *Ottone in Villa* in 1713, that is, one year after the publication of the first concerto collection; it ended in 1739 with *Feraspe*, one year before the composition of the last concertos whose date is fixed positively, those performed at the Pietà in the presence of Prince Frederick Christian of Saxony. The two activities therefore were pursued concurrently from the composer's youth until death was not far off, for nothing warrants us to conclude, with Mario Rinaldi, that dramatic composition in some years turned Vivaldi wholly away from instrumental music.

The natural result of this paralleling was an exchange, an interpenetration between the two genres, thanks to which the operas have the solidity of instrumental music and the latter, as much in inspiration as in treatment, is continually being affected by opera. This is so much the case that we may feel that one of the principal features of Vivaldi's originality is the way in which he transfers into his concertos the procedures and even the spirit of opera. We have noted this previously in the contrasts between fierce unison tutti and the gentle inflections of the solos; in the cantilenas of the slow movements which are barely supported by their accompaniments unburdened of all basses; in the aria with an opening motto *alla* Legrenzi; in the use of various ingredients—tremolo, mutes, and the like—whose abuse in opera is mocked at by Marcello in his *Teatro alla moda*. The third-act storm of *La fida ninfa* is hardly different from the descriptive concertos on the subject of "*la tempesta di mare*." The principle of the echo concertos is exploited as early as 1713 in his very first opera, *Ottone in Villa*, where two flutes and two violins playing on stage answer the bulk of the orchestra. The concertos of *The Seasons* date from 1725; earlier (1723), in *Ercole sul Termodonte*,

the little orchestral prelude that announces the aria *Onde chiare*
had anticipated them. Its almost physical impression of a cooling
stream with singing birds at its banks is given in less than twenty
measures by two on-stage violins without bass, then by a harpsichord solo, then by the combination of ripieno violins and violas
over a harpsichord bass of extreme thinness.

We have not discussed the other side of the matter and listed
the symphonic fragments in operas put together and written
down as concert sinfonie or as tuttis in concertos. Sometimes these
are exact transfers, in the same way that some arias are repetitions of concerto solos; an aria from the first act of *Il Giustino*
appropriates the theme of a Dresden violin concerto in *d*.

It seems, therefore, rather fruitless to compare the concertos
and the operas as to their musical substance, which is the same
in both genres. Let us admit that there is probably more waste
material in the operas, which the unlucky composer had to do,
as I have already indicated, in haste and confusion. Looking over
the sixteen scores preserved in the Turin library, Casella came
upon the same aria used in four different operas. Vivaldi, moreover, has given a most realistic picture of his working conditions
in the letters that he sent to Marquis Bentivoglio at Ferrara. Here
are some passages from the letter of December 29, 1736. He has
just told his patrons that he let the Abbé Bollani, who wanted to
stage some shows at Ferrara, worm a promise out of him to turn
over two operas, *Genevra* (*Ginevra*) and *L'Olimpiade*, to the
producer, "and readapting for his troop the recitatives of the
two at the miserable price of six sequins for each opera." He
continues as follows:

Having just returned from Ferrara, he [the abbé Bollani] pestered
me to turn out *Genevra* immediately. Forthwith I adapted the original
and had the parts copied, which I sent to Your Excellency as a token;
the parts for Moro and the tenor, however, are still in their hands.
Scarcely had this been done than a new order came; these gentlemen
[the patrons of the theater] no longer want *Genevra*, but *Demetrio*.
I go to look for it at the Grimani palace in order to have it copied,
but I see that out of six parts, five must be changed; hence it follows
that the recitatives come out all wrong. I therefore decided (Your
Excellency can form an opinion of my good will from this) to do
over all the recitatives. I ought to inform Your Excellency that in

addition to the six sequins, I concluded an agreement with the afore-said impresario that he would pay for all the copies of the vocal and instrumental parts. Thus, when *Demetrio* is completely put into shape again, I have the vocal and instrumental parts copied, I have all the singers learn their roles by heart, I hold three rehearsals, and I get everything set. I am sure that such delight had not been got from the opera before. All this being done, I tell him that between *Genevra* and *Demetrio* I have spent fifty lire for the vocal and instrumental parts. And although one opera alone cost him thirty lire, there are a good ten letters in which I entreat him to give orders to this Lanzetti for the payment of the other twenty, and he has never answered me on that score. Through a number of messengers he pestered me to send him *L'Olimpiade*. I arrange or, rather, spoil my original manu-script by patching it up. I have some passages copied under my very eyes, still without having received the order for it, because I believe it is in his interest by reason of the difference there is between one copyist and another. And then comes a new order; they no longer want *L'Olimpiade* but *Alessandro nell'Indie*. . . .

The composer was obliged at the same time to busy himself with discussing the tickets and with the recruitment of the com-pany and of its training. This was not easy; he had to catch up with his *première danseuse*, who had run away from the family home "to make her life" with a dancer "capable of every mistake and every extravagance." He had also to perform the various jobs that devolved on him as a teacher and *maestro de' concerti* at the Pietà. Hence it is understandable that very often he would be forced into acrobatics in which music might have to suffer.

Another stumbling block lay in the taste of the time—and the very special predilection of the Venetians—for historical or mythological plots set off with large scenic effects. (The French today relegate such spectacular displays to the Théâtre du Châtelet, from which the Académie Nationale de Musique in-cidentally sometimes borrows.) As an example, let us take *Il Giustino*, which Vivaldi had performed in 1724 in Rome in the Teatro Capranica.

The libretto of Niccolo Beregan (Berengani), which Legrenzi, Albinoni, and Lotti had already set and which Handel took up again in 1737, had as its point of departure the story of Justin I, a humble Illyrian shepherd who rose to be prefect of the Prae-torian Guard. He was elected East Roman Emperor, and reigned

from 518 to 527. It was his nephew, like him the son of country
folk, who under the name of Justinian made himself famous as
a lawmaker.

Berengani had prefaced his libretto with a statement of the
theme as follows: "At the time when Arianna, widow of Zeno,
named Anastasio emperor, Vitaliano the younger crossed vic-
toriously over the Bosphorus with a large army and besieged
Constantinople. At the same time Giustino forsook his plough to
go to war on behalf of the Greek empire, and took Vitaliano
prisoner. By way of recompense he was crowned with the imperial laurel. On these facts the drama has been constructed."

But he constructed it with great freedom and an excess of
dramatic doings added thereto, not without harm to the clearness
of the action. Giustino reaches glory, not because of having begun by demonstrating superior military qualities. Not at all;
he rescues Leocasta, sister of the Emperor Anastasio, from the
clutches of a bear who is pursuing her. (The bear was so commonly used as a character in the fantastic Venetian shows that
Marcello devoted a passage to him in his *Teatro alla moda*.)
Bewitched by the unhoped-for appearance of this deliverer,
Leocasta takes him for a god. Is he a man? Too bad. And yet not
so bad; she falls in love with him and brings him back to the imperial court to make a warrior of him. In the second act Giustino
exterminates a sea monster who is attacking the empress; she is
chained to a steep rock on the deserted shore. . . . It is also
necessary to relate the doings of the traitor Andronico, disguised
as an exiled princess, and to tell of Vitaliano's confusion when
lightning cuts in two the mountain in which there is a vault
where he has imprisoned Giustino, whom he is preparing to
assassinate. Next, voices issuing from the unexpectedly uncovered
tomb of the first emperor Vitaliano reveal to the would-be mur-
derer that Giustino is his brother who in infancy had been carried off by a tiger and whose right arm bears a mark attesting to
his ancestry. . . .

Let us not be too quick to scoff at these rather obvious contrivances. Handel's *Giustino*, which failed after five performances
in London in 1737, also had its sea monster episode. But it is still
found in 1781 in Mozart's *Idomeneo*. In Venice, where the

operatic monsters lived an especially durable life, the Englishman Burgh tells of having seen in 1792 an opera by Peter von Winter, *Il sacrificio di Creta*, in which the tenor playing Theseus exterminates the Minotaur at the end of his bravura aria. When the public demanded an encore, the Minotaur obligingly came to life again so as to be killed a second time.

The development of opera in the ninteenth and twentieth centuries has led us far from these spectacular shows. In them, moreover, conventions now forgotten also prevailed in the realm of musical construction. This is the main reason for the depreciation of Vivaldi's operas. An American musicologist, Donald Jay Grout, put it this way in *The Musical Quarterly* (October, 1946):

It has already been stated that opera is of all great musical forms the most sensitive to its environment. For this very reason opera is one of the most perishable forms of music. Every educated musician knows something about Vivaldi's concertos and Handel's oratorios, but comparatively few know much about Vivaldi's or Handel's operas. It is not that the music of these operas is any less worthy of remembrance, but rather that it is so clearly bound by a hundred subtle ties to a certain way of life that has now disappeared—to bygone fashions in psychology, in poetry, in drama, in dress, manners, and customs— that we can hardly revive it with convincing effect without reviving the whole culture from which it was nourished.

This means, therefore, that if we wish to judge Venetian opera fairly and to make an allowance for what is "of the time," and the result of the customs of a certain public and the servitude to which the composer was subjected, we ought to forget the malicious criticism of Benedetto Marcello, whose *Teatro alla moda* was aimed chiefly at the Red Priest. We ought also to pass over an observation by Tartini which may have been only an ill-considered outburst that is adequately refuted by the facts. All this we ought to do so that we may be free to examine only the music. An eminent composer and critic, Virgilio Mortari, has done this in the *Note e documenti* published following the Vivaldi Week of September, 1939, in Siena.

Mortari does not ascribe to his subject a revolutionary attitude in the matter of opera. He even shows some surprise in ascertaining that so imaginative a nature—a preromantic one, to tell the truth—did not deeply affect opera, pre-eminently the domain of restless spirits. He is responsive to the expressive power and the technical solidity of the music, but he goes further. He shows, in discussing *L'Olimpiade*, written for the Sant'Angelo of Venice in 1734 and repeated at Siena in 1939, that Vivaldi was capable of an unusual psychological penetration of characters in the course of the action. He analyzes, among others, the part of Megacle. "At the beginning of the opera, unaware of the tragedy that threatens him, he is completely happy in showing his gratitude to the friend who saved him from death; in the aria *Superbo di me stesso* there is force and a healthy pride. But his tone thereafter darkens, and accents of tragic emotion appear in the accompanied recitative of the second act and the aria that follows, *Se cerca, se dice*, one of the most intense and emotionally stirring moments in the opera." Likewise, the prince Licida is admirably delineated—impulsive and moody, by turns friendly and gentle (the aria *Mentre dormi*) and vehement and tragic (*Gemo in un punto e fremo*). The roles of Clistene, Aminta, Aritea, and Argene are no less well set off. In any Vivaldi opera whatever, even the most hurriedly composed, pages will be found whose beauty, truth of expression, and masterly technique make them worthy to survive.

With greater reason Vivaldi's sacred music is assured of finding a widening audience. Like the concertos and the operas, it was composed throughout his life; like them, it expresses the work of a lifetime. But in this domain the servitude that bore heavily on his dramatic music was absent. He did not have to be preoccupied either with the impresarios, with the recruitment of singers and their various demands and claims, or with magical settings that vied with the music for the audience's attention. His sacred music Vivaldi wrote in his own way and at the call of his own inspiration, for a group that he had at hand and from whom he might demand anything—the instrumentalists and singers at the Pietà.

What is its musical substance? Until the time when the providential holdings of Turin were disclosed, we were completely ignorant of it. It was rightly suspected that the Red Priest's functions involved supplying works designed for the religious offices and solemn ceremonies that were set in the Pietà. In the *Mercure de France* in 1727, mention is made of a *Te Deum* by him that was sung in Venice during the festivities given by the French ambassador on the occasion of the birth of the royal princesses of France. Today it has become possible to pass judgment on these *opere sacre* by what has been edited or recorded from the Foà and Giordano collections.

There is the same variety we have come to expect. A polyphonic talent asserts itself that the tuttis of some concertos and some movements in the sinfonie and concerti ripieni have given us a foretaste of. And then we have all the elements common to both his instrumental and his dramatic music—certain ways of writing, of construction, and of orchestration that are almost his signature. There are symphonic episodes, ritornellos that could just as well belong to a concerto or an opera overture, arias that would be just as appropriate with secular words. In this Vivaldi is like many other composers of his time. Recall the fact that Bach had the Blessed Virgin in the Christmas Oratorio sing a melody with which Pleasure had previously lulled Hercules to sleep. Vivaldi assumes the same liberties or their reverse, borrowing themes for his *La Primavera* concerto from his oratorio *Juditha*. But apart from these likenesses, the similarities of treatment and even of themes and rhythms are numerous and interesting. I am thinking of the opening chorus of *Juditha*, a chorus of warriors prefaced by a forceful fanfare that is built, like the chorus itself, upon the tonic chord. A more instrumental design could not be conceived; yet nothing could be more suitable to express the violence that the text breathes forth: *"Arma, caedes, vindictae, furores, angustiae, timores, precedite nos!* [Weapons, slaughter, vengeance, fury, distress, and terror go before us!]"

Likewise, in the *Gloria* in D for two solo women's voices, chorus, and orchestra, the charming *Domine deus* reflects the same spirit of the siciliano making up the slow movement of Opus 3, No. 11. It will be noticed, by the way, that such a page can stand comparison with the most beautiful arias in the Bach Passions without, for all that, causing us to wonder if one of the composers imitates the other. Very recently, Robert Stevenson

in his book *Music before the Classic Era* (1955) recalls the
admiration of Vivaldi that Bach had borne witness to by transcribing several of his concertos, and continues: "It may be in-
structive to compare the *Gloria* of the *B minor Mass* with Vivaldi's *Gloria Mass*. It will be found that Bach followed Vivaldi
not only in the division of the text, but also in the assignment of
certain sections to solo voices and others to chorus. Vivaldi split
up the *Gloria* into eleven different numbers, Bach into eight."
As a matter of fact, it seems unlikely that Bach was acquainted
with Vivaldi's sacred works, which were composed for use at
the Pietà and which hardly ever emerged from there. The co-
incidences cited are not very conclusive, but the fact that they
can be cited has its interest all the same.

An analysis or even a cursory examination of the forty-odd
sacred works, a volume almost equal to his dramatic output,
would go well beyond the limits of the present book. I shall
content myself with pointing out again the *Beatus vir* (a good
recording of which exists), in which we again meet the heir of
the Gabrieli, who a century before had displayed in San Marco
the splendors of double choruses answering one another from
either side of the nave. Nowhere can the fusion of three styles
that Vivaldi so often succeeded in achieving be better comprehended: the church style of the double choir in *Beatus vir qui
timet dominum;* the operatic style reflected in a duet for basses,
Potens in terra; and the style of the concerto, when, in *Gloria et
divitiae ejus manet*, two sopranos vie in virtuosity with the most
agile instruments of the orchestra—all infused with a religious
feeling that is not Bach's, that has neither quiet intensity nor
austerity, but that does kindle rapture. It is not to be doubted
that the "exaggeratedly devout" practices on Vivaldi's part, the
object of Gerber's jeers, were due to deep feeling. His music
is so thoroughly imbued with this feeling that it still moves the
listener of today.

III

Vivaldi's Music: Influence and Reputation

THE more precise our knowledge of the pre-Classical forms becomes, the greater appears Vivaldi's influence in these realms. This is dazzlingly clear where the concerto is concerned. Investigations as to the symphony are less far advanced, but it seems that they will lead to no less positive results.

Even with respect to the concerto, however, a possible ambiguity must be avoided. In discovering a "Vivaldi trait" distinctly present in such and such a work, it should be understood that what is seen there may be not a direct borrowing from Vivaldi, but just as probably a turn of which Corelli, Torelli, or the Venetians (most frequently Albinoni) may have bethought themselves before him; or it may be one that Vivaldi had merely transferred from vocal to instrumental music, from the opera to the symphony. Simply by having used some devices more constantly and with greater authority and brilliance than his predecessors, he alone made them integral parts of a style. Thus a certain Vivaldi tone prevails in a multitude of works from diverse sources, a tone as marked as the Beethovenian manner, or that of Franck or of Debussy in music nearer to our day. In this sense and to this extent we shall agree with Fausto Torrefranca, and hail Vivaldi as the "inventor [*scopritore*] of a new musical world."

INFLUENCE IN ITALY

It is in Venice that the first consequences of the Red Priest's innovations are to be sought. Perhaps it is there that they are hardest to measure with any precision, because there above all, beginning with the most interesting instance, that of Albinoni, is posed the problem of priority, to which I have just alluded.

The first of Albinoni's publications are earlier than those of Vivaldi. His *Sinfonie e Concerti a cinque*, Opus 2, appeared in 1700, and the themes of their tuttis already show the incisive vigor that is to enliven those of *L'Estro armonico*, just as their virtuoso passage work prefigures its instrumental dispositions and harmonic modulations. But the whole has a more skimpy form and a more cautious tessitura; there is a hardly perceptible differentiation of the tuttis and solos. The *adagios*, in Opus 2 at least, are conceived in the old way, simply as bridges between two fast movements.

Opus 5 (*ca.* 1707) gives more importance to the *adagio*. It is possible that as early as this, several years before their publication, Vivaldi's concertos were being circulated, and that Albinoni, through following their example, may have turned into the imitator of a younger man to whom he had once been a model. He would never match Vivaldi in either breadth or formal freedom and variety, but more than one detail in his last works indicates an effort to attain them—the use of the aria with a motto, of tuttis in unison, and of the superposition of rhythm (the presentation of ternary rhythm within the frame of quaternary time), as we have observed them in many of Vivaldi's works.

The great influence that Vivaldi had over his fellow citizens at the height of his fame after around 1720 can scarcely be doubted. Nevertheless, Albinoni had some difficulty following him in the domain of formal construction; he uses the opposition of tutti and solo, such a fertile area for expressive resources, in a much less adroit way. There was even regression in this regard from his Opus 2 (1700) to his Opus 5 (1707). In the first of these collections relatively well-developed solos are found; whereas in the second they seem to be reabsorbed.

The impress of Vivaldi's style is likewise pronounced in the instrumental compositions of other Venetians—the Marcello brothers, Alberto Gallo, and Giovanni Platti, who transferred these characteristics to keyboard music. Also in the harpsichord works of Baldassare Galuppi, who was a pure, Burano-born

Venetian, themes and developments abound that are inspired by violin writing, particularly Vivaldi's. To limit myself to an easily accessible example, I refer the reader to the beginning of the first two repeated sections in the *Seconda Sonata per Cembalo*, published by Ricordi (No. 537). Not only are we familiar with the theme and its recapitulation, the descending scales, and the arpeggios that follow; but as the themes are spun out, rhythms come in that descend in a direct line from *La Stravaganza*.

Be it said in passing that other harpsichordists outside Venice follow the same path, beginning with Domenico Scarlatti. In his works, samples of the so-called Lombard rhythm and of the unison tutti are to be found, contrasting with highly-wrought solos and sequential developments inspired by the concertos of Vivaldi.

But nearly all the symphonists of that time, in particular those of the Milan school, foremost among them Giovanni Battista Sammartini, are indebted to Vivaldi's concertos for their over-all plans. Many of them, including Sammartini, found useful suggestions in the matter of rhythm and in thematic elements such as those concise motives—the tonic triad, the hammering of octaves, the persistent repetition of a short ornamental formula—on which they built whole movements.

To return to the violinist-composers, there were few indeed among them whose personalities were strong enough to prevent them from being, if not wholly absorbed, at least altered, by so inspiriting a talent. Of this group perhaps Bonporti, that misunderstood composer, preserved his integrity with the most complete success. He made use of the concerto form, but with such originality and with a melodic, harmonic, and expressive style so personal that he scarcely seems to have had an inkling of the art whose home was a short distance from Trent and whose fame radiated so far.

Vivaldi's most famous contemporaries—Geminiani, Veracini, Locatelli, and Tartini—are not all equally in the Red Priest's debt; but all knew and heard him, and at the very least adopted the over-all economy of his concertos.

This was true of Geminiani. He was rather Corellian as a rule, but he framed most of his concerti grossi in three movements, fast–slow–fast; and, beginning with his Opus 2, gave a clear predominance to a solo violin. That he esteemed Vivaldi is known at least by the episode of his meeting with the Irish harpist Turlogh O'Carolan; on the spur of the moment he performed the fifth concerto of *L'Estro armonico* for the harpist, whereupon, to his great surprise, O'Carolan took up his harp and immediately played it over again from beginning to end.

Veracini, as we have seen, met Vivaldi at Venice in 1716. To him he owes more than rhythm and melody. In his *Sonate accademiche* some bird song imitations recall the nightingales of *The Seasons*. But the similarity does not go very far. His concertos published in 1717 (Le Cène No. 448, which contains works by several composers) indicate, from the formal viewpoint, a retreat rather than an advance; the tuttis and solos lose their specific characteristics, which impairs the concerto feeling.

In Locatelli's works, it is the rhythm that shows most clearly the results of his rather long stay in Venice, where he was a guest at patrician homes (see the dedication of his Opus 3 to Girolamo Michiellini). Some syncopated patterns of *La Stravaganza* (finale of No. 2) pass almost unchanged into his Opus 6 (*allegro* of the twelfth sonata). The whole of one tutti in his *Introduttioni teatrali*, Opus 4, refers back to the same source, not only with regard to its thematic elements, but with regard to its over-all structure as well. This is also true for the tutti of the 3/8 finale in the same concerto, and, again among many others, for the tutti that opens the concerto Opus 3, No. 12.

Tartini's concertos, although their distribution of movements is that which Vivaldi had just been asserting, are presided over by a more modern ideal. The earliest of them preserve certain points of similarity with Vivaldi's work in their conception of an opening tutti (a section made up of several motives, one of which may produce the solo theme), and in their conception of a slow movement (a cantilena of beautiful lines supported by a sober accompaniment in long time values). On the other hand, in his descriptive concertos Tartini is far removed from Vivaldi's narrative manner in *The Seasons*. The "program" that he adopts is intended less for the listener than for himself; what he looks for is not an outline, but a stimulant to inspiration and a source of poetic invention.

In the nature of his sonata and concerto themes, Tartini at the beginning of his career often imitated the nervous and nimble design of the typical Vivaldi phrase; later, he was to lean to the rococo, even getting himself reproached by good judges such as J. J. Quantz for an abuse of ornamentation. We are allowed to get a notion of his practices from the *Adagio varié* that J. B. Cartier gives as an appendix to his *Art du violon.*

In the works of less important composers, similarities to Vivaldi's style are everywhere, to the point where one suspects a kind of unconscious aping. I shall cite the following names, which are far from all that could be listed: Carlo Tessarini, who copied even the title of *La Stravaganza;* Giuseppe Valentini; Andrea Zani; and Casale Maggiore, whose sonatas, Opus 1, include purely Vivaldian characteristics side by side with work of a potent originality. These sonatas are dedicated to Princess Theodora, wife of the Landgrave of Hesse-Darmstadt, in whose service at Mantua, according to all probability, Vivaldi was from 1720 to 1723. Now, Zani's sonatas appeared in the same city in 1727, and there is a strong likelihood that the two musicians knew each other in the circle of the prince.

As to Mossi, Bitti, Salvini, Predieri, Rampini, and a few other composers, joint collections published by Roger and Le Cène around 1715–1720 contained some of their concertos side by side with some of Vivaldi's. Better proof cannot be given of the extent to which they submitted to Vivaldi's influence than the fact that it sometimes turns out to be impossible, when these concertos are not assigned by name, to decide if they are by the master or by his imitators.

Giuseppe Matteo Alberti, several of whose concertos appear in such collections, deserves to be considered separately. This Bolognese was a musician markedly superior to those just mentioned. Chronologically he was the first to have written works in Vivaldi's form that have a clear profile of their own despite somewhat unguarded thematic likenesses. And in his first works, from 1713, he employs ways of writing that are not to be met with in Vivaldi's work before Opus 6, ways that could very well have been inspired by him. (We know, however, that Vivaldi's concertos circulated for some years before being published.) Also, in his manner of orchestration and formal construction Alberti early appears inventive. An immediate and complete exploration of his merits cannot be too much desired.

BACH AND VIVALDI

It seemed logical to begin this review of musicians upon whom Vivaldi was able to exercise an influence with Italy. This alone prevented Johann Sebastian Bach from being taken up as by far the most important of them. The problem of the relationship between Bach and Vivaldi—the relationship between certain individual works, for the two men did not know each other—has often been discussed, and violently contradictory arguments advanced. This problem interests so many musicians that I believe I ought to reproduce almost the whole section that I devoted to it in my more detailed book on Vivaldi. Broadly, it is a question of deciding if, as Forkel asserts, familiarity with the Italian masters, Vivaldi foremost among them, made so great an impression on Bach that the subsequent development of his genius was greatly dependent on it; or if—Rühlmann's contention—Bach's encounter with Italy was only an incident too trivial to influence in any way whatsoever a personality of such scope and one that had, moreover, already arrived at maturity.

In 1802, when scarcely anyone was concerning himself with Bach, Johann Nikolaus Forkel, in discussing the composer's early career, wrote the following:

Bach's first attempts at composition, like all early efforts, were unsatisfactory. Lacking any special instruction that would have directed him toward a goal, he was compelled to do what he could in his own way, like others who have set out upon such a career without guidance. The common practice for all beginners is to run riot up and down the keyboard, to play as many notes as the five fingers of each hand can manage, and to continue in this wild course until some point of rest is reached by chance. Such people are merely finger composers (Bach in later years would call them "harpsichord hussars") who write what their fingers tell them to instead of telling their fingers what to play. Bach does not long follow this course. He early sensed that this endless rushing and leaping would lead to nothing. He realized that musical ideas need to be brought into order and logical relationship, and that, to attain this end, one needs a model. Vivaldi's violin concertos, just then being published, gave him the guidance he needed. He so often heard them cited as outstanding compositions that he thereby hit upon the happy idea of transcribing them as a group for the keyboard. Hence he studied the progression of the ideas and their relations, variety in modulating, and many other things. The process of adapting the ideas and phrases that were conceived for the violin and which were not suited to the keyboard taught him to think musically, so that, after completing his work, he no longer had to receive his ideas from his fingers but could draw them from his own imagination [*Über Johann Sebastian Bachs Leben, Kunst, und Kunstwerke*].

Although reservations will be made to these statements later, let us note here that Forkel had gathered their substance from Bach's two eldest sons, Wilhelm Friedemann and Carl Philipp Emanuel, with whom, he precisely sets down, he had "personal bonds of friendship and a regularly maintained correspondence." Let us remark in another connection that Forkel had no special reason to extol Vivaldi, a man long dead who was no longer spoken of; his music had been absent from programs for over a generation and in actual fact the musical texts were lost or considered so. It was the systematic disinterment of Bach's works that, as I remarked at the outset of this book, revived a certain interest in the Venetian; and it was the publication by Peters and then by the Bachgesellschaft of the sixteen harpsichord concertos and of the four organ concertos *"nach Vivaldi"* that led historians to seek out the originals. Their rediscovery is rather a long story; I shall summarize it a little further on.

An opinion opposed to Forkel's was set forth a fairly long time after his work was published. In 1867 Julius Rühlmann wrote for the *Neue Zeitschrift für Musik* a series of articles devoted to Vivaldi and his influence on Bach. Despite a fair number of errors, unavoidable because of the state of our knowledge at the time when he was writing, his study is not devoid of merit. His purpose is all too obvious, however—to minimize Vivaldi's contribution in two ways:

1) by caviling over the real value of the Italian master's concertos. Their *allegros*, based on themes to which he grants clearness and a certain magnitude, are poorly written and bear no trace of thematic working; the *adagios*, which are seldom sing-

ing—so Rühlmann maintains—but which rather are harmonically conceived, correspond to the definition that Quantz gives of slow movements of the old school: "Formerly *adagios* were often composed in a dry and flat style, and harmony more than melody was sought for in them."

2) by putting as late as possible in Bach's career his knowledge of Vivaldi's concertos. They must have been known in Germany only after the return of Pisendel from Italy; and Opus 1—Rühlmann undoubtedly wished to speak of the first collection of concertos, actually Opus 3—must have been published only in 1720. Accordingly, Bach must have written his original concertos, which undoubtedly date from the Cöthen period, before transcribing those of Vivaldi.

And here is what motivated those transcriptions. "Bach, a circumspect artist and a serious teacher, could not dispense with an exact knowledge of compositions that he had many a time heard great things of and that he had no right to be unacquainted with." He owed an extra amount of attention to novices ("*Neulingen*") and to their works. The concertos were published only in separate parts, which must be put into score; to avoid this drudgery, it might be satisfactory to carry over the essential material to a clavier part—the job being all the more easy in that many of the concertos were actually written for three voices with the *basso continuo* permitted to fill in the harmony. It was indeed "a truly artistic and pedagogic way of fathoming the Italian version of *style galant*, and at the same time it constituted very substantial study material for his sons and pupils," while being also a good exercise for the realization of figured bass.

Unfortunately, Rühlmann's chronology is not worth anything. It was not at Cöthen, much less at Leipzig, that Bach knew and transcribed Vivaldi's concertos, but at Weimar between 1708 and 1717 and nearer to the first date than the second. Opus 3, the famous *L'Estro armonico*, had been published around 1712; and we know that in this period publication came and crowned the success of works that had previously circulated in manuscripts, sometimes for years. Arnold Schering has pointed out that among the Bach transcriptions, the second harpsichord concerto and the third organ concerto are both based on Opus 7 and certainly precede its publication in book form; he also observes, following Count Waldersee (see below), that the fourth of Bach's harpsichord concertos transcribes Vivaldi's Opus 4, No. 6, and follows a very different text from that of the printed edition. I shall add to much the same end the instance of Bach's ninth harpsichord concerto. Only the source of the first movement has, to my knowledge, been discovered—namely, the first movement of Opus 4, No. 1. The last two movements have no correspondences with those of the violin concerto in its printed version; but they do agree with another version preserved in manuscript at Upsala (Cap. 617). The opening *allegro* of this is the same as the published one, while its *largo* and *finale* correspond to Bach's transcription.

Here Bach has again made a transcription following a text that could very well have circulated before the printed version.

There are the strongest grounds for believing that the task of transcribing dates from his stay at Weimar. Bach was engaged for the first time there in 1703 in a private orchestra of the young prince Johann Ernst, brother of the reigning duke. He remained only a few months. But he returned in July, 1708, to perform the functions of a chamber musician—as violinist, violist, and harpsichordist—and at the same time those of court organist. This time he remained on the scene long enough to become *Concertmeister* (that is, solo violinist and deputy director) in March, 1714. Perhaps it was resentment at not being named *Capellmeister* (principal director) at the death of his superior, Samuel Drese, that brought about the events leading to his permanently quitting the Weimar court in December, 1717. Until then, especially during the lifetime of Johann Ernst, who died prematurely in 1715 (he was scarcely nineteen years old), Bach was immersed in the most Italianate musical environment possible. The reigning duke with his little orchestra of sixteen players maintained a high consumption of instrumental music, and the young prince, doting on the violin and on composition, and gifted, moreover, as are few professional composers, was sufficiently influenced by Vivaldi to write concertos following his example. And until Schering's comparatively recent work three of these had been attributed to the Red Priest. Bach's friend and rather near relation, the organist J. G. Walther, was at the Weimar court at the same time as Bach; like him, Walther was a man curious about everything produced south of the Alps and a great transcriber for his instrument of violin concertos by Albinoni, Torelli, and Gentili.

It might be useful to recall here the attraction that northern Italy and, in particular, Venice exerted at that time on German artists and the courts to which they belonged. I have already discussed the trips of J. D. Heinichen and G. H. Stölzel. The result, not unexpectedly, was that the Italian models penetrated into Germany. Quantz recounts in his autobiography the deep impression that Vivaldi's concertos made on him in 1714 at Pirna.

Bach, as a violinist, as he was at this point in his career, necessarily came to take an interest in what was new and sensational in the repertory for bowed instruments—the advent of the solo concerto form, carried straightway to so high a stage of completion, if not wholly created, by Vivaldi. What is more plausible than that he should play in the orchestra the best numbers of Opus 3 and of the future Opus 4 and Opus 7, and that, having sampled them, he wished to put himself in a position to perform them alone and to analyze them more easily by transcribing them for the harpsichord or the organ?

Only fairly recently was the list of Bach's Vivaldi transcriptions fixed precisely. They are less numerous than had been thought at first. The large collections published by Peters and the Bachgesellschaft (Bg. denotes the Bachgesellschaft edition) include the following:

Sixteen concertos for harpsichord, after Vivaldi: Peters No. 217, Bg. XLII.

One concerto for four harpsichords and four-part string ensemble, after Vivaldi: Peters No. 260, Bg. XLIII, 1.

Four concertos for organ solo, after Vivaldi: Peters No. 247, Bg. XXXVIII, 2.

These editions were based on certain manuscripts in the Berlin Staatsbibliothek, originally from the Poelchau collection. Here is a list of these manuscript sources:

1) Ms. P. 280, containing the first eleven harpsichord concertos and the first one for organ under the title *XII Concerto* (sic) *di Vivaldi elaborati di J. S. Bach. J. E. Bach Lipsiae 1739* (J. E. signifies Johann Ernst, son of Johann Bernard Bach, organist at Eisenach);

2) P. 804, containing the harpsichord concertos Nos. 1–6 and 12–16;

3) P. 247, the concerto for four harpsichords, copied by Forkel and entitled *Concerto per IV Clavicembali accompagn. da 2 Violini, Braccio e Violoncello, composto da Giov. Seb. Bach;*

4) P. 288, the second organ concerto, with the title *Concerto per Organo ex A moll [composé par Mons. Teleman pour les Violons et transposé par Mons. J. Bach].* The words within brackets have been scratched out; it is in reality a question of a transcription of Vivaldi's Opus 3, No. 6;

5) P. 400[1], the same organ concerto entitled this time *Concerto del Sig^r. Ant. Vivaldi accomodato per l'Organo a 2 clav. e ped. del Sig^re. Giovanni Sebastiano Bach;*

6) P. 400[3], the third organ concerto (same title as P. 400[1]);

7) P. 286, the same work entitled *Concerto a 2 Clavier et Pedal di Johann Sebastian Bach*, and the fourth concerto under the title *Concerto del Illustrissimo Principe Giov. Ernesto Duca di Sassonia, appropriato all'organo a 2 Clavier e Pedal da Giov. Seb. Bach.*

Some of these manuscripts bear names other than Vivaldi's— Telemann and Prince Johann Ernst of Saxe-Weimar. However, the first editors of the above-mentioned collections seem not to have questioned a common origin for the seventeen concertos for one or more harpsichords and the four organ concertos "after Vivaldi" (a total of twenty works, because the fourth organ concerto is a retranscription of the thirteenth for harpsichord). The fact is that the identification came head on against the difficulty of discovering the text on which Bach worked.

These texts came to light again little by little. In 1850, C. L. Hilgenfeldt in his *Johann Sebastian Bachs Leben, Wirken und Werke* established that the four-harpsichord concerto led back to the tenth of *L'Estro armonico*. A little later, Julius Rühlmann traced the second harpsichord concerto to Vivaldi's Opus 7, Book 2, No. 2. Philipp Spitta (1873) and then Count Waldersee in the *Vierteljahrsschrift für Musikwissenschaft* (1885) supplied the sources for the first, fourth, fifth, seventh, and ninth harpsichord concertos, and the second and third organ concertos.

Pursuing a thorough inquiry, using both stylistic analysis and bibliographical cross-checking, Arnold Schering at last reached conclusions that may be considered definitive, at least insofar as Vivaldi is concerned. To him belong only the originals of nine concertos duly assigned by the four above-mentioned historians. The other pieces in the Peters and Bachgesellschaft collections are by other German and Italian composers, some of whom remain to be identified. Here, summarized, are the conclusions of Schering's studies, "Zur Bach-Forschung," in the *Sammelbände der internationalen Musikgesellschaft* (1902–04).

Harpsichord Concertos (Bg. XLII, under the title *16 Konzerte nach A. Vivaldi*):

No. 1 in D   Original: Vivaldi, Opus 3, No. 9

No. 2 in G   Original: Vivaldi, Opus 7, Book 2, No. 2

No. 3 in d   Original: Benedetto Marcello (for oboe). Here Schering's attribution occasioned extended discussion. S. A. Luciani ("Un Concerto di Vivaldi attribuito a Marcello" in *La Scuolo Veneziana*, Siena, 1941) tried to re-establish Vivaldi's claim, without furnishing formal proof. S. A. Luciani again, in the course of an exchange of views with Dr. Pietro Berri (in the Milan review *Musica*, July–September, 1949), put forth the hypothesis that this concerto was not by Benedetto but by Alessandro Marcello, a hypothesis taken up and confirmed by the English musicologist Frank Walker. (On this subject see one last report by Dr. Berri, "Posta in arrivo" in *Musica e Dischi*, Milan, August, 1953).

No. 4 in g   Original: Vivaldi, Opus 4, No. 6

No. 5 in C   Original: Vivaldi, Opus 3, No. 12 (original in E)

No. 6 in C   Original: an Italian composer, perhaps Benedetto Marcello

No. 7 in F   Original: Vivaldi, Opus 3, No. 3 (original in G)

No. 8 in b   Original: a German composer?

No. 9 in G   Original: Vivaldi, Opus 4, Book 1, No. 1 (original in B-flat)

No. 10 in c   Original: an Italian composer. Gregori, Torelli?

No. 11 in B-flat   Original: Prince Johann Ernst of Saxe-Weimar

No. 12 in g   Original: a German composer?

No. 13 in C   Original: Prince Johann Ernst of Saxe-Weimar

No. 14 in g   Original: Telemann

No. 15 in G   Original: a German composer. Telemann?

No. 16 in d   Original: Prince Johann Ernst of Saxe-Weimar

Concerto for four harpsichords and strings (Bg. XLIII) in *a*. Original: Vivaldi, Opus 3, No. 10 (original in *b*).

Concertos for organ solo (Bg. XXXVIII, 2):

No. 1 in G   Original: a German composer. Telemann?

No. 2 in *a*　　Original: Vivaldi, Opus 3, No. 8 (Waldersee erro-
　　　　　　　　neously indicates No. 6)
No. 3 in C　　Original: Vivaldi, Opus 7, Book 2, No. 5 (original
　　　　　　　　in *D*)
No. 4 in C　　Original: Prince Johann Ernst (transcription of
　　　　　　　　the thirteenth harpsichord concerto)

That is, nine concertos transcribed are certainly from Vivaldi.
Among the attributions that remain in doubt, one at least might
possibly be re-awarded to Vivaldi—No. 10, for which Schering
names Torelli or Gregori as conjectural sources. This is the unqualified opinion of a recent transcriber, W. Kolischer, who published a new piano version (1934) of the Bach transcription
under Vivaldi's name, although its original is no more known
to him than to Schering. The main reason he gives is the similarity
between the theme of the second movement, *vivace*, and that of
the fugue of Opus 3, No. 11.

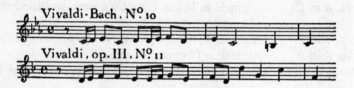

If one has before one's eyes no other document than W.
Kolischer's "*libera trascrizione*" (how very free!), any evidence
other than this fleeting thematic likeness will scarcely be seen.
His work is actually a total misconception aesthetically, a height-
ening of the procedures of Stradal, whom we will meet a little
further on. In Bach's work, the original string writing, the
monodic writing, and the polyphony where each voice has its
complete melodic meaning are easily identifiable. In Kolischer's
transcription, however, the most innocent garland of sixteenth
notes is transmuted into a patchwork of bulky chords with each
sixteenth note supported by a column of four or five tones, the
bass steadily doubled. All polyphony is dissipated in this confusion. A single example: in Bach's transcription the first move-

ment begins with one voice alone and exposed; in the second measure the second voice enters at the third below; in the third measure the bass enters along with a fourth, filling voice. In Kolischer, from the outset there is a heavy and extremely low bass sounded in octaves, while in the right hand chords of three tones appear throughout.

But when we consider only the older transcription—that of Bach—the similarities to Vivaldi again become perceivable. Nothing denies the fact that the theme of the initial *allegro* and the development of its modulation (measures 20 to 34) are from the suggested original. As for the second movement, the significance of the fugal motive cited above needs no further comment; and later some progressions recall very closely the obbligato cello of Opus 3, No. 11. The andante alternates between tuttis of marked chords and melodic solos whose chromaticism is familiar to us as is the harmonic framework. The finale evokes, among others, that of Opus 3, No. 9.

The reasons for which Arnold Schering ruled out the attribution of this concerto to Vivaldi were two: first, the original has not been found; second, Vivaldi, beginning with Opus 4, no longer wrote any concertos that were not in three movements (this one is in four), and he banned the fugal style. If the first reason has lost none of its weight, the other has been conspicuously weakened since the discovery of the Turin manuscripts, which abound in movements written in the fugal style and concertos with the most varied constructions. And, moreover, what prevents this concerto No. 10 from having been composed at the same time as *L'Estro armonico?* It is seen that doubt remains permissible, with rather strong presumption in favor of Vivaldi.

If the conclusions of Schering be accepted for the twenty-one above-mentioned concertos, it is in any case necessary to add to his list a tenth concerto by Vivaldi-Bach that neither the Bachgesellschaft nor the great Peters edition had taken into consideration and that has been identified only recently.

In 1844 F. K. Griepenkerl published an organ concerto by Wilhelm Friedemann Bach that came from Forkel's estate. A piano version of that work by A. Golde appeared in 1865. In

1897 (reprinted in 1906) a piano version by August Stradal was published to which was added a descriptive summary: the concerto was the drama of a storm within a soul "undermined by grief, tortured by a passionate desire," which accounts for, if it does not justify, the excess of cadenzas, the dishevelled passage work, and the thundering bass lines to which this arrangement owes its many years of vogue. And this is not to speak of the "variants of variants" conceived by Emil Sauer nor of the reversed order of movements, the fugue being moved forward to follow the *largo*. The dauntless arranger describes the latter movement as "mournful and very free." The hyperromanticism of this transcription is manifest even in the frontispiece, where we see a tree uprooted by the storm, with a gloomy cathedral in the background menaced by lightning and encircled by a flight of ravens.

Four years later, in 1910, the Munich musicologist Ludwig Schittler noticed that this piece was in fact a paraphrase—and not a free one—of Vivaldi's concerto, Opus 3, No. 11; and Max Schneider, in the *Bach-Jahrbuch* of 1911, by a study of the manuscript in the Forkel estate which the Berlin library had meanwhile acquired, restored the credit of the first transcription to Johann Sebastian Bach. It is indeed an autograph of the Leipzig Cantor, on the first page of which Wilhelm Friedemann has written in a wavering hand, "*di W. F. Bach . . . manu mei Patris descriptum* [of W. F. Bach . . . written down by the hand of my father]." On this basis the son was charged with having wanted to appropriate his father's workmanship, as apparently it occurred to him to do on other occasions. It is, however, as natural to suppose that "*di*" had in his eyes only a possessive sense, and that he meant, with complete honesty, "belonging to W. F. Bach."

This inventory being set straight, what is the true scope of Bach's transcriptions, in what spirit were they conceived, and what is their worth in comparison with the originals? It might be convenient to adopt J. W. von Wasielewski's views without discussion—that by the side of its transcription by Bach, an original by Vivaldi is only a "dried skeleton." It is presumed, as he puts it in his *Die Violine und ihre Meister* (1893), that "like magic, a border of poor grass was transformed into a cheerful bed of flowers."

But a less frankly chauvinistic answer demands, in the first place, a precise comparison of the texts. This has been done with care, although on a limited basis, by Rühlmann, and much more fully by Count Waldersee, who worked on all of the series except the pseudo-concerto of W. F. Bach. I shall not reprint his long and minute collating, to which the reader may easily refer. It is enough for us to see in what degree it supports Rühlmann's conclusions, or, on the contrary, denies them.

According to Rühlmann, it is obvious that Bach owes scarcely anything to Vivaldi. He may have drawn inspiration from the tripartite form of the concertos, nothing more. Besides, Rühlmann states, his transcriptions are later than the original works that he composed in the same form (this is an error as we now know). Examining the transcriptions of merely the two works that he had recovered, Opus 7, Book 2, No. 2, and Opus 3, No. 10, Rühlmann considers them clearly very superior to their models.

As to the first, he acknowledges that Bach observes a certain restraint in the *allegros*. The right hand faithfully reproduces the first violin part, aside from the filling in of the tutti and some added ornaments in the solo, in conformity with the tradition. The left hand realizes the bass without changing its harmonic meaning, in the same way that an experienced accompanist, whether or not assisted by figures, would do it.

It is in the slow movement that the superiority of the transcriber appears. The writing of the original, which is in two parts only—the melody of the solo violin accompanied by all the strings in unison (the violins written in the F-clef)—appears incomprehensible to Rühlmann. "Such harmonic poverty," he wrote, "is scarcely tolerable"; and he wondered if, despite the *tacet* expressly indicated for the harpsichord, it ought not to be assumed that the harpsichordist at that point improvised *ad libitum*. And one may call to witness the counterpoint interpolated by Bach between Vivaldi's two voices:

It is certain that Vivaldi's text would have been inadmissible
if it had been transcribed for the harpsichord in its original form
as just a melody and a bass; the latter would have been reduced
to a simple pizzicato. But the sober, almost stark bass line is ac-
ceptable when played in unison by bowed instruments. We have
seen such layouts above, and we know the reasons why they were
written—to give the soloist all possible independence, and to bring
about a double contrast, first between the opulence of the ornamented melody and the austerity of the bass, and, second between the brilliant sound of the *allegros* played by the full orchestra, and the meditation of the slow movement that is framed
by them. This is a place which echoes the opera.

Today we can no longer look for an explanation of such bare
writing in Vivaldi's supposed inability to think polyphonically.
His first collection of concertos, Opus 3, includes rather fine
specimens of contrapuntal writing. In the fugue of its eleventh
concerto, Bach altered nothing; he merely omitted the figuring
for the bass, useful to the harpsichordist of an orchestra who is

charged with consolidating an ensemble, but superfluous in a reduction for organ alone. The soundness of this fugue has long since been observed. Ten years after the death of its composer, at the time when his reputation had started to ebb, the English theorist Charles Avison harshly criticized Vivaldi's compositions as "being equally defective in various harmony and true invention" (*An Essay on Musical Expression*, 1753). Dr. William Hayes, professor of music at Oxford, answered with a vigorous and pointed reply. After conceding that Vivaldi is sometimes as light and mannered as Tessarini, Alberti, and Locatelli, he states his decision to set him well above them.

An essential difference must still be allowed between the former [Vivaldi] and the latter [Tessarini, etc.]; inasmuch as an original is certainly preferable to a servile, mean copy. That Vivaldi runs into this error, I take to be owing to his having a great command of his instrument, being of a volatile disposition (having too much mercury in his constitution), and to misapplication of good parts and abilities. And this I am more inclined to believe, as in the eleventh of his first twelve concertos he has given us a specimen of his capacity in solid composition. For the generalities, in the others he piques himself upon a certain brilliance of fancy and execution, in which he excelled all who went before him, and in which even Geminiani has not thought him unworthy to be imitated [Hayes' footnote: *Vide* the first of his second set of concertos]. But in the above concerto is a fugue, the principal subjects of which are well invented, well maintained, the whole properly diversified with masterly contrivances, and the harmony full and complete [*Remarks on Mr. Avison's Essay on Musical Expression*, 1753].

Hayes could have added that the finale is also, here and there, contrapuntal in a lively and ingenious way. (Its opening, an often imitated passage that became a sort of commonplace, may have been borrowed from the overture to Badia's *Ercole vincitore di Gerione* of 1708.) And if he had wished to extend the comparison to the slow movement, which is in the rhythmic pattern of a siciliano, nothing would have prevented him from noting that Vivaldi had achieved a sonorous balance that no arrangement could ever surpass.

To return to Vivaldi as a contrapuntist—the greatest severity with regard to him is shown on this subject, but it must be admitted that he has nearly always been underestimated. The Dresden and Turin manuscripts, which I have cited so many times, show that he made extensive and frequent use of the imitative style. He did not blaze out with the constant mastery of a Bach, and it can be confidently maintained that he did not aspire to. He wrote with an obvious care to please a certain public, to save time, and to satisfy his taste for theatrical effects even in purely symphonic forms—none of these being preoccupations that encourage a scrupulous polishing. Moreover, he used two kinds of counterpoint. Most of the time, with his pen outrunning his thoughts, he dashed off the beginnings of wonderful canons and fugues, which have dynamic intensity and yield rich sonorities but which are not free of certain impurities that fiery performances probably concealed. After a little while, usually at the end of a tutti, these stray impulses of learning vanish, to be succeeded by homophonic writing. But he was capable of much fuller texture and of a more elaborate and lofty style; the fugue of Opus 3, No. 11, and the choral fugue *Cum sancto spiritu* in the *Gloria* testify to the solidity of a culture he could have displayed had he the desire and the leisure.

In the light of these statements, less credence will be given to Rühlmann and to those who follow at his heels. The most conspicuous of these followers, because of the attention to minutiae with which he conducted his comparisons, is Count Waldersee. Through his detailed analyses he establishes that Bach sometimes gives us explicitly the manner of performance that Vivaldi indicated schematically; he demonstrates that some added inner parts follow from the original figuring. He shows how Bach abandoned certain repetitions, adorned some bass parts, restored others in passages where Vivaldi had silenced them, adapted the specifically violinistic passage work to the style of the harpsichord, and seasoned some too abridged harmonies with dissonances. When he rises to an over-all opinion, he states, with an obvious concern for fairness, "Vivaldi writes his parts in a very melodious style, his harmonic progressions are simple and clear but occasionally stiff and bare, and it may be questioned whether he reaches the highest forms of art—the highest forms of charming thematic work, yes, but not of development. No great wealth of musical ideas and an abundance of rosalias show that the well whereat he drinks is not deep. However, with regard to the rosalias it is fitting to remember the period in which he wrote."

In the writing of most Bach exegetes, more or less exact echoes of these opinions are found. However, with the restoration to their original versions of a number of Vivaldi's concertos, and with the recent possibility of hearing them at concerts, on records, and over the radio, this orientation is beginning to change a little. When André Pirro wrote his masterpiece, *L'esthétique de Jean-Sébastien Bach*, published in 1907, he did not have at his disposal the exact chronological details with which he might have defined precisely Vivaldi's influence. But at least he brought out the intrinsic worth of his contribution. Before being acquainted with Vivaldi's work, Bach could have found models for the tutti-solo alternation, the principle that generates the concerto form, in Italian opera arias; but after knowing Vivaldi's work, he could "admire in this music without words a freer development of the purely musical idea, a richness not confined by a text, and an enemy to vague lyricism. This speech has logic as well, and it gratifies the mind. Less rich in nuances than is the language modulated according to motives determined by a vocal line, this language has a kind of life of its own. Without evoking exact images when considered separately, the themes, nevertheless, by their continuation, their movement, their repetition, and their progression, in short, by their fertility, arouse notions of grandeur and unwearying energy. Recognizable in these Latin works are the eloquent garrulity, the skill in saying nothing, the inexhaustible loquacity, the plenitude, the *copia* of the ancient orators and rhetoricians. Everything sparkles and swirls about, in a magnificent display of sonority." "A magnificent display of sonority"; here perhaps is the principal discovery—and also the point on which Bach is inferior compared to his predecessor; for only blindly fetishistic admiration would assert that the transcriber's slight alterations had been unerringly felicitous in this respect. The assignment to the harpsichord of slow movements conceived for the violin (even when Bach transcribes his own works, for that matter) surprises and occasionally shocks us as a kind of profanation. I have mentioned above the siciliano of the concerto in *d,* which has so vocal a line; Bach's transfer of the violin solo, note for note, to the harpsichord can only be considered to be a makeshift, so much are the *legato* bowing and what it permits in the way of undulating sonority a part of such a melody. Much the same thing has been said of more than one passage in the four-harpsichord concerto. Hans Engel, in his *Das Instrumentalkonzert* (1932), terms as *"etwas monströse"* the substitution of the harpsichords for the violins not only in melodic phrases, but also at some points where Vivaldi uses the violins in an unusual way—such as in the *larghetto,* where each of them employs a different form of arpeggio. While having a marvelous knowledge of instrumental timbres, an extraordinary competence in proportioning them, and an inquisitiveness always on the watch in matters concerning them, it does seem that Bach was not moved sensuously by their arrangement as the Italians could be. In an introduction to the Eulenburg score of Opus 3, No. 10, which he edited,* Alfred Einstein also, with a vigor hardly curbed by the scruple not to breach the dogma of Bach's infallibility, indicates that the correct worth of Vivaldi's concertos appears when a performance of one of them is juxtaposed to one of its transcription. The impression of the Italian prototype remains striking; "This is due to the magnificent sonority of the strings, for which the work was originally conceived. It is one of the most important stages on the road of discovery leading to a new world of sound, in which the exalted art of the old classics reaches its height and the intoxication of which may even today be experienced. If this were comprehended, 'rosalias' and 'paltry figurations' would not be spoken of, and the way in which the primitive or naïve character is essential to this music would be discerned." Unquestionably the transcriber enriches his model, even from the standpoint of pure sonority, when he enlivens with new contrapuntal parts what had been left in outlined form. Still, it may be regretted sometimes that—in Hans Engel's words—"this complexity alters the clear and simple style of Vivaldi."

These remarks are not aimed at disputing the general superior-

* Einstein also edited the following Vivaldi concertos published as miniature scores: Opus 3, Nos. 6, 8, and 11; Opus 6, No. 1; Opus 10, No. 3 (F. XII, 9; *Il Cardellino*), Leipzig, Eulenburg, 1927–1932.

ity of Bach's transcriptions over the originals of Vivaldi. We wish only to confirm what we have said in the preceding chapter of this book—namely, that the concertos that excited Bach's interest were not the stammerings of a beginner (the "*Neuling*" of Rühlmann), to which the labor of the adapter alone gave life, but true works of art, works that at least in one sense brought more to the transcriber than they received from him.

Let us reread Forkel. His statements, reduced to their essentials, could be summarized as follows: to Vivaldi Bach owes a plan, a form according to which he could organize his thoughts; he learned the art of instrumental composition from him. Some commentators, even when not over familiar with the music of the Venetian, and when moved by a certain malice towards him, recognize this educational worth. These writers include Sir Hubert Parry, who wrote as follows in his article "Arrangement" in *Grove's Dictionary of Music* (1904 edition):

Vivaldi's concertos are excellent in form, but his ideas are frequently crude and unsatisfactory, and their treatment is often thin and weak. Bach's object being to have good illustrations of beauty of form rather than of substance, he did not hesitate to alter the details of figures, rhythms and melodies, and even successions of keys, to amplify cadences, and add inner parts, till the whole is transformed into a Bach-commentary on the form-principles of the Italians, rather than an arrangement in the ordinary meaning of the term.

A more attentive reading of the concertos in question might make the historian aware of what exaggerations lie in such an interpretation. Actually the arranger does not deviate so much from his subject; some transcriptions are almost literal, whole movements being reproduced without any thematic modification. With few exceptions, the transcriber's interventions are limited to upholstering a somewhat thin web of sound, enriching the ornamentation, and, more rarely, giving a little relish to the harmonies. The plan is not changed, and the essential nature of the music is not altered. Indeed, Bach found a formal model there. One is convinced of this in examining what he wrote for instruments prior to the years 1710–12. Neither the *Capriccio* on the departure of his beloved brother, nor the first chorale fantasias give presage of the logical and sturdy structures that multiply themselves after

Weimar. From the very beginning of Bach's work, music spurts out as from a spring, and the contrapuntal language is of incomparable distinction; but the proportions remain curt and arbitrary. Albert Schweitzer has pointed it out in better words than Forkel while materially upholding the same position. "At Weimar," he writes, "the sonatas and the concertos of the Italians revealed to him what the Buxtehudes and Böhms had not been able to teach, because they were ignorant of it themselves—musical architecture. This discovery enraptured him, and he straightway applied himself to studying Vivaldi, Albinoni, Legrenzi, and Corelli. In the *Canzona* (*Orgelwerke*, Peters edition, Vol. 4, No. 10) and in the *Allabreve* in D (*Ibid.*, Vol. 8, p. 72) he gives himself up completely to the charm of the Italian creations. In this way he proves to have made a large step forward instantaneously. Leaving the German masters far, far behind, he attained perfection in one bound" (*J.-S. Bach, le musicien-poete*, 1905).

The direct result of this initiation was, first of all, the creation of the harpsichord or organ concerto without accompaniment, in which the property of registration allows the basic tutti-solo opposition to be retained. J. G. Walther at Weimar, and the blind organist De Grave in Holland were undoubtedly undertaking such reductions at very nearly the same time. But it was Bach's mastery that established the genre, and it was he who some years later, in 1735—this time freed of all direct imitation—produced the perfect model of it in the Italian Concerto.

It goes without saying that the original concertos for one or more harpsichords and orchestra, or for one or two violins and orchestra (they were written for the most part at Cöthen) are likewise of Vivaldian stock, although the distribution of the tuttis and solos may be more subtle and the writing more compact. If one examines, for instance, the harpsichord concerto in *d* (Bg. XVII), the only one that pianists have currently embraced, one will find innumerable Vivaldi touches. The tuttis of the first and second movements are Bach-like in their thematic elements, but the unison writing and the orchestral color stem from the Italian model. Matters more directly inspired by him are the extended passage work in octaves, which is only slightly contrapuntal when at all so, and which modulates with a nonchalant ease, as well as other passages copied from the *bariolages* of the violin—all make evidences of the work's lineal descent. The Brandenburg Concertos Nos. 2, 4, and 5 are cut from the same pattern; Nos. 1, 3, and 6, which are allied in their outward shape to the Corelli concerto grosso, nevertheless show more than a trace of Vivaldi's influence.

In the violin concertos, not only certain themes (for example, that of the concerto in *E*) but the developmental procedures as well sometimes hark back to the Italian prototype. In the concerto in *a*, the rather dry formula of sequential repetition without appreciable alteration recalls certain of Vivaldi's moments of empty chattering. Let us hasten to add that Bach does not for long allow himself the facile rhetoric to which Vivaldi was doomed by the chronic speed with which he wrote. Yet we may perceive Vivaldi close at hand in the unison tutti of the *allegros*. As to the slow movements, they are cantilenas in the Italian manner, with scarcely any counterpoint and with ornamentation that Bach has taken the trouble to write out exactly but that is conceived in an exuberant style decked out with improvised *abbellimenti*.

Vivaldi's imprint appears outside the concertos, in other instrumental works and in the purely instrumental portions of the cantatas. André Pirro remarked that Bach had recourse—one might say instinctively—to Italian themes when he did not intend to depict or evoke definite feelings, "when he wants to write only for the sake of music, to free himself from his emotions, and to live only by the intellect." He gives a description of a good many similarities, for instance, between the opening motive of the two-violin concerto in *d* and the beginning of one of Vivaldi's sonatas preserved at Dresden. This resemblance had already been mentioned by Schering; and a good many more have been turned up by Pirro, Alfredo Casella, and others in vocal music as well as in such instrumental works as the suites for violin alone and the inventions.

From all this we may without rashness conclude that the transcription of Vivaldi concertos constituted for Bach something other than an occasional pastime or a teaching stint in the sense that Rühlmann meant—that is, study material designed to teach others what an Italian concerto was or how to realize a thorough-bass. Rather it is necessary to admit that at Weimar, at the dawn of his career, at the time when he would be most receptive to external impressions and influences, he had the good fortune to live for several years in contact with musical forms that were new to him. He was able to read, perform, and direct instrumental works not only by Vivaldi, but by his imitators, Telemann and the prince Johann Ernst of Saxe-Weimar. Like the French whom he had known at Celle, these Italian or Italianate composers contributed characteristic rhythms and melodic conformations. Above all, they revealed to him—to come back to the opinion of Schweitzer and Forkel—a method of formal construction that he was to turn to very great account. That he progressed far beyond them in both refinement and power is not to be doubted. Yet he does not remain less their debtor on that score, and he owes Vivaldi more than any of the rest.

INFLUENCE IN GERMANY, FRANCE, AND OTHER LANDS

Among music historians there is a firmly rooted custom of never discussing J. S. Bach without immediately bringing into the picture the no less commanding figure of George Frideric Handel. Therefore, let us see, more briefly, to what extent Handel may have been affected by the art of Vivaldi. As apt as anyone could be in turning everything to advantage, he did not make several sojourns in Venice without getting certain benefits. It is established that he strove to assimilate the taste that then prevailed there. What is more, with *Agrippina* (1709), he succeeded in composing a heroic-comic opera almost as Venetian as those of his local models, Pollaroli and Legrenzi. In the matter of instrumental music Vivaldi represented a more modern current, and he must have had a more direct effect on Handel's sensibilities than did his old master Legrenzi. Corelli unquestionably eclipses both of them at this juncture; the form of the Handel concerto and that of the sonatas and trio sonatas come straight from him.

In his youth, however, shortly after his stay in Venice on the occasion of the presentation of *Agrippina*, Handel for a time interested himself in the Vivaldi solo concerto. In an unfinished concerto, which Chrysander dates around 1715, he grants the first violin absolute pre-eminence throughout the opening movement; the soloist pours forth rapid figurations, diatonic runs, and arpeggios, accompanied by an orchestra that is systematically unobtrusive, although over and above the four-part string ensemble it includes two horns, two oboes, and a bassoon.

The sonata *a cinque* that Hans David published not long ago (1935) and that dates from around 1710 is, despite its title, an authentic violin concerto with the accompaniment of the orchestral quartet of strings. Effects borrowed from opera, after the manner of Vivaldi—unisons, tremolos in sixteenth notes, and such—characterize the tuttis. The themes and the breadth of the solos very quickly give away their derivation. Later, after he decides on the concerto of Corellian design, Handel more than once hit upon Vivaldi's melodic spirit and his rhythm.

But it cannot be a question of comparing Vivaldi's influence on the composer of *The Messiah* with that exerted on J. S. Bach. To Bach, Vivaldi brought a new conception of form, and inspired a series of transcriptions that in turn generated wholly original works modeled on the scheme of the Italian concerto. For Handel the encounter was only one episode among many, for he was accustomed to scrounge freely. An unrepentant plagiarist if held to the letter of the law (actually he borrowed openly with the license of his century, and he transformed what he touched), he took less from Vivaldi than from Stradella, Clari, or Muffat. We may only be certain that Handel could discover in Vivaldi, beyond characteristic rhythms and themes, a precedent for logical and solid form, for clear writing, and for orchestral exploitation of a new sense of sonority.

As much may be said of most of the German composers in his generation and the succeeding one. The historiographer of the German concerto grosso, Walther Krüger, has very well said that everything within this form that came from beyond the Rhine hails from Corelli or from Vivaldi or occasionally from both at once. Such a follower of Corelli as Telemann nevertheless welcomed the innovations that Vivaldi brought into the structure as well as the substance of the concerto; so it was also with Christoph Graupner and J. M. Molter.

More purely Vivaldian are G. H. Stölzel, J. F. Fasch, J. D. Heinichen, J. J. Quantz, the Graun brothers, and the whole Czech school, from which we may single out four composers—Jan Dismas Zelenka; Franz Benda, who founded the Berlin violin school; Joseph Mysliveček, who is known chiefly because of his connection with Mozart, but who merits recognition on his own account; and finally Frantisek Miča, who cannot be fairly passed over since the recent appearance of Vladimir Helfert's studies. This writer deems Miča the precursor and, in the matter of formal construction, the probable inventor of the bithematic sonata *allegro*—before C. P. E. Bach, before the Viennese preclassical composers M. G. Monn and J. K. Wagenseil, even before Giovanni Platti, so determinedly brought forward for this honor by Fausto Torrefranca. *Capellmeister* and first *valet de chambre* of the Counts Questenberg and their purveyor of music for the dramatic shows that they staged at their chateau of Jaromeřice, Miča had employed that new form in his opera and oratorio overtures as early as 1730.

Here what interests us most is the nature of his themes. Vladimir Helfert declares them to have been inspired chiefly by those of Monn, Wagenseil, and the Italians who wrote for Vienna, Caldara foremost among them. Is it not more natural, in anything that relates to the sinfonie, to refer the origin back to the character of Vivaldi's themes? After all, he had already transferred to instrumental music various elements—themes, rhythms, orchestral colors—appropriated from operas by such composers as Caldara, Pollaroli, and Ziani. This seems all the more plausible since Vivaldi maintained close ties with the Austrian capital; he went there at the time of his fame, the Emperor was on friendly terms with him, and he returned there to die. The incipits of some of Miča's themes will be enough to convince us that Vivaldi may have had an influence on him.

Allegro (Sinfonia, 1729)

Presto (Sinfonia, 1730)

Allegro (1735)

Miča's orchestration, rich in Vivaldian effects—unison passages, elimination of the cellos, and the like—corroborates the impression of a kinship in methods; so does his customary musical expansion, which consists not of deducing from the principal themes germs of secondary themes, but of inserting simple decorative motives, repeated sequentially, between the principal themes.

Johann Georg Pisendel (1687–1755) brings us back to the German musicians investigated by Walther Krüger. The cordiality of his relations with Vivaldi are known to us; it is confirmed again by the series of works Vivaldi dedicated to the Saxon violinist—a sinfonia, four sonatas, and six concertos. Their manuscripts, which are lodged in Dresden, carry the words "*Fatto per il Sigr. Pisendel*" as the whole autograph endorsement.

At the time of the composers' first acquaintance in Venice in 1717, the pupil was ready to make the best possible use of the instruction that he was going to get. He had previously profited

from Torelli's teaching at Ansbach; he had had access to the
great Bach at Weimar; he had heard the Frenchman Volumier,
and he had taken some lessons at Rome with Montanari. He absorbed the new style perfectly enough to ornament his teacher's
adagios in a way that leaves the reader unable to determine the
precise extent of the collaboration. In his own concertos it is
Vivaldi's manner that he adopts, filling it out, however, with a
more studied counterpoint. Like J. S. Bach, due allowance being
made, he achieves an excellent synthesis of the German and
Italian tastes.

In that which relates to J. J. Quantz (1697–1773), we do not
have to seek very far for evidence of his adherence to the Vivaldi
aesthetic. He supplies it himself, first, in the passage in his autobiography, quoted above, where he relates the deep impression
made on him at Pirna in 1714 by the first concertos that he heard
there, probably from *L'Estro armonico;* second, in the chapters
in his *Versuch* where he furnishes a theory of the concerto that
is most accurately that of the concerto as conceived by Vivaldi.
His 320 or so concertos for flute are precise illustrations of this
conception. The first *allegro* nearly always includes five tuttis
framing four solos; the tuttis and solos are in opposition to each
other as in *L'Estro armonico,* the tuttis containing the essential
part of the melodic and rhythmic substance, the solos, decorative
on the whole, aiming above all at enhancing the virtuosity of the
performer. The spirit of the finale differs only in its resolve to
leave the audience with an even more light and gay impression.
The middle movement, on the contrary, seeks to be moving. His
texture corroborates his remarks made during a trip to Italy in
1724, when he avowed his firm resolution to leave to one side "the
aridity and barrenness of studied contrapuntal refinement" in
order to sing forth as freely as possible.

J. A. Hasse has been called "the Italian composer of the most
popular operas in the Germany of the south." Romain Rolland has
him belonging to the Neapolitan school, Fausto Torrefranca to the
Venetian, at least as regards instrumental music. The truth is perhaps less simple, but certainly his ties with Venice are numerous.
He sojourned there for a long time; at least ten operas and two
oratorios by him were given there between 1730 and 1758. His

wife, Faustina Bordoni, was born there of a patrician family, and was credited with having been a Vivaldi pupil. His choice of musicians in the orchestra he led indicates clearly where his sympathies lay; at the Dresden opera in 1734 his solo violinist was Pisendel, his first flutist, J. J. Quantz.

More than these historical particulars, an examination of the scores will reliably bear this out. An Italianate quality, often a purely Venetian quality, appears in certain descriptive overtures, in the structure of his concertos, and in the famous Hasse syncopations. From the same source may come a number of themes (even for French overtures) among those that Karl Mennicke has brought together in his book (1906), the standard work on Hasse and the Graun brothers.

It is known that C. H. Graun lived for several months in Venice in the course of the years 1740–41, and that he wrote there at the very least his descriptive concerto for the harpsichord *La Battaglia del Re di Prussia*. He has likewise left some descriptive concertos. Several themes of his *Catone in Utica* (1744) are typically Vivaldian, as are many tuttis in concertos by his brother, Johann Gottlieb. Although the latter, a pupil of Tartini, adopts a more modern method of composing and already employs the systematic opposition of two contrasting themes, he remains faithful to the Venetian thematic character, more sinewy and less encumbered with ornaments than that of his teacher. The two influences co-exist in almost all his instrumental music, without prejudice to purely German influences.

When traces of Vivaldi's style—traces by no means negligible —that are found in the works of a good many Vienna and Mannheim composers (Wagenseil, Christian Cannabich, Eichner, M. G. Monn, and others) are considered, one recognizes the vogue of the Red Priest to have been, when all is said and done, more lasting in the Germanic countries than in Italy. In 1767 at the court of Braunschweig, *Il Siroe*, a pastiche in which arias from his operas were incorporated, was still being performed. In 1792 Gerber stated in his *Lexicon* that for more than thirty years Vivaldi had set the fashion for concerto composers, especially in Berlin. Right up to Joseph Haydn, certain characteristics of concertos preserve a little of his tone; for example, the finale of the concerto in C *"fatto per il Luigi Tommasini."* And Schering perceives it in a concerto for four violins by Louis Maurer, performed at the Leipzig Gewandhaus in 1844.

Gerber's remark may be extended to the German Swiss. The Collegium Musicum of Basel opened its first meeting in 1755 with a Vivaldi symphony. The same year an anonymous traveler was present at a concert in a large Swiss town, believed to be Basel. He left behind an account of that event that is delicious in its naïveté (Karl Nef has quoted it in his book [1897] on the Collegia Musica). He is enraptured by imitations of the nightingale and the cuckoo; he recognizes the sound of the hurdygurdy and the accents of the *Ranz des vaches*. He asks the friend who brought him whose music this could be, "because nothing so pretty was ever heard before." To this his guide answers, "It is *La Primavera* by Vivaldi [Herr Wivaldi]."

In Holland the circulation of the publications of Roger, Le Cène, and Witvogel could not help but have an influence on the national composers. It is Willem de Fesch who testifies most eloquently to this. Moreover, Vivaldi confirms this connection by directing the performance of a sinfonia by Fesch at the festivities in Amsterdam in 1739.

It may be stated that in France between 1715 and 1750 there was not only a craze, but nearly a cult, as regards Vivaldi. At the beginning of the century Corelli had been the great man for the Italophiles of Paris. Less than twenty-five years later *L'Estro armonico* eclipsed the too sober splendors of Corelli's famous *"Cinquième Opéra."* The change may have been given impetus by Lyon, the natural stopping place en route to the capital for maestri from beyond the Alps. As early as 1713–18 the Lyon Académie des Beaux-Arts inscribed the concertos of Vivaldi in its repertory. Chancellor d'Aguesseau knew them when, at about the same time, he drew up the fourth of his Instructions, which he intended for his son. High society took an interest in their creator. From Venice the abbé Conti informed his correspondent Madame de Caylus on the composer's actions and conduct. From Venice once again word is sent to the *Mercure de France* (October, 1727) of the performance of his *Te Deum* as sung in the previous month to celebrate the birth of the royal princesses of France. It has been seen how—this the crowning favor—Louis XV in 1730 mobilized an amateur extemporaneous orchestra around Guignon in order to give *La Primavera* a hearing.

The following year La Pouplinière, who represented the most wide-awake portion of the public, attested to a similar predilection. Recounting his arrival in Calais at the home of one Monsieur Parthon, he wrote, "We were received there like the gods in the operas, with a symphony for many instruments. It was by Vivaldi; I thank heaven for it."

An "air italien de Vivaldi" was sung at one of the Lille concerts, on December 17, 1733. Opus 3 likewise appears listed in 1739 in the library of the Lille orchestra. Many were the collections—Parisian and provincial, public and private—that owned either that work or Opus 8 (definitely the two opuses most esteemed in France), or some symphonies or arias.

The poets contributed their praise, sometimes in doggerel. For instance, Serré de Rieux wrote in 1734 as follows:

> *Vivaldi, Marini, par de brillans ouvrages*
> *De nos sçavans en foule obtiennent les suffrages.*

[By their brilliant works, Vivaldi and Marini get the approval of the multitude of our connoisseurs.]

The historians, the memorialists, and the aestheticians, even those who resist any bias in favor of Italian music, had to take into account the "*brillans ouvrages*" in question. Here are the words of Titon du Tillet: "I shall confess . . . that our music pleases and moves me more than Italian music, which I also regard highly and which during a year that I spent in Italy I heard with pleasure performed by the most skillful musicians, such as Vivaldi and Somis for the violin . . ." (*Suite du parnasse françois jusqu'en 1743*). D'Aquin in his *Siècle littéraire de Louis XV* (1753) says that only *The Seasons* is worthy of sustaining a comparison with the music of Corelli. Dom Caffiaux in his manuscript *Histoire de la musique* places Opus 3 and Opus 8 beyond compare. He does not hesitate to put Vivaldi on the same plane with Handel, Hasse, and Telemann. "Be Vivaldi, Locatelli, Handel,

Hasse, and Tellemann Italians, Germans, Englishmen, Turks, or
Chinese, since they have good things, we are justified in profiting
from them." It is probably Caffiaux who, in the *Mémoires de
Trévoux* (1746), an anonymous answer to Boullioud de Mermet's
essay *De la corruption du goust dans la musique françoise* (1746),
reprints this list accompanied by a more detailed commentary.
Boullioud de Mermet had objected to French composers who
imitated the Italians, among whom only Corelli seemed to him a
possible guide. The anonymous author retorts, "The author ex-
cepts Corelli. Thirty years ago perhaps he was not excepted.
Corelli was then completely Italian because we were completely
French. Is this not because he is himself to this extent Italian?
And were not Valentini and Scarlatti and Buononcini of the same
time? And as to Vivaldi, Locatelli, Hendel, Hess, and Tellemann,
and many other foreigners who have the freedom of the city in
Paris, they may indeed smack of the soil of Italy, of Germany, or
of England for those who find them too difficult to play, read, lis-
ten to, or appreciate."

In concerts, where it was the custom for virtuosos to perform
only a few compositions not their own, the rare departures from
this practice that are recorded are almost all to Vivaldi's profit.
This has already been seen with regard to *The Seasons;* but other
concertos also benefit from this privileged treatment. On May 15,
1749, Pagin, although devoting himself above all to the fame of
his teacher Tartini, presented the *Tempête di Mare* (sic) *del
Signor Vivaldi* at the Concert Spirituel; on August 15th the
younger Taillart played one of his flute concertos.

The publishers exploited the success of *La Primavera* by offering it in all sorts of forms. But they did not offer only transcriptions to their customers. They also reprinted or imported a
good many works in their original texts. The Vienna Nationalbibliothek owns an edition of Opus 1, sonatas for two violins and
bass, put out by the younger Le Clerc under the Privilège Gén-
éral of 1714. Later, in Le Clerc's catalogue are Opus 8, Opus 13
(*Il Pastor fido*) and, of course, Opus 3, the famous *L'Estro
armonico*, which he spells *Les Troharnonico*.

After that, if we look for music composed in France at the
time when Vivaldi's influence was prevalent, we are bound to

expect to come across him fairly often—less often than in Germany and with a less profound likeness because, setting aside the taste for description in music, French art was at that time in the act of orienting itself away from Italy. Before Jean Marie Leclair's vigorous personality asserted itself, the clavecin took precedence over the violin among the French. The style imposed by François Couperin denied the larger impulses of Italian eloquence. The nature of the themes was more spare and pallid, the ornamentation more definite, being seldom if ever confided to the whim of the performer, and clarity was more esteemed than pathos. In general it was an autonomous instrumental style, hardly touched by the recent developments in opera.

Some French composers, nevertheless, came under the spell of the Italian style, filled as it was with youthful energy, among them, obviously, the transplanted Italians, such as Guignon and the elder Canavas. The concertos of Guignon are in three movements. The first concerto has an opening *allegro* built on a single theme entrusted to a tutti, while virtuoso passage work falls to the soloist; the second has an initial bithematic *allegro* whose subordinate theme is set forth by the soloist. Both these schemes come from Vivaldi, as does the handling of the main instrument. Guignon interpreted Vivaldi's music, particularly *The Seasons*, frequently enough for the vocabulary and the syntax to come of themselves to his mind and from his pen. Opus 1 and Opus 2 of the elder Canavas, both entitled *Sonates pour le Violoncelle avec la B. C.* present several characteristic movements: in Opus 1 the *andante* of the first sonata and the *allegro* of the third; in Opus 2 the opening movement of the first and the siciliano of the fourth.

Among purely French composers, several of whom travelled in Italy and took lessons from Italian teachers, François Francoeur is the earliest whom we should note. The first of his works to appear, *Sonates à violon seul et basse* (1720) has themes modeled on Vivaldi's, and some sequential developments of a decorative nature fashioned in his way.

So it was also with the works of J. M. Leclair, well before the appearance of the concertos in which he openly employed the Vivaldian outline and at the same time enlarged it. In his first book of sonatas (1723), typical figuration can already be found.

The slow movements are often of a fairly marked Italian character, although this is never maintained throughout the whole of a
piece. Rhythms from *La Stravaganza*, which also influenced Locatelli (the sonata, Opus 6, No. 12), appear in Leclair's first concerto. In his opera *Scylla et Glaucus*, which is in a purely national
tradition, the orchestration in more than one spot seems to draw
profitably upon Vivaldi's experiments. This is especially true of
the writing for the orchestral quartet of strings, which is
vigorous and rich, without excessive display of instrumental
virtuosity. Finally, certain descriptive passages would not be what
they are were it not for the precedent of *The Seasons;* the storm
in the prologue brings in passage work that is similar to that of
the concertos *L'Estate* and *L' Inverno.*

The younger Quentin uses themes founded in the tonic triad
and the diatonic scale, in the Italian manner. Boismortier, with his
concertos of 1727 for five transverse flutes or other instruments
without bass, was the first to introduce the three-movement concerto form into France. The nature of his themes is very French,
but here and there some motives have the square phraseology of
the Italian prototypes.

What others had accomplished in a more or less casual way,
Jacques Aubert carried out deliberately. In the preface or
Avertissement of his *Première Suite de Concerts de Symphonies*
(1730), he expresses his firm resolve to reconcile the concerto
style of "Corelli, Vivaldi, and some others with the charm, the
clarity, and the beautiful simplicity of the French taste." His
work comes up to this stated purpose quite well. As regards
Italian qualities, he did not go beyond the aesthetic of the concerto grosso of Corelli in this work. On the other hand, his first
book of concertos, Opus 17 (1734–35), marks the progress of the
Vivaldian tendency, both in the thematic elements and in the
predominance of the first solo violin, which monopolizes the
virtuoso passage work, of an admittedly not very demanding
character, and again in certain orchestral effects such as the tutti
of the second concerto where a unison is maintained for sixteen
measures.

Many other French composers—Mondonville, Balbastre, Guille-
main, the younger Cupis, and others—show an unquestionable

acquaintance with the works of the Prete Rosso, but in too fleeting a way for it to be at all worth dwelling on. However, as late as 1753 a promising beginner, Gossec, was guided by him. A comparison of particular passages from the trios, Opus 1 (1753) and from the symphonies, Opus 5 and Opus 12, with some portions of Vivaldi's Opus 4 and Opus 8 brings out a kinship not only of constructive method and melodic inspiration, but of taste in the matter of ornamentation (see in particular those light *gruppetti*, the *Vögelchen* of Mannheim, that Vivaldi lavishes on his concertos of *The Seasons*).

We might close this list on an illustrious name, that of Pierre Gaviniès, the last of the great French interpreters of *La Primavera*. In his Opus 4 (1764) he constructs tuttis on Vivaldi-like motives, and makes use of the Lombard rhythm. The finale of No. 6, with its pastoral theme, its leaping over strings, its tremolos with higher sparkling notes, would not disfigure *The Seasons*. In his extreme old age, writing *Les vingt-quatre matinées*, Gaviniès attests his loyalty to formulas that he goes back to, if the truth be told, in order to carry them to the highest degree of virtuosity—*bariolages*, extensions, arpeggios. Above all, he signs these keepsakes by his fondness for the Lombard rhythm, which had become obsolete, but which he still strews about in profusion.

This didactic influence of Vivaldi is not an isolated example in French eighteenth century pedagogy. Witness Michel Corrette, who cites him in his *Méthode de violoncelle* of 1741, and forty years later, in 1782, in *L'art de se perfectionner dans le violon*.

Vivaldi's popularity in England was evident in the eagerness with which the London publishers reprinted, with permission or without, the Amsterdam editions, or drew up new collections. Walsh alone published Opus 2, 3, and 4, as well as the collections *Harmonia Mundi*, *Select Harmony*, and *Two Celebrated Concertos*.

The *Cuckoo Concerto*, of which no edition other than the English is known, was played so often that connoisseurs joked about it; it ended by being relegated to the repertory of provincial concerts. Geminiani's playing of a Vivaldi concerto before the harpist O'Carolan may be recalled. Yet this *Cuckoo* piece must have somewhat annoyed him, because in writing his *Art of Playing on the Violin* (London, 1751) he warns the reader that he will not find there a way to imitate "the cock, cuckoo, owl and other birds. . . . Such tricks rather belong to the professors of legerdemain . . . than to the art of music."

The penetration of Vivaldi's music had started much earlier. Walsh's publications began three years after the Dutch editions of *L'Estro armonico* (1712). In April, 1720, Dubourg (Monsieur Duburge) is described by the journal *The Post Boy* as having played a concerto from *La Stravaganza*. In 1723 a young violinist chose for his London debut in the Haymarket Theater a Vivaldi concerto, on which the advertising laid stress. The announcements were worded, according to Burney, as follows: "[Concert given] by particular desire of several ladies of quality, for the benefit of John Clegg, a youth of nine years of age, lately arrived from Ireland, with several solos and concertos by the youth, particularly a concerto of Vivaldi." And in 1773 Vivaldi was still being sung at Covent Garden Theater in a potpourri concocted by Kane O'Hara from arias by Italian, English, and French composers.

This rather wide diffusion of his music, which lasted for a fairly long time, did not have the repercussions on the national composers that might be expected. During the period that preceded the coming of the great classics, all those musicians who were revolving around Handel adhered, as he did, to the old-style concerto grosso of Corelli-like form and inspiration. A one-time student of Corelli, Geminiani, strengthened that influence during his long stay in the British Isles. Yet here and there reminders of Vivaldi crop up in pieces by John Stanley, John Alcock, and more clearly in the work of a musician of some scope, Michael Christian Festing, who though not a brilliant performer was a sound and occasionally inspired composer. In the seventh concerto of his Opus 3 of 1734 (which is, as a whole, a collection of concerti grossi), aside from the first measure, that being an almost literal quotation from the beginning of Albinoni's concerto Opus 2, No. 2, the whole tutti reflects the spirit of the sixth concerto of *L'Estro armonico;* the second measure is transposed note for note; and other instances occur later on that result from a deep permeation rather than from a premeditated intention to plagiarize.

In contrast to this, in the concertos brought back from Italy by the idiosyncratic William Corbett there are not found the Vivaldi imitations that the title of his collection, published in London in 1728 on his return from the peninsula, leads one to hope. I reprint the whole of the title because of its oddness: *Le Bizzarie universali a quattro cio Due Violini, Viola e Basso continuo Concerto's in four Parts for two Violins, Tenor e Thrôbase for ye Harpsichord. Humilissimo Dedicato a Sua Maestà Christianissima and Composed by William Corbett Delitante* [*sic*] *on all the new Gusto's in his Travels thro Italy Opera VIII. N. B. These Concertos may be play'd in 3 parts, 2 Hautboys, Flutes, or German Flutes.*

The dozen concertos that make up this work are entitled, respectively, No. 1 *alla Germana*, No. 2 *alla Turinese*, No. 3 *alla Parmegiana*, No. 4 *alla Olandese*, No. 5 *alla Cremonese*, No. 6 *alla Venetiane*, No. 7 *alla Todesca*, No. 8 *alla Modonese*, No. 9 *alla Pollonese*, No. 10 *alla Spagniola*, No. 11 *alla Paduana*, and No. 12 *alla Francese*.

The promises of these titles are unfortunately deceiving. The style of the nation or city is scarcely evident, with the exception of the German style (*alla Todesca*), which is symbolized by a rather indeterminate counterpoint, and also the French, which is represented by a little pseudo-Lully overture with inflections of a fair likeness. The concerto in the Venetian manner recalls neither Marcello or Albinoni; no more are we reminded of Vivaldi, who may sooner be perceived in the so-called *alla Parmegiana* and *alla Cremonese*.

Finally, we shall note that in Spain in 1726 Juan Francisco de Corominas, "first violin of the great University of Salamanca," in a lampoon entitled *Aposento anti-critico* . . . , extols Vivaldi as "a performer of good taste praised by all, whose *Extravagancias* speak well of the high degree of competence to which he has risen in this kind of composition."

ECLIPSE AND RE-EMERGENCE

Vivaldi's fame and the influence that he exerted on so many musicians, composers, and virtuosos of different schools and ages, were followed without transition, as it were, by silence concerning a name that had excited all musical Europe—an extraordinary reversal that it is indeed obligatory to record. It was in Italy that Vivaldi was most quickly forgotten. For him the curtain fell there as soon as his active career had ended. His death passed unnoticed; the announcement of it is only to be found much later and in foreign publications. For nearly a century no further mention is made of him, not even in Arteaga's *Rivoluzioni del teatro musicale* (1785, second edition), which, nevertheless, lists such minor composers as Lanzetti and Chabrun although the Prete Rosso with his forty-odd operas had a far better claim to his interest. Vivaldi is not referred to in Perotti's serious work (1812), nor in that of Pietro Canal (1847), nor in even the most copious biographical compilations until the middle of the nineteenth century. Only one monograph on music in Italy, which in other respects is of no great standing, does accord him two pages; it is the *Essai sur l'histoire de la musique en Italie* by a Russian author, Count G. V. Orlov, which was published in Paris in 1822.

There proves to be more justice in Germany, where no lacuna, as it were, occurs between the already quoted texts from Quantz, J. A. Hiller, and Gerber, which take us from 1750 to the very end of the century, and the works of Forkel, then of Hilgenfeldt and others, who were put on the trail of *L'Estro armonico* and the Dresden manuscripts by their Bach researches.

In England, before oblivion overtakes the composer of the *Cuckoo Concerto,* so lately a favorite, some at least take the trouble to attack him. In 1753 Charles Avison, a theorist and at the same time the composer of some rather poor music, states that the time has come to treat as they deserve the composers who get lost in "the most unnatural modulations." After having ruled out those who, according to him, do not even merit the honor of mere mention, he undertakes to classify the rest. He then ranks

Vivaldi, Tessarini, Alberti, and Locatelli in the first and lowest category. Their works lack at one and the same time harmonic variety and genuine invention; they are, at best, good for "the amusement of children." Hawkins is scarely less severe. After him and Burney, who is favorable but very summary, the silence was not broken for a long time except by William Bingley, who shamelessly plagiarized Hawkins in his *Musical Biography* (1834, second edition).

We have seen how the active vogue for Vivaldi in France maintained itself up to the time of Corrette and Gaviniès. This constancy dies out at the close of the century. It is astonishing that the magnificent collection brought together by J. B. Cartier in his *Art du violon* (1798) contained only one sonata *largo* by Vivaldi in contrast to six examples of Corelli, five of Tartini, and as many of Leclair. In 1801 Michel Woldemar, in his *Méthode de violon*, which he had the temerity to present as a translation of Leopold Mozart's, gets along with a double-edged encomium of Vivaldi, without quoting a line of his music, though he is prodigal with examples drawn from composers unworthy to be put in the limelight. "Corelli," he writes, "is regarded in Italy as the founder of the art of the violin. Nevertheless, he does have a rival named Vivaldi or the Red Priest, whose light style contrasted with Corelli's beautiful playing." But Vivaldi's name does not even appear in *La Méthode de violon* established for the Paris Conservatory by Baillot, Rode, and Kreutzer (1803), or in Baillot's *Art du violon*, either.

French historians and lexicographers were less forgetful than the pedagogues. I have already cited, from the period 1750 to 1780, Jacques Lacombe, C. H. Blainville, J. B. de Laborde, and some others. Ginguené's article, "Concerto," for the *Encyclopédie* (1791) expatiates at some length on Vivaldi—in so biased and vague a way, it must be added, that it may be suspected that Ginguené limited himself to plagiarizing from Hawkins; thus may be explained that black-and-white charge of Vivaldi's seeking out less "melody and harmony than brilliant, difficult, and occasionally bizarre passage work," and, with regard to *La Stravaganza*, of his appearing to be "more taken up with the cares of astounding the ear than with those of enchanting it." It is this paragraph that Fétis, without indicating the source, copied word for word in his *Revue Musicale*.

In 1810 François Fayolle's interesting *Notices sur Corelli, Tartini, Gaviniès, Pugnani et Viotti* was published as a precursor to an "unpublished work entitled *L'histoire du violon,* in which the biography of each famous violinist is accompanied by his portrait." The comprehensive work announced in this fashion unfortunately never did come out. But it is known that a chapter was to have been devoted to the Prete Rosso, because the portrait engraved for this purpose is extant; it is the one by the younger Lambert (after de La Cave's engraving), which had been drawn separately, and has the format and the exact style of those pictures that illustrate the *Notices*.

For nearly a century, in France and elsewhere, the biographers would have hardly any other source than an article in the *Dictionnaire historique des musiciens* (1811) of Choron and Fayolle, inspired chiefly by Gerber. This is all until the time when contact was again made with Vivaldi's works—first with *L'Estro armonico* and a few manuscripts, then with all the published collections and the manuscripts at Dresden, and finally and very recently, with the huge contribution of the Turin holdings.

Putting these riches back into circulation did not lead right away to a radical alteration of old opinions. Quite a long while after the stage of the first discoveries had been passed—discoveries fragmentary enough for their finders to have good reason for not comprehending their precise significance—writers continued to formulate appraisals that had become traditional, and in which an almost complete ignorance of the works is betrayed.

The name of Vivaldi had taken on importance, and it was thought necessary to speak of him. Since the republications up to 1920 were rather sparse and the original texts dispersed and hard to come by, those who did not rely on their dusty predecessors and made risky judgments from these specimens were no more than soothsayers.

This may be verified, surprisingly, in England, where the old instrumental music enjoys such favor, where so many excellent historians study it, and where the public and private libraries abound in it. However, in the substantial *Oxford History of*

Music, Sir Hubert Parry—in 1902, it is true—returned to the Corelli-Vivaldi comparison worked out in terms that remind us of the disputatious pamphlets of another century. "The contrast," he wrote, "is notable in this respect between his work [Corelli's] and that of some of his contemporaries, such as Vivaldi, whose works, though more lively and brilliant, have failed to maintain any hold upon the world, because they are musically so much more empty and devoid of deeper qualities of expression and interest of texture."

Whom are we to believe? A virtuoso and musicographer of German extraction, Florizel von Reuter, set forth opinions that are not only different but diametrically opposed. Having allowed a real inventive capacity to his subject, he continues, "His creations suffer from an excess of pedantic strictness. In each piece we are conscious of the intellectual and the teacher. . . . A wonderfully correct counterpoint and noble themes overflowing with rhythm, an austere and elevated lyricism—such are the elements of this music; but what cements them together is pedantry carried to an extreme." And yet Spitta claimed that Vivaldi's themes were nearly always poor and his form excellent.

In France until quite recently no less astounding views were advanced. But the fact is that they no longer in any way correspond to the present state of opinion. Quite abruptly, in about forty years, the Red Priest has again emerged after an eclipse of a hundred years.

First of all, the better-informed historians and those who more readily grasped the musical contents of the texts that they deciphered were all agog over his work. Arnold Schering was foremost among these; writing in 1905 in his *Geschichte des Instrumentalkonzerts*, he centered the whole first part on Vivaldi. Despite the dearth of biographical documents and the fact that he did not yet have the Turin manuscripts at his disposal, he really grasped the essential points about the composer's role in the creation of the solo concerto and in the enlargement of the concerto grosso. As for the symphony, it did not come within the frame of Schering's book, and the reader of the foregoing pages will be able to verify that on this score the added contributions of the Foà and Giordano collections were needed to call into question the priority of the Milan or Mannheim composers.

Since Schering many researchers have investigated the path that he laid out. What matters even more than this fervor on the part of the scholars—to persons who feel that one of the essential jobs of musicology is a duty to contribute to the flowering of music—is the restoration of a large repertory that came from it.

Here the modern transcribers come in. When the discovery of the concertos by Bach adapted from Vivaldi led to the tracking down of the string originals, a few pianists continued indeed to adapt some of them for the piano; but good sense demanded that they be instead returned to the instruments for which they were conceived. That is what Moffat and Nachez did in publications that did not always exhibit scholarly accuracy, but which never went against the spirit of the works; then, much more faithful to that spirit came Borrel, Bouvet, Dandelot, Einstein, Gentili, Landshoff, and others. Perhaps the most beautiful realizations are those of Claude Crussard (they are unpublished, and some have been made public only in records), which arrive at that equilibrium, so difficult to achieve, midway between bare, literal harmonization and anachronism resulting from excessive freedom. At the present time Ricordi is in the process of putting out under the direction of G. F. Malipiero the complete edition of the Turin manuscripts, and perhaps the complete works. Recordings follow publication; sometimes they are linked with it, and sometimes actually precede the printed book. And I shall take care not to forget the impressive series of Vivaldi publications made possible by the munificence of Count Chigi of Siena and the untiring industry of Miss Olga Rudge, secretary of the Accademia Chigiana.

Thanks to this trend, which every day increases, the public, both at concerts and over the radio, has been able to hear music of an unsuspected accent, of a direct and vehement style (interpreters do not always bethink themselves of this) with themes that launch out at one bound; though they swerve, sometimes going astray in more conventional roulades and in passage work whose interest has lost its keenness, we put up with these shallow moments when we know what usage—what servitude—they mirror. And then inspiration flashes out again; it is not unusual for indifferent rosalias to give way to an unforeseen modulation and for a sudden impetus to seize us again and carry us away.

Before summing up, by way of conclusion, the characteristics of Vivaldi's work, which this whole book has tried to unravel and to analyze, there remains one last, essential characteristic to be pointed out, which cold research cannot account for—the *life*, the staying power of a spirit which during two centuries and more has not grown barren, of an inspiration still capable of affecting mind and heart despite the fact that when this music two centuries old is performed, it confronts us with secrets whose meaning has been last forever.

In concerts devoted to works from past centuries the listener often can have no other attitude than the kind of historical admiration which is the next thing to a yawn. Some ideas, however ingenious, weary us through their routine unfolding. Some counterpoint is too noble, and some Alberti basses are too trivial; they unite to cause that gloomy state of resignation which inhibits any outburst of applause.

Nothing like this is true for Vivaldi. With Bach and Handel, Domenico Scarlatti, François Couperin, and a few others in his generation (the list of whom would not be long), he escapes from this chilly if respectful response. Let the tutti of one of his concertos sound forth and all torpor vanishes in a flash. We no longer ask ourselves whether or not it is a question of "old music." Music is there, a thing that outlives its creator, that preserves its vitality and its efficacy, that does not have to excuse itself on account of the date of its origin.

Several times recently a suggestive experiment has been revived by juxtaposing on the same program a Vivaldi concerto and its transcription by Bach. The result has not been that which the comments of Rühlmann, Spitta, and Waldersee would lead us to expect. The difference in temperaments shines forth, strengthened by the irreducibly opposed natures of the solo instruments. One does not feel that the Venetian is inferior to his transcriber; the brilliance of his orchestral writing amply compensates for his lack of refinement in this or that contrapuntal line.

This is a question of a clearly circumscribed realm—that of the concerto. Far be it from me to think of likening Vivaldi with J. S. Bach generally; but to be able to stand comparison with him even for a moment is quite a handsome claim to glory. He has another claim in that he opened to Bach a field of activity in which the latter in his turn became renowned.

And it goes without saying that Vivaldi's influence was exerted well beyond the few examples enumerated above. Aside from the precise influences that the texts bring out, there are others just as plain, which go further than thematic and rhythmic similarities; they are matters of over-all structure, or of spirit, or of both at once. One is aware of this in encompassing the whole of his work in a synthetic view. Whether or not the nature of his compositions was prepared for by such predecessors as Legrenzi, Torelli, Corelli, and Albinoni, whether or not it originated in the music of the theater, it still set in motion a double revolution in instrumental art. In regard to form, it established a scheme that prefigures that of the sonata and the Classical symphony; in regard to substance, it marked the coming of a modern lyricism, it was the harbinger of romanticism.

It is of course true that the new lyric tendency was in the air, in Venice more than anywhere else. In the first half of the eighteenth century all art produced in this city was disposed to it. Mario Tinti, in studying the paintings of Guardi, observes in them the completely new intrusion of an individual element, an emotion, a sensibility, which confers on them an autobiographical value. He notes a second characteristic that could refer just as well to Vivaldi—an obvious pre-eminence granted to hasty and nervous outlines in what is a spacious and decorative painting of large dimensions and vast architectural counterpoints.

Promotion of individual feelings and rapidity of execution—these are to be found at every turn in the works of Vivaldi. In this he cuts the figure of the pre-romantic, as his favorite procedures bear out. He writes tuttis of great passion; he instigates conflict between the soloist and the orchestra drawn up in aggressive unison. His slow movements have pages of contemplative rapture, but now and then contain brusque outbursts, almost dramatic apostrophes, which are comparable to the most violent operatic recitatives. His instrumental coloring, dazzling in the *allegros,* is willingly attenuated in the *largos,* sometimes being veiled with mutes or deprived of the rumblings of the bass, and sometimes being reduced to the confidings of a scarcely accompanied melody. None of these characteristics belong to him alone; but no one else in his time brought them together in a form in which the clarity of each is so highly developed. And only a success such as that which welcomed his output could have spread it outside his own country with enough persuasive power to engender a "style."

In the development of forms he played a similarly decisive role by carrying throughout Europe the tripartite model of the Italian overture which, through the enlargement of the slow movement, he had brought to its ultimate equilibrium. By virtue of this, Eitner sees in him the actual creator of the Classical sonata, derived not from the suite, but from the concerto.

Fausto Torrefranca ascribes to him the same role in the development of the symphony. "It is commonly said that the symphony takes its origin from the concerto grosso. If it is really necessary to construct an evolution, we ought to say that the concerto grosso gave rise to the new concerto without fugal parts and with free thematic developments, the Vivaldi concerto, which Leclair took for his model, which J. S. Bach transcribed for harpsichord, which Quantz heard with such deep emotion. From the Vivaldi concerto came the fresh blossoming of the harpsichord sonata, semidramatic and semifugal, exemplified by the Venetian school; from it spread the preference for the new style, which revitalized the dramatic sinfonia. The symphony of Sammartini and of Stamitz afterwards takes on the new animation that music had acquired, and starts to broaden its meaning."

The concerti ripieni and the sinfonie of Turin, which were not known at the time when Fausto Torrefranca wrote these words, make this parentage even more plausible. Because of this, Sammartini loses a large part of the importance that had been attributed to him as a link in the historical growth of the genre. And when, very close to us, contemporary composers, bored with their own subtleties, turn back to the eighteenth century in order to find "pure" forms, when Igor Stravinsky seeks to establish the possibly chimerical model of the concerto or the sonata "in itself," who then is their exemplar, outside of J. S. Bach, if not the old Venetian master?

He was a model to Bach. He popularized and, we may hazard, virtually invented, not only a form, of which *L'Estro armonico* furnished the first masterpieces, but a whole new instrumental style. He was the precursor of the symphony and—it may now be presumed—the composer of dramatic and sacred music impressive by its quality no less than by its quantity. Due to all these accomplishments Vivaldi continued, even at the time when his name had been most completely forgotten, to contribute mightily to the progress of technique.

But above all we must be grateful that he was, in the most immediate way, a creator, a poet. When I long ago undertook my study of Vivaldi, I told my plans to André Pirro, who was the most musical of musicologists in spite of the apparent chilliness that went with limitless erudition. He replied by spiritedly encouraging me, and his letter closed with a panegyric to a master "in whom some perceive only facile talent when it is his lyrical power that ought to be extolled."

Assuredly so. That power is such that, with an indulgence seldom granted to bygone composers, there is no type of listener who is not stirred by it. What vitality this revived musician possesses, and how quickly he has regained his place in the sun, so unlike those composers fit for archives and museums. (For the latter—I borrow the phrase of Dr. Pietro Berri, one of the best Vivaldi scholars in Italy—"exhumation will be more to the glory of him who exhumes them than to their own.") And it is not the least paradoxical of Vivaldi's strange fortunes that this potent survival occurs when everything in the musical development of today conspires to alienate us from that form of art which he so superbly, so completely, embodies.

IV

Bibliography

The following is a list of the most important relevant eighteenth-century sources, and of some of the more available specialized studies. A nearly complete bibliography up to its date of publication will be found in Marc Pincherle, *Antonio Vivaldi et la musique instrumentale*, Paris, 1948 (Vol. 1, pp. 302–310). Also in this work (Vol. 2, pp. 70–74) will be found a musical bibliography of the scattered modern publications and transcriptions, up to 1939, of Vivaldi's works.

Altmann, Wilhelm. "Thematischer Katalog der gedruckten Werke Antonio Vivaldis," in *Archiv für Musikwissenschaft*, 4:262–279 (1922).

Antonio Vivaldi, note e documenti sulla vita e sulle opere (ed. S. A. Luciano). Siena, 1939.

Berri, Pietro. *Indice discografico vivaldiano*, Milan, 1953.

Burney, Charles. *A General History of Music* (second edition). London, 1789 (new edition [Frank Mercer], 1935).

Engel, Hans. *Das Instrumentalkonzert*, Leipzig, 1932.

Gentili, Alberto, "La raccolta Mauro Foà," in *Rievista Musicale Italiana*, 34:356–368 (1927).

Kolneder, Walter. "Die Klarinette als Concertino-Instrument bei Vivaldi," in *Die Musikforschung*, 4:185–191 (1951).

———. "Vivaldi als Bearbeiter eigener Werke," in *Acta Musicologica*, 24:45–52 (1952).

———. "Il concerto per due trombe di Antonio Vivaldi," *Rievista Musicale Italiana*, 55:54–63 (1953).

———. "Zur Frage der Vivaldi-Katalogue," in *Archiv für Musikwissenschaft*, 11:323–331 (1954).

———. "Noch einmal: Vivaldi und die Klarinette," in *Die Musikforschung*, 8:209–211 (1955).

———. *Afführungspraxis bei Vivaldi*. Leipzig, 1956.

267

Lebermann, Walter. "Zur Besetzungsfrage der Concerti Grossi von Vivaldi," in *Die Musikforschung*, 7:337–339 (1954).

Mattheson, Johann. *Das neu-eröffnete Orchestre*, Hamburg, 1713.

——. *Der vollkommene Capellmeister*, Hamburg, 1739 (facsimile edition, 1954).

Marcello, Benedetto. *Il teatro alla moda*, Venice, 1720. New edition (Andrea Tessier), 1887; English translation (R. G. Pauly) in *Musical Quarterly*, 34:371–403 (1948), and 35:85–105 (1949).

Newman, William. "The Sonatas of Albinoni and Vivaldi," in *Journal of the American Musicological Society*, 5:99–113 (1952).

Preussner, Eberhard. *Die musikalischen Reisen des Herrn von Uffenbach*, Kassel, 1949.

Quantz, Johann Joachim. *Versuch einer Anweisung die Flöte traversière zu spielen*, Berlin, 1752. New edition (Arnold Schering), 1906.

Rinaldi, Mario. *Antonio Vivaldi*, Milan, 1943.

——. *Catalogo numerico tematico delle composizioni di Antonio Vivaldi*, Rome, 1945.

Rudge, Olga, ed. *Lettere e dediche di Antonio Vivaldi*, Siena, 1942.

Schering, Arnold. *Geschichte des Instrumentalkonzerts* (second edition), Leipzig, 1927.

Terenzio, Vincenzo. "Temi vivaldiani," in *La Rassegna Musicale*, 23:30–37 (1953).

Torrefranca, Fausto. "Problemi vivaldiani," in *Internationale Gesellschaft für Musikwissenschaft, Kongressbericht* (Fourth Congress), Basel, 1949, 195–202.

Index

---

[1] See page 29*n* for explanation of F. numbers.
[2] See page 29*n* for explanation of P. or Pincherle numbers.

THE NORTON LIBRARY

Lunt, Dudley C. *The Road to the Law.* N183

Mackenzie, Henry. *The Man of Feeling.* Introduction by Kenneth C. Slagle. N14

Mackinder, Halford J. *Democratic Ideals and Reality.* New intro. by Anthony J. Pearce. N184

Moore, George. *Esther Waters.* Intro. by Malcolm Brown. N6

Morey, C. R. *Christian Art.* With 49 illustrations. N103

Morrison, Hugh. *Louis Sullivan:* Prophet of Modern Architecture. Illustrated. N116

Ortega y Gasset, José. *History as a System.* Tr. from Spanish by Mildred Adams. N122

Ortega y Gasset José. *Man and Crisis.* Tr. from Spanish by Mildred Adams. N121

Piaget, Jean. *Play, Dreams and Imitation in Childhood.* Tr. by C. Gattegno and F. M. Hodgson. N171

Pincherle, Marc. *Vivaldi: Genius of the Baroque.* Tr. by Christopher Hatch. N168

Richardson, Henry Handel. *Australia Felix (The Fortunes of Richard Mahony:* 1). N117

Richardson, Henry Handel. *The Way Home (The Fortunes of Richard Mahony:* 2). N118

Richardson, Henry Handel. *Ultima Thule (The Fortunes of Richard Mahony:* 3). N119

Richardson, Samuel. *Pamela.* Introduction by William M. Sale, Jr. N166

Rilke, Rainer Maria. *Sonnets to Orpheus.* Tr. by M. D. Herter Norton. N157

Rilke, Rainer Maria. *Translations from the Poetry* by M. D. Herter Norton. N156

Rostow, W. W. *The Process of Economic Growth.* New intro. N176

Russell, Bertrand. *Freedom Versus Organization.* N136

Russell, Bertrand. *The Scientific Outlook.* N137

Salvemini, Gaetano. *The French Revolution.* Tr. by I. M. Rawson. N179

Simms, William Gilmore. *Woodcraft.* Introduction by Richmond Croom Beatty. N107

Sitwell, Edith. *Alexander Pope.* N182

Spender, Stephen. *The Making of a Poem.* New intro. N120

Stauffer, David. *The Nature of Poetry.* N167

Stendhal. *The Private Diaries of Stendhal.* Tr. and ed. by Robert Sage. N175

Stovall, Floyd, Editor. *Eight American Authors.* N178

Strachey, Lytton. *Portraits in Miniature.* N181

Stravinsky, Igor. *An Autobiography.* N161

Ward, Barbara. *The Interplay of East and West:* Points of Conflict and Cooperation. New epilogue. N162